The Law and Policy of Toxic Substances Control

The Law and Policy of Toxic Substances Control

A Case Study of Vinyl Chloride

DAVID D. DONIGER

/||

Published for Resources for the Future
By The Johns Hopkins University Press
Baltimore and London

Library of Congress Catalog Card Number 78-24624

ISBN 0-8018-2234-3
      0-8018-2235-1 paper

TABLE OF CONTENTS

FOREWORD

This book on the law and public policy of toxic substances control is the second product of a modest grant made in 1976 by RFF to the *Ecology Law Quarterly*, Boalt Hall School of Law of the University of California at Berkeley. Our grant supported the extra expenses involved in preparation and publication of a special issue of the *Quarterly* on "Hazardous Substances in the Environment." This ambitious issue was published in the summer of 1978, just as the continuing public debate on this most important topic was heating up.

In reviewing the special issue, several of us at RFF concluded that the paper by David Doniger constituted such an excellent introduction to this evolving field that its wider circulation could be very useful. Accordingly, we have arranged to bring out this study alone, with the hope that it will be used in legal, economic, and other courses on environmental problems. The publication may also serve as an announcement of RFF's interest in this field for, while several staff members have written individually on toxic substances, a formal program on toxic substances problems is now developing here under the direction of Allen V. Kneese.

Doniger is currently an attorney with the Natural Resources Defense Council and was formerly with the Environmental Law Institute, both in Washington, D.C. He holds a J.D. and a master's degree in city planning from the University of California at Berkeley. While at Berkeley he was special issue editor of the *Quarterly*. In organizing the project, he had the support and cooperation of Richard H. Cowart (editor-in-chief 1976/77), Karl E. Geier (managing editor 1977/78), and members of the board of editors. For readers whose interest goes beyond this paper, we have reprinted the complete table of contents from the journal issue on page 179. Copies of the entire issue are available for $10.00 from the *Ecology Law Quarterly*, School of Law (Boalt Hall), University of California, Berkeley, California 94720.

The case study of vinyl chloride regulation, the observations about the federal agencies' coordination efforts, and the analysis of the developing administrative law in the area of health and environmental regulation carry through April 1978. Naturally, as the government and the courts continue to work on these problems, there are further developments constantly. Nonetheless, it is likely that the basic structure and background this paper provides will remain valid for some years.

November 1978   Clifford S. Russell
Senior Fellow
Resources for the Future

INTRODUCTION

On January 22, 1974, the B.F. Goodrich Company revealed that three workers at its plant in Louisville, Kentucky, recently had died of angiosarcoma of the liver, an extremely rare and incurable cancer, and that a fourth had died of the same illness five years before.[1] The plant converts vinyl chloride, a petrochemical gas, into polyvinyl chloride, the second most widely used plastic in the United States.[2] The grouping of these rare cancers at this plant immediately raised the suspicion that vinyl chloride was the cause. This suspicion was soon confirmed by reports from other companies that some of their workers exposed to the chemical had developed the same cancer, and by disclosures that since 1970 vinyl chloride had induced a wide variety of cancers in experimental animals.[3]

Within a week of the Goodrich disclosure, the Occupational Safety and Health Administration and the National Institute for Occupational Safety and Health began preparing a workplace standard for vinyl chloride.[4] This marked the beginning of the still incomplete regulation of this pervasive chemical, an endeavor that has involved five major federal agencies operating under 15 separate health and environmental statutes.

---

1. These events are summarized in Occupational Safety and Health Administration, *Standard for Exposure to Vinyl Chloride*, 39 Fed. Reg. 35,890, 35,890-91 (1974) [hereinafter cited as *OSHA Permanent Standard for VC*]. *See also Hearings on Dangers of Vinyl Chloride before the Subcomm. on Environment of the Senate Comm. on Commerce*, 93d Cong., 2d Sess. 39-42 (1974) (testimony of Dr. Marcus Key, Director, National Institute for Occupational Safety and Health) [hereinafter cited as *VC Hearings*].
   2. See text accompanying notes 81-82 *infra*.
   3. See text accompanying notes 124-129, 139-141 *infra*.
   4. Dep't of Labor, *Possible Hazards of Vinyl Chloride Manufacture and Use, Request for Information and Notice of Fact-Finding Hearing*, 39 Fed. Reg. 3874 (1974) [hereinafter cited as *OSHA Hearing Notice*].

This Article examines the federal regulation of vinyl chloride, and through that experience, the complex law and policy of toxic substances control in the United States. Attempts to control toxic substances were begun seriously only in the 1970s. The law and policy in this area are in rapid growth and transition and are still deeply disorganized. The vinyl chloride problem is one of several chemical crises that has strongly influenced the growth of the field.[5]

Vinyl chloride gas (VC) and polyvinyl chloride plastic (PVC) permeate modern American living. PVC has hundreds of widely different uses, some very important and others completely frivolous. PVC is a major construction material, used in products such as water pipe, floor tile, and exterior siding. It is a major food packaging material. PVC is used to make consumer products ranging from household furniture to auto interiors, from credit cards to baby pants. Ironically, it provides a valuable coating for pollution control equipment, due to its resistance to corrosion. VC gas itself has been used as an aerosol propellant and a refrigerant. It was once even tested for use as a general anaesthetic.[6]

Hundreds of thousands of people are exposed to VC at their places of work. Millions are exposed to VC from living and working near the factories where it is made and processed, and near the routes over which it is transported between factories. VC leaches from many of the PVC products with which the consumer is in contact daily—from packaging into food, from pipe into drinking water, from latex paint into indoor air, and from many other sources.[7]

The primary threat from VC is to the workers. To date there have been at least 68 known cases of liver angiosarcoma among the roughly 30,000 workers most heavily exposed to the chemical in the three decades prior to 1974. The illness is occurring in these workers at a rate as much as 3,000 times higher than in the general population. VC is also suspected of causing an equivalent number of more common cancers in these workers. Moreover, many other workers are expected to develop liver angiosarcoma and other cancers as a result of their exposure in the 1950s, 1960s, and early 1970s.[8]

---

5. There have been several other studies of the regulation of VC: Krause, *Environmental Carcinogenesis: Regulation on the Frontiers of Science*, 7 ENVT'L L. 83 (1976); N. Ashford, E. Zolt, D. Hattis, & J. Katz, The Impact of Governmental Restrictions on the Production and Use of Chemicals: Draft Final Report (appendices concerning regulation of VC in the workplace and as a food additive) (Dec. 1976) (report prepared for the Council on Environmental Quality); G. Adams, Toxic Substance Control: Vinyl Chloride (unpublished master's thesis, Washington University, St. Louis, Mo., Dec. 1976).

6. For a more thorough description of the uses of VC and PVC, see text accompanying notes 84-87 and Figure 1 *infra*.

7. For a more complete description of the sources of exposure, see text accompanying notes 148-167 *infra*.

8. See text accompanying notes 98, 125-135 *infra*.

Most of the victims known to date have been exposed to VC at levels far higher than those experienced by most workers, consumers, and others. But even low doses of a carcinogen are a matter of serious concern. Presently, it is not possible to identify safe levels of exposure to carcinogens, and some scientists believe that as little as a single molecule of such a chemical, interacting with the appropriate portion of the genetic material of a susceptible cell, can cause a fatal cancer many years later.[9]

The adverse effects of VC are not limited to cancer. At relatively high doses it causes a variety of degenerative symptoms. At low doses it may cause birth defects and mutations.[10]

Unfortunately, VC is not an oddity. It is representative of thousands of chemicals that are capable of causing cancer, other long-term illnesses, and many subtle adverse environmental effects. Like VC, many of these chemicals were once thought to be safe, are important components of significant industries, and are manufactured, transported, consumed, and discarded in vast quantities. Nearly everyone is exposed to them in complex, possibly interactive combinations; nearly everyone is at some degree of risk.[11]

These hazardous substances are only a fraction of the estimated 65,000 chemicals in commerce and the more than four million chemicals that are known.[12] But in absolute terms toxic substances are large in number, and they are responsible for a substantial portion of the illnesses, deaths, and environmental insults experienced today.[13] The vast number of chemicals to be tested, evaluated, and regulated makes toxic substances control in many respects the major challenge of the health and environmental movement.

One focus of this Article is the staggering complexity and fragmentation of the federal programs to control these toxic substances. About 20 separate health and environmental statutes empower five major agencies to regulate such substances. (See Table 1) The patchwork of statutes grew incrementally, mostly over the last two decades, as Congress perceived additional, relatively narrowly defined needs for controls. Together the laws cover virtually all the avenues through which people can be exposed to dangerous chemicals, and most of the avenues through which such substances can harm natural systems.[14]

---

9. See text accompanying notes 22-80, 148-167 *infra*.

10. See text accompanying note 138 *infra*.

11. On the vast number of hazardous substances needing regulatory attention, see Slesin & Sandler, *Categorization of Chemicals Under the Toxic Substances Control Act*, 7 ECOLOGY L. Q. 359 (1978); Page, *A Generic View of Toxic Chemicals and Similar Risks*, 7 ECOLOGY L. Q. 207 (1978). As an example of the numbers problem, see NATIONAL INSTITUTE FOR OCCUPATIONAL SAFETY & HEALTH, SUSPECTED CARCINOGENS (2d ed. 1976), which identifies 1,500-2,000 chemicals that animal experiments have implicated as possible carcinogens.

12. Maugh, *Chemicals: How Many Are There?* 199 SCIENCE 162 (1978).

13. Between 60 and 90 percent of human cancers are estimated to be caused, wholly or in part, by chemicals in food, water, workplaces, cigarette smoke, and the general environment. *See* COUNCIL ON ENVIRONMENTAL QUALITY, SIXTH ANNUAL REPORT 32-33 (1975). *See also* text accompanying note 33 *infra*.

14. Two possible exceptions are the components of cosmetics and of substances harmful

TABLE I

FEDERAL AUTHORITY OVER VINYL CHLORIDE EXPOSURE

AGENCY STATUTE	YEAR ENACTED	USES OR SOURCES OF EXPOSURE COVERED
Occupational Safety and Health Administration		
Occupational Safety and Health Act	1970	Exposure in factories and in transportation (workers only)
Environmental Protection Agency		
Clean Air Act	1970	Factory emissions
Federal Environmental Pesticide Control Act	1972	Insecticide aerosols
Federal Water Pollution Control Act	1972	VC discharges to water
Safe Drinking Water Act	1974	VC in drinking water, PVC water pipe
Resource Conservation and Recovery Act	1976	PVC sludge wastes
Toxic Substances Control Act	1976	Possible to use in lieu of multiple separate actions under other laws
Food and Drug Administration		
Food, Drug, and Cosmetic Act	1938	Cosmetic aerosols, PVC cosmetic packaging
Food Additives Amendment	1958	PVC food packaging, PVC water pipe
New Drug Amendments	1962	Drug aerosols, PVC drug packaging
Medical Device Amendments	1976	PVC medical devices
Consumer Product Safety Commission		
Federal Hazardous Substances Act	1966	Household aerosols, household plastics and paints
Department of Transportation		
Hazardous Materials Transportation Act	1975	Rail and truck tank vehicles
Federal Rail Safety Act	1970	Rail tank cars and roadbed
Ports and Waterways Safety Act	1972	Barges and tank vessels
Dangerous Cargo Act	1940	

But although the coverage of these statutes, taken together, is nearly complete, it is highly fragmented. As noted above, to address all of the sources of human exposure to VC would require action by all five agencies acting under 15 of the statutes. Few chemicals are as widely used as VC, and therefore few will fall under so many authorities. Nonetheless, there are already more than 20 chemicals undergoing regulation by two or more agencies.[15] This is likely to be the rule rather than the exception, at least for chemicals currently well established in commerce.[16]

A serious problem is that in many cases the boundaries between agencies' jurisdictions are not clear. Sometimes authorities overlap, empowering two agencies to regulate a given source of exposure.[17] In some areas where two agencies have abutting jurisdiction—*i.e.*, where together their statutes cover a type of hazard without overlap—the dividing line is uncertain, and it is uncertain into which bailiwick a particular source falls.[18] Jurisdictional complexity and confusion often discourage agencies from stepping forward to deal with a problem; each waits for another to act.

Even when jurisdictional issues are resolved, the fragmented system discourages comprehensive assessment and balancing of all of a substance's risks and benefits. No agency has the responsibility to consider the net social gain or loss from different levels of control. Such a holistic consideration might yield a different result than the sum of partial analyses. Moreover, in the case of VC, some risks have been seriously understated and some control costs seriously exaggerated because of the fragmentation of assessment of both hazards and economic benefits.[19]

The final drawback to the current balkanized system is the duplication of decision making. Many separate, essentially identical proceedings must be held. The duplication wastes the resources of all concerned—government, regulated industries, and health and environmental groups. Some industries may prefer the fragmentation because it slows the speed with which the government places controls on the profitable use and sale of

---

to the natural environment which are components of food and drugs. *See generally* Page & Blackburn, *Behind the Looking Glass: Administrative, Legislative, and Private Approaches to Cosmetic Safety Substantiation*, 24 U.C.L.A. L. REV. 795 (1977); EPA, *Fully Halogenated Chlorofluoroalkanes, Proposed Rule*, 42 Fed. Reg. 24,544, 24,545 (1977).

15. *See* Interagency Regulatory Liason Group, Joint Regulatory Developments, March 1, 1978, *reprinted in* 1 BNA CHEM. REG. REP.—CURR. REP. 1916-21 (1978) [hereinafter cited as IRLG List of Substances of Common Concern]. The list includes VC. For some of these substances, such as VC, some regulations are already in effect and more are under consideration.

16. The problem may be avoided for new chemicals, which under the Toxic Sustances Control Act (TSCA) must be tested by manufacturers and evaluated by the Environmental Protection Agency prior to their entry into commerce. TSCA § 4, 15 U.S.C. § 2063 (Supp. V 1975).

17. See text accompanying notes 672-674, 753-771, 793-795 *infra*.

18. See text accompanying notes 557-561, 608 *infra*.

19. See text accompanying notes 347-348, 470-472, 803-804 *infra*.

hazardous substances. But in many cases uncertainty over the ultimate scope of regulation probably outweighs the industries' advantages in delay.

In response to problems encountered in the control of VC and several other substances through this fragmented system, the agencies recently have begun efforts to coordinate their many programs and to increase the consistency of their actions. The promise and pitfalls of these efforts are surveyed at the end of the Article, on the basis of the lessons of the VC experience.[20]

The second focus of this Article is how agencies cope with problems of uncertainty and competing, dissimilar interests that are inherent in toxic substances control decisions. As is explored in Part I, the regulation of any of these substances involves complex decision making under uncertainty and controversial value judgments concerning the weighing of health and environmental values against economic interests. The VC case study permits one to see how the many statutes and agencies approach these problems, in a relatively constant scientific, technological, and economic context.

Part II, the case study, makes up the major portion of this Article. It begins with a survey of the uses of VC and PVC, the technology and economics of associated industries, and what is known of VC's toxicity. This is the factual background for all the regulatory proceedings; additional data peculiar to individual areas is given in those discussions.

The next three sections in Part II analyze in depth the actions taken to date respecting three of the major sources of VC exposure. The first section considers the development of a standard for workplace exposure by the Occupational Safety and Health Administration (OSHA). The second addresses standard setting for emissions from factories to the surrounding air, by the Environmental Protection Agency (EPA). The third considers the proposal by the Food and Drug Administration (FDA) to regulate the use of PVC food packaging. Each of these sections illustrates central legal and policy problems in toxic substances control and a range of responses by agencies and interested parties. Considered together, the OSHA and EPA actions also illustrate the underweighting of risks that can result from jurisdictional fragmentation.

The extremes of jurisdictional complexity are illustrated in the next two sections, on VC-propelled aerosol products and the transportation of VC between factories. Authority over aerosols is divided among three agencies: FDA, EPA, and the Consumer Product Safety Commission (CPSC). Authority over hazardous material transportation is divided among OSHA and three agencies within the Department of Transportation (DOT). Because very small economic interests were at stake over aerosols, regulation proceeded relatively smoothly. However, the aerosol episode reveals the potential for serious jurisdictional conflict in those future cases when more money

---

20. See text accompanying notes 836-868 *infra*.

is at stake, when decisions are more difficult, and when the results for a given product might depend on which statute and agency it falls under. In the transportation area the economic interests are greater and the balancing of risk and benefit is more difficult. The jurisdictional lines also are unclear. Moreover, historically none of the agencies concerned has regulated the movement of carcinogens and other substances with long-term or subtle effects. Each is reluctant to assert its authority vigorously and is content to wait for another to step forward.

The last section of the case study briefly surveys the authorities for controlling the remaining sources of VC exposure. Principally, these are exposure routes connected with water, consumer products, packaging other than for food, and medical devices. The agencies involved are EPA, FDA, and CPSC. No controls of these exposure sources have yet moved beyond the proposal stage. The control of these sources leads to several more examples of jurisdictional overlap, of underweighting of risks, and of conflicting statutory responsibilities.

The final section also considers how the Toxic Substances Control Act,[21] administered by EPA, relates to the control of VC and to future instances in which authority over a dangerous chemical is seriously fragmented. The Act was passed only in 1976, after some standards for VC already had been set under prior laws or had been proposed, and therefore it is of minimal use to control this chemical. But EPA might use the Act in the future to reduce the number of separate, fragmented actions that are needed to regulate similar substances.

Part III of this Article has two purposes. First, in light of the VC episode and similar experiences, it surveys past and ongoing efforts to deal with jurisdictional fragmentation and to coordinate federal action and policy on toxic substances control. It discusses the agencies' internal coordination efforts, interagency agreements, cooperative regulation of particular substances, and two new interagency groups created to foster broader forms of cooperation. Serious coordination efforts are only just beginning.

Second, Part III of the Article confronts the capacity of certain characteristics of the legal framework for toxic substances regulation to deal with the other central policy problems noted above: decision making under uncertainty and balancing of dissimilar, competing interests. The statutory formulations, which are analyzed individually in detail in the appropriate sections of the case study, are considered here in general terms.

From the case study it becomes clear that in view of the problems of factual uncertainty and conflicting values, each agency faces a wide range of rational choices in setting exposure limits and other standards, but no one choice can be said to be objectively "correct." Each agency must make judgments about what to assume when the true facts are uncertain and about

---

21.   15 U.S.C. §§ 2601-2629 (West Supp. 1978).

which interests to favor among competing ones. The policies or norms that drive these judgments are difficult to state clearly and difficult to apply precisely to the circumstances at hand.

The statutes that delegate responsibility to the agencies for making these judgments provide certain limitations, along with some measure of guidance for decision making. The statutory formulations differ in many particulars, but certain themes and basic alternatives emerge clearly.

First, virtually all the statutes are precautionary; *i.e.*, they direct the agencies to act on the basis of uncertain, suggestive indications that a substance is dangerous. Because many substances can be shown definitively to be harmful only after serious harms have already occurred, these statutes reject the view that control measures must await proof of actual, past harm.

On the balancing problem there is substantial division among the statutes. Most of the statutes require agencies to weigh health and environmental concerns against economic considerations, but several statutes prohibit agencies from considering anything but health factors. Depending upon which approach is used, the results of regulation will differ dramatically. Because of the severe results of the health-only rule, the prohibition is acknowledged more often in the breach than in the observance.

The toxic substances control statutes also differ in the allocation of the burden of persuasion. Most place the burden of showing that a substance should be regulated on the government. Several important statutes, however, place the burden of showing that a substance should be allowed in commerce on the proponent of use. The difference in the burden of persuasion can affect fine judgments at the margin, such as where an agency is deciding between alternative levels of exposure.

Finally, the statutes call for searching judicial review of agency decisions, although ultimately they leave to the agencies a large measure of discretion. Although the statutory formulations regarding standards of judicial review vary, the courts are developing consistent principles for scrutinizing decisions.

Through these devices the statutes give some guidance and offer some control, but they leave the agencies a wide range of legitimate choices. This Article contends that these legal tools are not instruments of finely-tuned control, and that the agencies and advocates waste considerable energy in unproductive attempts to draw from the statutory differences fine distinctions in the agencies' obligations. Ultimately, regulations emerge from the interplay of available facts, the advocacy of interested parties and the predispositions of the agencies. The dynamics of this process are best seen in operation, as in the VC case study. Before analyzing the actions of the agencies in the regulation of VC, it is necessary to examine the central policy problems of uncertainty and balancing that the agencies have had to face. These problems are considered in the next section.

I

BASIC POLICY PROBLEMS IN TOXIC SUBSTANCES CONTROL: DECIDING UNDER
UNCERTAINTY AND BALANCING INCOMMENSURABLE INTERESTS

Two cardinal problems are endemic to any scheme for regulating
substances that cause cancer or other long-term, serious health or environmental effects of relatively low probability. First, all decisions must be
made under substantial uncertainty about the medical and ecological risks,
technological difficulties, and economic costs associated with different
degrees of exposure. Second, all decisions involve trade-offs among groups
with interests that are not readily comparable. These two problems form
serious "boundaries of analysis" that prevent regulatory agencies from
making exact, objective, and noncontroversial decisions.[22] This section
explores the problems of uncertainty and balancing generally, as a preface to
the exploration of agency response to the VC hazard, and to the discussion
of the legal framework within which the agencies make decisions.

Cancer is the primary adverse effect of VC, and the disease is the
chemical hazard most on the public mind. For these reasons, this section
explores the nature of scientific uncertainty in the management of hazardous
substances through the example of cancer risk assessment. This section also
discusses the technological and economic uncertainties of estimating the
difficulty and cost of toxic substances control. Finally, the section examines
the difficulty of determining what risk-benefit trade-offs are acceptable to
individuals and to the society as a whole. Only with an understanding of the
boundaries of our scientific, technological, economic, and ethical knowledge is it possible to evaluate fairly the analytical efforts and normative
choices of the agencies that have regulated VC.

A.   The Limits of Cancer Risk Assessment

Cancer is a group of illnesses characterized by the unrestrained multi-
plication of cells that somehow have lost an essential self-regulatory mechanism.[23] The uncontrolled growth of these cells eventually threatens the life
of the host organism. Presently, cancer is the second leading cause of death
in the United States.[24] One American in four is expected to contract some
type of cancer,[25] and one American in five is expected to die of it.[26]

---

22.   The quoted phrase is taken from the title of a study of water project planning and,
more particularly, from an article on similar issues in cost-benefit analysis in that context. *See*
Bradford & Feiveson, *Benefits and Costs, Winners and Losers* in BOUNDARIES OF ANALYSIS:
AN INQUIRY INTO THE TOCKS ISLAND DAM CONTROVERSY 125, 144 (H. Feiveson, F. Sinden, & R.
Socolow eds. 1976).

23.   *See* COUNCIL ON ENVIRONMENTAL QUALITY, SIXTH ANNUAL REPORT 13 (1975) (ch. 1,
Carcinogens in the Environment) [hereinafter cited as CEQ SIXTH ANNUAL REPORT]. For
explanations of the essentials of cancer directed to the lay reader, see M. SHIMKIN, SCIENCE
AND CANCER 1-6, 45-54, 87-98 (1973) [hereinafter cited as SCIENCE AND CANCER]; Cairns, *The
Cancer Problem*, SCIENTIFIC AMERICAN, Nov. 1975, at 64 [hereinafter cited as *The Cancer
Problem*].

24.   CEQ SIXTH ANNUAL REPORT, *supra* note 23, at 9, table 2.

25.   *Id.* at 12.

26.   *The Cancer Problem, supra* note 23, at 66.

Most forms of cancer are difficult or impossible to cure; less than one-half of all cancer patients survive longer than five years from the discovery of their illness.[27] The elusiveness of cures largely is due to the fact that cancer's basic biological mechanisms at the cellular level are not well understood.[28]

The causes of cancer are, however, somewhat better understood than the cures. Studies of cancer incidence in particular groups have shown strong statistical connections between exposure to certain chemical substances and particular cancers. The connection between tobacco smoke and lung cancer is the most widely known.[29] Markedly elevated cancer rates are also found among certain occupational groups in the United States and in other highly industrialized countries.[30] Cancer rates are elevated where air and drinking water are contaminated with industrial organic chemicals.[31] In general, cancer rates are higher than average in American urbanized areas.[32] From comparisons of different rates of different cancers throughout the world, the World Health Organization and other prominent institutions and individual experts have concluded that 60 to 90 percent of all human cancers are caused by exposure to chemical substances (and, to a lesser extent, radiation) present in our air, workplaces, food, water, and the rest of our environment.[33]

The causal relationships underlying the statistical connections observed in humans have been confirmed for many substances by controlled experiments on animals. With one possible exception, all substances related to cancer in humans have been shown to cause cancer in animals.[34] In addition, animal experiments have implicated 1,500-2,000 other chemical substances

---

27. CANCER PATIENT SURVIVAL, REP. NO. 5, U.S. DEP'T HEALTH, EDUC., & WELF. PUB. NO. (NIH) 77-992, at 3 (1976).

28. *The Cancer Problem, supra* note 23, at 72.

29. See Hammond, *Tobacco* in PERSONS AT HIGH RISK OF CANCER: AN APPROACH TO CANCER ETIOLOGY AND CONTROL 131 (J. Fraumeni ed. 1975) [hereinafter cited as PERSONS AT HIGH RISK OF CANCER].

30. CEQ SIXTH ANNUAL REPORT, *supra* note 23, at 23-26; Cole & Goldman, *Occupation* in PERSONS AT HIGH RISK OF CANCER, *supra* note 29, at 167.

31. EPA, *Interim Drinking Water Regulations: Control of Organic Chemical Contaminants in Drinking Water*, 43 Fed. Reg. 5756, 5758 (1978), *citing* NATIONAL ACADEMY OF SCIENCES, DRINKING WATER AND HEALTH (June 1977); Pike, *Air Pollution* in PERSONS AT HIGH RISK OF CANCER, *supra* note 29, at 225.

32. CEQ SIXTH ANNUAL REPORT, *supra* note 23, at 19; Hoover, Mason, McKay, & Fraumeni, *Geographic Patterns of Cancer Mortality in the United States* in PERSONS AT HIGH RISK OF CANCER, *supra* note 29, at 343-44 & table 1, at 345.

33. CEQ SIXTH ANNUAL REPORT, *supra* note 23, at 17; Higginson, *Importance of Environmental Factors in Cancer* in ENVIRONMENTAL POLLUTION AND CARCINOGENIC RISKS 15, 17 (C. Rosenfeld & W. Davis, eds. 1975) [hereinafter cited as ENVIRONMENTAL POLLUTION]; Boyland, *The Correlation of Experimental Carcinogenesis and Cancer in Man*, 11 PROGRESS IN EXPERIMENTAL TUMOR RESEARCH 222, 223 (1969); Epstein, *Environmental Determinants of Human Cancer*, 34 CANCER RESEARCH 2425 (1974). *See also* R. DOLL, PREVENTION OF CANCER: POINTERS FROM EPIDEMIOLOGY (1967) [hereinafter cited as PREVENTION OF CANCER].

34. CEQ SIXTH ANNUAL REPORT, *supra* note 23, at 30-32. The apparent exception is arsenic.

as potential human carcinogens.[35] Many of these substances are synthetic organic chemicals that have been in commercial use only since the 1930s. Because cancer is a latent disease that typically manifests itself only 15 to 40 years after exposure begins, it is too early to know the effects of chemicals that have been in widespread use for only this short period.

This evidence suggests that cancer rates could be cut significantly by reducing human exposure to the disease's chemical causes. Even though it may be quite expensive, preventing human exposure to carcinogens often is a more effective and economically efficient method of reducing cancer rates than attempts to cure patients who already have the disease.[36] In order to make the best use of the resources available to prevent cancer, precise data on which substances are carcinogenic and on how dangerous they are at various levels of exposure would be helpful. Unfortunately, the causal relationship between a chemical and cancer is often difficult to establish. Even where a qualitative relationship is visible, precise quantitative estimates of risks to humans cannot be made reliably, particularly for low risks on the order of one case in 10,000 or more subjects.[37]

In the first place, not enough is known about how chemical carcinogens operate, especially at the cellular level. There is general agreement that the substances cause changes in the genetic material of an individual cell or in the mechanisms through which the genetic material controls a cell's behavior, inducing it to multiply wildly.[38] There is uncertainty and disagreement on whether only one such "hit" need occur or whether a certain sequence of independent hits by the same or different substances is needed.[39] Further uncertainty stems from the complexity of cellular metabolism—the system of chemical and physical processes that occur within a living organism. Opinions differ on whether there are chemical reactions that detoxify certain amounts of a carcinogen by converting it into a harmless substance, or that repair genetic changes after they have occurred.[40] The metabolic "pathway" of a substance from its point of entry (*e.g.*, lungs, skin, or digestive system) to its point of damage is also often uncertain.[41]

---

35. Occupational Safety and Health Administration, *Identification, Classification and Regulation of Toxic Substances Posing a Potential Occupational Carcinogenic Risk*, 42 Fed. Reg. 54,148 (1977).

36. Schneiderman, *Sources, Resources, and Tsouris* in PERSONS AT HIGH RISK OF CANCER, *supra* note 29, at 451, 452, 459.

37. *See generally* Schneiderman, Mantel, & Brown, *From Mouse to Man—Or How to Get from the Laboratory to Park Avenue and 59th Street*, 246 ANNALS N.Y. ACAD. SCI. 237, 243 (1975) [hereinafter cited as *From Mouse to Man*].

38. SCIENCE AND CANCER, *supra* note 23, at 45-54, 87-92.

39. *See generally* Mantel & Schneiderman, *Estimating "Safe" Levels, a Hazardous Undertaking*, 35 CANCER RESEARCH 1379 (1975) [hereinafter cited as *Estimating "Safe" Levels*].

40. *See* Cornfield, *Carcinogenic Risk Assessment*, 198 SCIENCE 693 (1977) [hereinafter cited as *Carcinogenic Risk Assessment*].

41. *See, e.g.*, Watanabe & Gehring, *Dose-Dependent Fate of Vinyl Chloride and Its Possible Relationship to Oncogenicity in Rats*, 17 ENVT'L HEALTH PERSPECTIVES 145 (1976).

Whether or not there are defense or repair mechanisms has profound implications for strategies for cancer prevention. If the "one-hit" model is accurate, and if there are no detoxification, repair, or other defense mechanisms, then as little as one molecule of a carcinogenic substance, interacting with the appropriate portion of the susceptible cell, can cause an irreversible cancer. If multiple hits by different substances are needed, any one substance alone may not be carcinogenic (or may be only weakly so) but together these substances may be potent causes of the disease. If detoxification or repair mechanisms or other defenses exist, there may be safe doses—"thresholds"—below which no cancers will be caused. More important than the question of whether a threshold exists is the question of what risks to expect from a range of doses. Different propositions about cancer causation lead to different conclusions about the rate of cancer to expect from each dose.[42]

The second major source of uncertainty is a result of the limitations of available research techniques. Current methods for investigating the carcinogenicity of substances do not permit the verification or disproof of alternative theories of cancer causation. The methods are themselves also the subject of great controversy. Observation from direct human experiences is of limited utility. Purposeful experimentation on humans is ethically unacceptable, since the results often would be fatal. Human evidence of carcinogenesis usually comes from observation of occupational groups exposed, often unwittingly, to chemicals in the industrial economy.[43] Some connections can be drawn in the general population, but for the most part humans are exposed to too many different substances at unknown doses for unknown periods to permit statistically reliable conclusions to be drawn.[44] Moreover, there are synergistic and antagonistic interactions between chemicals that drastically complicate drawing conclusions about the effects of each chemical. Finally, because latency periods run 15 to 40 years or

---

42.   Some assumptions lead to the conclusion that threshold doses exist and that the risk at doses approaching the threshold declines to zero. *See* Kotin, *Dose-Response Relationship and Threshold Concepts*, 271 ANNALS N.Y. ACAD. SCI. 22, 25-27 [1976]. *See also Carcinogenic Risk Assessment, supra* note 40; *DNA Repair: New Clues to Carcinogenesis*, 200 SCIENCE 518 (1978). Other models decline to decide whether there are thresholds. One major model has dose and response in a logarithmic relationship, with risk declining more rapidly than dose at low doses. This model yields higher risks for given doses than those which posit thresholds. *See Estimating "Safe" Levels, supra* note 39.

Other researchers argue that the dose-response relationship at low doses is likely to be linear, *i.e.*, that decreases in risk are probably proportional to reductions of dose. This approach yields a risk for a given dose higher than the risks estimated by the other two approaches at least at low doses. *See* Crump, Hoel, Langley, & Peto, *Fundamental Carcinogenic Processes and Their Implications for Low Dose Risk Assessment*, 36 CANCER RESEARCH 2973 (1976) [hereinafter cited as *Fundamental Carcinogenic Processes*].

The issues are summarized briefly in NATIONAL ACADEMY OF SCIENCES, PRINCIPLES FOR EVALUATING CHEMICALS IN THE ENVIRONMENT 86-88 (1975) [hereinafter cited as PRINCIPLES FOR EVALUATING CHEMICALS].

43.   CEQ SIXTH ANNUAL REPORT, *supra* note 23, at 23-26.

44.   *Id.* at 26-28.

longer, definitive studies of effects on humans are impracticable.[45]

Studies on rodents are the major source of data on the carcinogenicity of chemicals.[46] Their response characteristics are considered essentially similar to those of humans, so that a substance carcinogenic to one is likely to be carcinogenic to the other.[47] But although the qualitative inferences are quite sound, there are limitations on the ability of the animal tests to indicate the magnitude of human risks. It is difficult both to detect small risks in test animals and to translate risks for animals into risks for humans.

The difficulty in detecting small risks is statistical in nature. For practical and financial reasons, nearly all experiments on animals involve small numbers of subjects, usually no more than a few hundred.[48] In so small a group, a chemical must cause an effect at a relatively high rate for the relationship to be confidently distinguished from random occurrences of the same event.[49] The dose of a substance that induces cancer at rates detectable in such tests is often far higher than most people experience.[50] The critical question is whether lower doses cause cancer, and at what rates. An effect occurring at a very low rate stands a good chance of not being observed in so small a test group, so that the failure to observe an effect in such a test is not a reliable indication of the substance's safety for a larger population.[51] Thus, no test has confirmed the existence of any threshold or detoxification mechanism or resolved any other basic aspect of the theoretical controversies discussed above.[52]

45. *Id*. If the effect is mutation rather than cancer, the effect will not manifest itself for one or more generations.
For a general description of the nature of epidemiological evidence and of the uses and limitations of such research, see PREVENTION OF CANCER, *supra* note 33, at 15-29.
46. CEQ SIXTH ANNUAL REPORT, *supra* note 23, at 28-32; In re Shell Chem. Co., 6 ERC 2047, 2052 (EPA, FIFRA Docket, 1977); PRINCIPLES FOR EVALUATING CHEMICALS, *supra* note 42, at 135-39; T. LOOMIS, ESSENTIALS OF TOXICOLOGY 206 (2d ed. 1974) [hereinafter cited as ESSENTIALS OF TOXICOLOGY].
47. CEQ SIXTH ANNUAL REPORT, *supra* note 23, at 30-32; *Estimating Safe Levels, supra* note 39, at 1381.
48. *See From Mouse to Man, supra* note 37. On the trade-off between the sensitivity and cost of tests, see Bates, *Laboratory Approaches to the Identification of Carcinogens*, 271 ANN. N.Y. ACAD. SCI. 29, 30-32 (1976).
49. For an explanation for laymen of the statistical issues, see W. LOWRANCE, OF ACCEPTABLE RISK 60-64 (1976) [hereinafter cited as OF ACCEPTABLE RISK].
50. This is not always the case, however. Some carcinogens are potent enough to cause cancers in experimental animals when administered at the dose levels to which people have been exposed. See text accompanying notes 133-146 *infra*.
51. Three examples illustrate the point. In a test involving 100 animals each in an experimental and a control group, if no tumors are detected in either group, there is a 1.0% chance that the real rate of cancer is as high as 4.5%. With 1,000 animals in each group and no tumors, there remains a 1.0% chance that the real rate is as high as 0.46%, or 4.6 animals out of each 1,000. If only ten animals are used in each group and the results show no tumors, the potential error increases drastically; there is a 1.0% chance that the real rate is as high as 37.0%. *See* OF ACCEPTABLE RISK, *supra* note 49, at 62.
52. For a clear discussion of these points, see Saffiotti, *Comments on the Scientific Basis for the "Delaney Clause,"* 2 PREVENTIVE MEDICINE 125 (1973) [hereinafter cited as *Comments on the Scientific Basis for the "Delaney Clause"*]. *See also* World Health Organization, Assessment of the Carcinogenicity and Mutagenicity of Chemicals, Technical Report Series, No. 546. at 9-11 (1974); *Estimating "Safe" Levels, supra* note 42, at 1382-83.

To investigate the effects of low doses directly would require experiments involving enormous numbers of animals. To demonstrate with 95 percent confidence that a given low dose of just one substance causes fewer than one cancer in a million subjects would require a test involving at least *six million* animals. Such "mega-mouse" experiments generally are considered impracticably expensive and vulnerable to laboratory errors that can destroy the statistical reliability of the results.[53]

Limited to observations at unrealistically high doses in unrealistically low numbers, the scientist's recourse is to use mathematical models of dose-response relationships to extrapolate from experimental results downward to the effects of low doses. However, like the theories on which they are based, the models yield widely divergent estimates of the risk associated with each low dose. The extent of the differences is astounding. For example, the major models differ by a factor of *100,000* on the size of the dose that creates a risk of one cancer in a million subjects.[54] The models do provide credible outer limits for the risk associated with each dose,[55] and they do permit the ranking of carcinogens in rough order of their potency. But they cannot provide the regulator with precise estimates of the risks of low doses.

More uncertainty is added to risk estimates by our ignorance of how to translate dose-response data across species lines. There simply is not enough known to determine if humans are more or less sensitive to a given dose of a carcinogen than the test animals.[56]

Several new techniques for assessing carcinogenicity are developing, but these do not yet hold out the promise of yielding quantitative risk estimates or of answering the basic questions about how cancer is caused. There are "quick" tests—such as the Ames test—of chemicals' abilities to mutate bacteria or other single-celled organisms. There is a high correlation between the ability to cause such mutations and carcinogenicity.[57] Currently, however, the value of the "quick" tests is primarily qualitative; they may be able to distinguish strong from weak carcinogens, but cannot give more precise risk estimates.

One important consequence of the uncertainty about the size of small risks is that a regulator agency does not know the *marginal* risk at each

---

53. *Estimating "Safe" Levels, supra* note 42, at 1383. *See also From Mouse to Man, supra* note 37, at 241.

54. *Carcinogenic Risk Assessment, supra* note 42, at 694.

55. For example, Schneiderman and his colleagues estimated on the basis of the animal experiments on VC completed by May 1974 "that a dose as low as 1 ppm [part per million] is almost certain to have a risk of less than 1 in 10,000" for animals. *From Mouse to Man, supra* note 37, at 241-42.

56. *See* Rall, *Problems of Low Doses of Carcinogens*, 64 J. WASH. ACAD. SCI. 63 (1974).

57. McCann & Ames, *A Simple Method for Detecting Environmental Carcinogens as Mutagens*, 271 ANNALS N.Y. ACAD. SCI. 5 (1976). *See also* Note, *From Microbes to Men: The New Toxic Substances Control Act and Bacterial Mutagenicity/Carcinogenicity Tests*, 6 ENVT'L L. REP. 10,248 (1976).

dose; that is, the agency does not know how great a difference in risk is caused by small changes in dose. If there is a large difference, then small increments in the allowable exposure will have a significant impact on human health and must be considered carefully. If the difference is small, the increments are not so important, and extensive efforts to obtain compliance with a small change in a standard might not be worthwhile.

Purely scientific problems of risk assessment are aggravated to some degree for regulatory agencies by their incomplete access to information. Most toxicological research is carried out or sponsored by the industries that make or market the substances being evaluated; industrial researchers have incentives to withhold negative information or to perform poorly designed and executed experiments incapable of revealing negative information.[58] To some extent, this behavior can be controlled by the use of standard test protocols and other means.[59] The problem of unequal access to data and of incentives to misinform or misrepresent is more serious with regard to the assessment of costs.[60]

In sum, because the nature of chemical carcinogenesis is unknown, and because available research techniques are limited in their ability to predict human risks from exposure to carcinogens, the only conclusion that may be drawn with complete certainty is that no level of exposure to a chemical that causes cancer in animals is sure to be safe. Neither experimental nor theoretical analysis can give the agencies precise estimates of the risks associated with low doses of substances that are known to cause cancer in humans or animals at higher doses. Nor can regulators be sure how sensitive risks are to changes in dose. At present, the best available techniques produce only broad estimates of the outer limits of risk.

B.   The Limits of Economic and Technological Assessment

The costs of controlling exposure to a toxic substance are shrouded in

---

58.   *See* NATIONAL RESEARCH COUNCIL, DECISION MAKING IN THE ENVIRONMENTAL PROTECTION AGENCY 54-57 (1977) [hereinafter cited as DECISION MAKING IN EPA].

59.   As an example of standard protocols for cancer testing, see Sontag, Page, & Saffiotti, Guidelines for Carcinogen Bioassay in Small Rodents, National Cancer Institute, Carcinogenesis Technical Report Series No. 1 (1976), *summarized in* Shubik & Clayson, *Application of the Results of Carcinogen Bioassays to Man* in ENVIRONMENTAL POLLUTION, *supra* note 33, at 241, 242. *See also* PRINCIPLES FOR EVALUATING CHEMICALS, *supra* note 42, at 134-55.

One other means for controlling the quality of data is to certify laboratories that meet minimum standards for their performance. *See* DECISION MAKING IN EPA, *supra* note 58, at 54-57. In addition, there are penalties in certain of the regulatory statutes for a company's misrepresenting or withholding toxicological data. Currently, the Food and Drug Administration is developing such certification procedures as part of "Good Laboratory Practice" regulations, and the agency has referred at least one case involving misrepresentation of data to the Justice Department with a recommendation for criminal prosecution. *See Creative Penmanship in Animal Testing Prompts FDA Controls*, 198 SCIENCE 1227 (1977). In addition, Velsicol Chemical Corporation has been indicted for withholding data from EPA regarding animal cancer tests on heptachlor/chlordane. *See Indictment Charges Velsicol, Six Persons, Withheld Chlordane, Heptachlordane Data*, 1 BNA CHEM. REG. REP.—CURR. REP. 1413-14 (1977).

60.   See text accompanying notes 67-71 *infra.*

as much uncertainty as the risks of the exposure. The difficulty of determining the costs of regulation arises from several compounded problems. At the simplest level, it is difficult to predict the technological problems and direct economic costs of meeting exposure limitations that may be only a fraction of the levels once thought to be safe. It is a more complex task to assess the wider economic consequences of changes in the price or availability of a substance. Finally, it is difficult to know whether the use of substitute products and other secondary responses to regulation will themselves harm health or the environment.[61]

As a general rule, as the degree of exposure control increases, the marginal costs of each additional increment of control increase.[62] Simple and inexpensive measures to reduce exposure will be taken before complicated and costly ones. Of equal importance in the regulation of toxic substances, as the degree of control increases, the cost of control grows more uncertain; the range of effects becomes more difficult even to identify, let alone quantify.[63] Additional improvements will require research and development of new control techniques; it will be uncertain what results can be achieved, how long the research and development process will take, and how much the new controls will cost to develop, install, and operate. In the extreme case, the necessary control means may defy invention, and until some completely unpredictable technological advance occurs, compliance will be impossible without closing the factory.

An increase in the cost of producing a regulated substance will have secondary economic consequences, depending on the profit margins of the producers, the degree of economic concentration of the industry, and the availability of substitute products. The evaluation of costs and benefits in the regulation of toxic chemicals is complicated by uncertainty as to the magnitude of these secondary effects in any given case. If close substitutes are available at prices nearly equal to a substance's preregulation price, producers will not be able to raise prices significantly to recoup the costs of compliance.[64] In such cases the producers' profit margins will decrease, or production will decline. In other cases, the product may have unique and

---

61.   *See generally* NATIONAL ACADEMY OF SCIENCES, DECISION MAKING FOR REGULATING CHEMICALS IN THE ENVIRONMENT 150-62 (1975) [hereinafter cited as DECISION MAKING FOR REGULATING CHEMICALS]. This study points out a fourth category of costs, effects of a regulation on market structure. A single decision or set of decisions may have the consequence of increasing concentration in an industry or of establishing barriers to entry, or may change the rate of innovation. *Id*. at 156. This topic is not addressed in this section. It is possible to argue, however, that other governmental mechanisms exist (*e.g.*, anti-trust regulation and research and development spending) to deal adequately with any such impacts. *See generally* R. NOLL, REFORMING REGULATION 29 (1971) [hereinafter cited as REFORMING REGULATION].

62.   The general rule is illustrated in A. FREEMAN, R. HAVEMAN, & A. KNEESE, THE ECONOMICS OF ENVIRONMENTAL POLICY 86-87 (1973).

63.   The increasing uncertainty is illustrated in W. ROWE, AN ANATOMY OF RISK 234 (1977) [hereinafter cited as AN ANATOMY OF RISK].

64.   The economic term for this relationship is elasticity of demand.

valuable features, and consumers may be willing to pay prices that reflect most or all of the cost increases. Finally, in some situations, human exposure to a toxic substance may be an intentional or unavoidable event, not reducible to safe levels without banning the substance. For such regulations, there is not much uncertainty as to the costs and technological means of control. There remains, however, the difficulty of determining the economic loss to society as a whole, including the adverse impacts of the use of substitutes.[65]

The last major element of uncertainty in the assessment of the costs of regulation is whether any of the substitute responses to regulation will themselves have an adverse health or environmental impact. If the substitutes are readily forseeable, something may be known of their toxicity. On the other hand, their effects may not yet be known,[66] and the effects of substitutes not yet identified cannot be predicted. This dimension of uncertainty, like those discussed above, becomes more significant as regulation becomes more severe, because increasingly stringent regulations will be more likely to result in substantial substitutions taking place.

The uncertainty in estimates of the costs of regulation is compounded by the fact that the regulated industries, the government, and other interested parties have unequal access to data and different incentives governing their approaches to estimation. To begin with, the parties tend to disagree on the emphasis to be placed on short-term, as opposed to long-term effects. Consumers require some time to react to price increases or diminished supply of the regulated substance; the location and utilization of substitutes cannot take place immediately. Plant shutdowns and production cutbacks may cause localized increases in unemployment in the short term, but this may be compensated for by increases in production and employment in the manufacture of substitute products. Thus, emphasis on the short-term "dislocation costs" of a regulation will commonly overestimate the regulation's long-term impact. At the same time, the long-term effects are much more difficult to estimate, particularly if potential technological advances in the production of substitutes are not known at the time regulation of a particular product is proposed.

---

65. The prime example of this problem is the continuing debate over whether the nearly complete ban on the use of DDT in the United States was a sensible or foolhardy decision. Much of the controversy concerns differences over the safety of the substance and differences between the parties on the acceptability of risks. In large part, however, the controversy concerns differences over the magnitude of the economic effects of the ban. *See* OF ACCEPTABLE RISK, *supra* note 49, at 155-73.

66. The recent history of aerosol products provides an example of the secondary adverse health consequences of a health-motivated regulation. Before 1974, VC was used in combination with fluorocarbons in some aerosols. When this use of VC was banned in 1974, no consideration was given to the possible adverse consequences of using a greater quantity of fluorocarbons. Subsequently, fluorocarbons were discovered to threaten the ozone layer in the upper atmosphere, and the use of this chemical in aerosol products will soon be ended. Thus the effect of regulating this use of VC was to aggravate the fluorocarbons problem, albeit for only a short period. On the regulation of VC in aerosols, see text accompanying notes 551-611 *infra*.

The problem of uncertainty is further aggravated by the fact that often the parties with the most accurate information on the costs and effects of regulation have an incentive to withhold or misinterpret that information. In general, the regulated industries have better access to information and more expertise concerning the technological difficulties and direct costs of exposure control than do the regulatory agencies, the unions, or the consumer and environmental groups.[67] To some extent, the industries also have the same advantage regarding the economic value of their substances.[68] The industries also have strong economic and institutional incentives to exaggerate the difficulties and costs of a potential regulation, with the hope of limiting its strength. Subsequent experience often reveals the industries' predictions to have been inflated in this manner.[69]

The imbalance is difficult to rectify. Whereas toxicological research can be regularized and made more reliable by the use of standard test protocols and evaluative techniques, no standard protocols for economic assessments have yet been developed or agreed upon. Governmental agencies are developing analytic capabilities of their own,[70] and they can compel industries to submit necessary data. These capabilities, however, require larger staffs and budgets, and significant legal barriers remain to obtaining the necessary information.[71]

Another means of coping with the imbalance is to discount the industries' representations as to the difficulties and costs of control and as to the economic value of the regulated substance. The shortcoming of this rule is that it does not encourage an end to exaggeration, and it may in fact lead industries to "cry wolf" all the more.[72] On the assumption, however, that industries will continue to overstate their problems under any rule, this rule is an effective way to improve the government's bargaining position.

---

67.   *See, e.g.*, DECISION MAKING IN EPA, *supra* note 58, at 52-54, 57-58. The industries are also better organized to participate in regulatory decisions than is the generally affected public. The general public's interest in a particular decision may be more weighty than an industry's, but there is a considerable cost to organizing. *See generally* M. OLSON, THE LOGIC OF COLLECTIVE ACTION 9-16 (1965). This organizational imbalance has been overcome only partly by the participation of environmental and consumer groups and labor unions in legislative and administrative proceedings.

68.   *See generally* DECISION MAKING FOR REGULATING CHEMICALS, *supra* note 61, at 134-36.

69.   See especially the misrepresentations of the VC and PVC industries regarding the impact of the OSHA standard, discussed at text accompanying notes 272-274, 325-338 *infra*.

70.   *See* DECISION MAKING IN EPA, *supra* note 58, at 51-54, 57-63. For example, OSHA and its companion research agency, the National Institute for Occupational Safety and Health, have been improving their capabilities to assess control possibilities and costs. *See* Hickey & Kearney, Engineering Control Research and Development Plan for Carcinogenic Materials, Research Triangle Institute, Research Triangle Park, North Carolina (Sept. 1977) (draft of study on contract from NIOSH).

71.   Much of the necessary information is withheld from the government or the public on the grounds of trade secrecy claims. There is a great deal of controversy over how trade secrets will be treated in toxic substances regulation.

72.   The rule penalizes an industry which presents data without exaggeration, because the data will be discounted rather than taken at face value.

In sum, the regulatory agency's data concerning the costs of regulation are as imprecise as its information about risks. The technological limits to present control capabilities are uncertain, and the limits to future capabilities are even more so. Only the costs of the readily forseeable controls can be calculated with much confidence. The wider economic and health consequences of regulation are difficult to identify in advance, especially if the regulated substance is in widespread use and if the regulation is stringent. As the agencies approach the task of balancing competing health and economic interests, they have only limited knowledge of the relative economic values at stake.

C. The Balancing Problem: Dilemmas of "Socially Acceptable Risk"

The greatest difficulties in the toxic substances area are in the selection of a level of risk that is somehow acceptable in light of its economic benefits. Even if risks and costs are known with certainty, they still are not fully comparable. Lives cannot be fully valued in dollars, and no satisfactory method exists for expressing one in terms of the other. Furthermore, as the people exposed to harm are not identical to those who bear the costs of control, any control measures transfer resources from the latter to the former. Both of these problems raise value-laden questions of fairness.

Several approaches to the problem of comparing health interests with economic interests have been suggested. One view is that no price can be put on a human life and that no economic benefit justifies causing a person's death. This view does not comport with everyday human behavior, however; people routinely drive automobiles, for example, placing their own and others' lives at risk.[73] Concluding that some trade-off between health and economic interests is socially and ethically acceptable, some theorists have attempted to derive economic values for individual human lives. For example, the "human capital" approach sets the value of a life at the individual's future earnings, or at the individual's net future contribution to the economy.[74] This technique has the obvious disadvantage of failing to value those aspects of life and personality that are not rewarded in the marketplace.

The approach currently in favor among economists and policy analysts focuses on the fact that while people are unwilling to name a dollar sum worth their own death, they apparently are willing to trade economic benefits for increases or decreases in the risk of death for each individual in a large group. A number of studies have examined individuals' "willing-

---

73. *See* Schelling, *The Life You Save May Be Your Own* in PROBLEMS IN PUBLIC EXPENDITURE ANALYSIS 127, 129-33 (S. Chase ed. 1968) [hereinafter cited as *The Life You Save May Be Your Own*].

74. This discussion is derived mainly from *id.* and from Mishan, *Evaluation of Life and Limb: A Theoretical Approach*, 79 J. POLITICAL ECON. 687, 687-90 (1971) [hereinafter cited as *Evaluation of Life and Limb*]. The issues are summarized in DECISION MAKING IN EPA, *supra* note 58, at 219-34.

ness-to-pay" for changes in the risk of death, particularly in hazardous categories of employment.[75] Some have asserted that risk-benefit combinations can be derived from these studies that are socially acceptable and that should be used as benchmarks for legislative, regulatory, and judicial policy making about toxic substances.[76]

Yet there are problems with the basic premise that socially acceptable risk-benefit relationships can be derived in this manner. It is questionable whether *observed* risk-benefit relationships of this kind should be treated as *norms* for toxic substances control or other programs of safety and health protection. For one thing, it is unlikely that the subjects of such employment risk studies were fully informed about their risks; at least not precisely enough to make subtle distinctions that can be extrapolated to larger populations. Second, it is possible that employees in hazardous industries are less adverse to taking risks than the general population. Finally, workers in most hazardous job categories may not have sufficient alternative employment opportunities or sufficient bargaining power to be able to insist on risk premiums that accurately reflect the perceived value of increased risks to their health and safety.

The problems of balancing health and economic values are compounded by the distributional impact of any toxic substances control measures. Although there may be no sharp division between the class of people who obtain the economic benefit of chemical use and the class of people who bear the health risks, some people gain or lose more than others. The employee exposed to vinyl chloride or other toxic substances in the workplace runs greater risks than the investor who never enters the plant. The farmworker exposed to dangerous pesticides bears a higher risk than food-company investors or the consumers of food. One who lives near a plant that emits toxic chemicals to the air or drinking water bears greater risks than another living far away. Which groups are subsidizing which others is often a matter of one's point of view and political values.[77]

A similar distributional issue exists because of the delayed impacts of many toxic substances. In the use of toxic chemicals, the economic benefits accrue quickly, but the adverse health and environmental effects are often delayed by many years. It may be tolerable for one generation to subject

---

75. *The Life You Save May Be Your Own, supra* note 73, at 129-33, 142-44; *Evaluation of Life and Limb, supra* note 74, at 693-95. *See* DECISION MAKING IN EPA, *supra* note 58, at 232-34. *See also* Thaler & Rosen, Value of Saving a Life: Evidence from the Labor Market (unpublished 1975), cited in Kneese & Schulze, *Environment, Health, and Economics—The Case of Cancer,* 67 AM. ECON. REV. 326, 331 (1977) [hereinafter cited as *Environment, Health, and Economics*]. Thaler and Rosen estimate the value of an additional 0.001 risk of death at $260 per year, and consequently put the value of a life at $260,000.

76. *The Life You Save May Be Your Own, supra* note 73, at 158-62. *See generally* Starr, *Benefit-Cost Studies in Socio-technical Systems* in NATIONAL ACADEMY OF ENGINEERING, PERSPECTIVES ON ENVIRONMENTAL RISK DECISION MAKING 17 (1973).

77 *See* Coase, *The Problem of Social Cost,* 3 J. L. & ECON. 1 (1960).

itself to future harms in exchange for present benefits, but severe equity problems are raised if the adverse effects span generations.[78]

D. Summing Up the Decision Problem

Toxic substances regulation, as we have seen, is characterized by ubiquitous problems of technological, medical, and economic uncertainty and by the difficulty of balancing incommensurable interests in standard-setting. It might seem, therefore, that factual analysis is a waste of resources for agencies and other parties affected by regulation. In reality, this is not so. First, although there is a wide range of decisions that an agency may make without being clearly wrong on a factual basis,[79] medical, technological, and economic research serves to eliminate relatively quickly a great number of clearly unsupportable regulatory possibilities. In addition, rough estimates of the health threats and economic significance of a number of chemicals, even though they may be uncertain, permit an agency to set priorities for regulation. Finally, continued pressure for more effective and precise information will continue to stimulate advances in the state of knowledge on these subjects.

Public debate on questions of acceptable risk has been markedly unsophisticated. Some commentators and some statutes call for absolute freedom from exposure to carcinogens regardless of cost.[80] Others emphasize the economic costs of environmental regulation, discounting impacts on health and the environment. For the most part, however, the toxic substances statutes represent a national political judgment that a middle ground should be reached. Those statutes establish ''rule of reason'' balancing tests that will support agency decisions favoring health interests over the economic interests that would result from an unregulated market.[80a] These stan-

---

78. See the chapter on equity considerations in Decision Making for Regulating Chemicals, *supra* note 61, at 121-29.

79. This is the thrust of most discussions of principles for judicial review of agency action regarding health and environmental hazards. *See, e.g.*, Ethyl Corp. v. EPA, 541 F.2d 1, 34, 8 ERC 1785, 1809-1811 (D.C. Cir. 1976). Judicial review is discussed in text accompanying notes 950-998 *infra*.

80. *See, e.g.*, the Delaney Clause in the Food Additives Amendment to the Food, Drug, and Cosmetic Act, 21 U.S.C. § 348(c)(3)(A) (1970), which prohibits the intentional addition to food of any amount of a substance determined to be carcinogenic in man or animal, and § 112(a)(3)(B) of the Clean Air Act, 42 U.S.C. § 7412(a)(3)(B) (West Supp. 1978), which states that a hazardous air pollutant standard must assure ''an ample margin of safety'' to protect health. See text accompanying notes 369-373, 492-494 *infra*.

80a. *See, e.g.* § 6(b)(5) of the Occupational Safety and Health Act, 29 U.S.C. § 655(b)(5) (1970), which specifies that standards protect health ''to the extent feasible.'' This provision, as well as certain others, has been held to be ''technology-forcing,'' *i.e.*, to allow an agency to set standards whose requirements are somewhat beyond the conceded control capabilities of regulated industries, in order to stimulate the development of new devices and to counter the industries' underestimation of present capabilities. See text accompanying notes 213, 322-324 *infra*. *See also* Portland Cement Ass'n v. Ruckelshaus, 486 F.2d 375, 384-85, 5 ERC 1593, 1599 (D.C. Cir. 1973) *cert. denied* 417 U.S. 921 (1974), 423 U.S. 1025 (1975), *reh. denied* 423 U.S. 1092 (1975) (interpreting the technology-forcing character of Clean Air Act § 111, 42 U.S.C. § 7411 (West Supp. 1978).

dards, however, give virtually no guidance on the relative weight to be accorded health and environmental interests in comparison to economic ones, and to date, the agencies' actions reflect Congress's lack of consensus on the issue of acceptable risk.

A measure of guidance to decision makers in the face of uncertainty and lack of consensus is provided by the observation that regulatory decisions involve moral as well as economic values. We may begin with the observation that the sacrifice of an individual for the benefit of a group is acceptable if the benefit served is the group's survival or the fulfillment of some other basic need. The sacrifice is morally unacceptable, however, if it is for no more important benefit than the provision of the luxuries of our consuming society. That some must die so that all can eat is one thing; that some must die so that all can have see-through food packaging is another.[80b] Particularly where non-essential products are concerned, the long-term goal of toxic substances control and the long-term effect of each regulation should be to channel economic growth away from industries hazardous to health and towards safer products and forms of employment.

As the case study in Part II shows, the problems of deciding under uncertainty and of balancing incommensurable interests have pervaded the regulation of VC. Reluctance to face these difficult problems accounts in part for the fact that in more than four years the agencies have set standards for only two of the major sources of exposure to VC. While the standards that have been set and the proposals that have been put forward are by no means totally deficient, there have been significant instances in which the agencies have made factually or logically insupportable conclusions, or in which they have ignored evidence and failed to draw conclusions the evidence virtually demands. In all instances, the agencies have held back from imposing standards that would require any significant economic change in the regulated industries. The industries' profits, volume of production of the regulated substances, and future growth prospects have been virtually unaffected. One may question whether the benefits of VC production and use are substantial enough to justify such extreme deference to the

---

80b. Many value judgments are not so easily made as the distinction between food and food packaging. Typically, economists take the position that neutrality is required at all times in this regard, because of the difficulty of making so many of these value judgments. *See, e.g.*, *Evaluation of Life and Limb, supra* note 74, at 695-96, 703. But the difficulty of making the hard decisions does not require us to avoid making the clearcut ones. And one need not accept the view that the values of a society must be regarded as inviolate. They change in a manner not fully understood, but certainly not free from the influences of groups, such as the business community, with strong financial interests in promoting the materialistic, consuming behavior of the public. As Professor Tribe puts it: "[W]e cannot simply assume that we must stand mute when confronting the ultimate question of whether we want our children, and their children's children, to live in—and *enjoy*—a plastic world." Tribe, *Ways Not to Think About Plastic Trees* in WHEN VALUES CONFLICT 61, 70 (L. Tribe, C. Schelling, & J. Voss eds. 1976) (emphasis in original). *See also* Dorfman, *An Afterword: Humane Values and Environmental Decisions*, in *id.* at 153-73.

industries' market position. This question is pursued in the sections that follow, each detailing the regulatory situation with regard to one or more of the many sources of human exposure to VC.

II
VINYL CHLORIDE CASE STUDY

A. An Introduction to Vinyl Chloride

In the previous section the problems of deciding under uncertainty and determining socially acceptable risks were discussed as they apply to toxic substances regulation generally. In this case study, these problems are considered as they have affected agency decision making with respect to the regulation of vinyl chloride. The case study begins with essential background material on the applications of VC, on the industries which create, transform, and use it, and on its deadly properties. Subsection 1 surveys the chemical's uses and the industries associated with them. Subsection 2 surveys VC's toxicity and the sources of human exposure to it.

1. Vinyl Chloride's Uses and the Associated Industries

The carcinogen vinyl chloride is the basis of the second most widely used plastic in the United States.[81] VC, a gas, is made from petrochemicals and chlorine. When polymerized into polyvinyl chloride, a solid, it is fabricated into a phenomenal array of products. VC was first manufactured commercially in the United States in 1939;[82] by 1976, VC production exceeded 5.5 billion pounds.[83]

The wide variety of uses of PVC is testimony to its adaptability. The major use of PVC is in construction products; other important uses are packaging and consumer products of all kinds. Figure I summarizes the applications of PVC in 1974. Woods, metals, glass, other plastics, and other materials can substitute for nearly all of PVC's uses, but PVC is preferred because of better performance or lower cost.[84] However, there are only a few uses for which no direct substitutes exist.[85]

Several direct uses of VC gas itself once existed, but these have been discontinued. In the late 1940s, VC was tested for use as an anaesthetic, but

---

81. *See Thermoplastics Poised For a Good Five Years*, CHEM. & ENG'R NEWS, Nov. 8, 1976, at 15. Polyethylene is the highest volume plastic. *Id.*

82. *OSHA Permanent Standard for VC, supra* note 1, at 35,890.

83. *Key Chemicals: Vinyl Chloride*, CHEM. & ENG'R NEWS, Aug. 23, 1976, at 13.

84. *Second Thoughts On Using PVC*, CHEMICAL WEEK, July 31, 1974, at 19.

85. U.S. Environmental Protection Agency, Standard Support and Environmental Impact Statement: Emission Standard for Vinyl Chloride 7-4 (Oct. 1975) [hereinafter cited as EPA EIS]; U.S. Environmental Protection Agency, Preliminary Assessment of the Environmental Problems Associated With Vinyl Chloride and Polyvinyl Chloride, Report on the Activities and Findings of the Vinyl Chloride Task Force at app. 1, table 2 (Sept. 1974) [hereinafter cited as EPA Task Force Report].

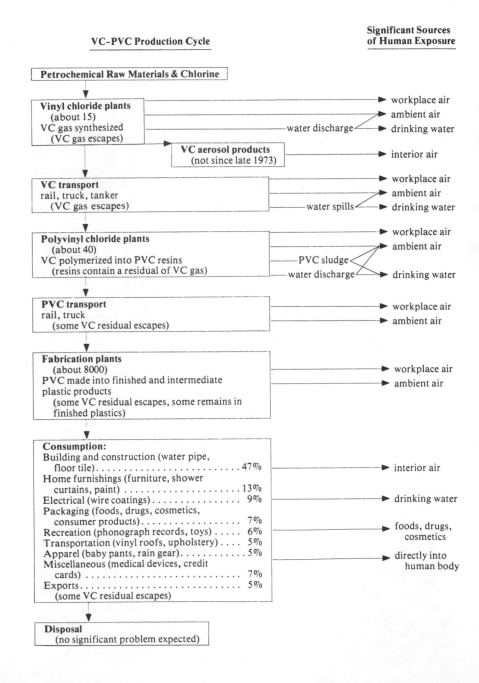

FIGURE I
THE LIFE CYCLE OF
VINYL CHLORIDE–POLYVINYL CHLORIDE

it was rejected because it upset cardiac function.[86] There are also indications that VC was once used as a refrigerant in cooling equipment.[87] Until late 1973, a small percentage of the VC produced was used as an aerosol propellant in some cosmetics, drugs, pesticides, and other consumer products. In 1974, when VC's carcinogenicity became generally known, millions of VC-propelled aerosols were still on the market or in consumer hands. The use of VC in aerosols has since been prohibited.[88]

Figure I illustrates the cycle of VC's creation, transformation, use, and disposal, and the routes of human exposure. There are three industries of central importance. The VC industry produces VC from petrochemicals. The PVC industry polymerizes the gas into the solid plastic, known in its raw form as resin. The fabrication industry converts PVC resins into finished products ready for consumer use or for incorporation into products of other industries. It is in these three industries that the workers are most heavily exposed to VC, and that the known human cancers have occurred.

Outside of these plants, additional people are exposed to VC in two major ways. First, VC emissions escape from factories to the surrounding air.[89] Second, since the polymerization process is imperfect, some VC remains a gas trapped in PVC materials. This residual escapes from the plastic in later production in fabrication plants and beyond, and in subsequent use and disposal.

As one moves through the production cycle of VC and PVC, the number of plants and companies increases, and plants become smaller and more labor intensive. The VC industry is composed of 10 companies operating 15 plants; in 1973, Shell, Dow, and Goodrich together held 56 percent of capacity.[90] In 1975, 23 companies operating 37 plants comprised the PVC industry. Goodrich is the major PVC producer with 15 percent; Firestone, Conoco, Union Carbide, Borden, Diamond Shamrock, and Tenneco each produce between five and nine percent.[91] There are about 8,000 fabrication companies of all sizes.[92] Beyond this point industries cease to be identified primarily by their use of VC.

---

86. Oster, Carr, Krantz, & Sauerweld, *Anesthesia XXVII: Narcosis with Vinyl Chloride*, 8 ANESTHESIOLOGY 359, 361 (1947).

87. 2 F. PATTY, INDUSTRIAL HYGIENE AND TOXICOLOGY 813 (1963).

88. The fate of these aerosols is discussed in the text accompanying notes 551-556 *infra*.

89. Most VC escapes directly into the air. Some leaves the plants in effluent water; most of this VC evaporates into the air. Some, however, enters drinking water. *See* EPA Task Force Report, *supra* note 85, at 5, 10, Appendices at 13; ENVIRONMENTAL PROTECTION AGENCY, PRELIMINARY ASSESSMENT OF SUSPECTED CARCINOGENS IN DRINKING WATER (REPORT TO CONGRESS) 7, 26-30, 35-39 (1975) [hereinafter cited as EPA PRELIMINARY REPORT ON DRINKING WATER CARCINOGENS].

90. OFFICE OF RESEARCH AND DEVELOPMENT, U.S. ENVIRONMENTAL PROTECTION AGENCY, SCIENTIFIC AND TECHNICAL ASSESSMENT REPORT ON VINYL CHLORIDE AND POLYVINYL CHLORIDE 20 (June 1975) [hereinafter cited as EPA SCIENTIFIC AND TECHNICAL REPORT].

91. *Id*. at 21-23.

92. EPA EIS, *supra* note 85, at 1-23.

As the above figures indicate, the VC and PVC industries are substantially concentrated. They are also vertically integrated. In 1972, 34 percent of VC produced was sold to PVC plants owned by VC companies, although this figure had dropped from 61 percent in 1962 as the industries grew.[93]

The fact that the VC and PVC industries contain only a small number of relatively concentrated and integrated firms has made it easy for the industries to speak with one voice in regulatory proceedings regarding the limits of their technological and economic capabilities to control VC exposures. The industrial market structure also makes it difficult to analyze the true costs of control measures and to determine the incidence of those costs on product prices, profits, wages, and other inputs.

Most VC plants are open-air, resembling oil refineries. They are located in populated areas in warm states—principally Louisiana, Texas, Kentucky, and California.[94] PVC plants are enclosed, but still emit VC, and they too are located mostly in populated areas. In addition to the above states, New Jersey, Ohio, and Massachusetts are major PVC-producing states.[95]

Only about one-third of total VC production is polymerized at the site at which it is produced. Most VC must be transported between VC and PVC plants, mainly by rail tank car, and also by tank truck and barge. In addition, PVC resin must be transported between the PVC and fabrication plants; this is done primarily by train and truck.[96]

VC and PVC plants are highly mechanized and employ a relatively small number of workers. At any one time, there are only about 1,000 employees in the VC industry, and only about 5,500 in the PVC industry.[97] Taking into account the normal turnover of workers, about 30,000 employees are estimated to have worked in these industries since 1939.[98] Fabrication plants are more labor intensive. The number of fabrication workers is estimated at 350,000.[99] These workers are subject to much lower exposures of VC than the workers in VC and PVC plants, as the exposure of the fabrication workers comes only from escaping VC residual.[100] The size of the group, however, gives rise to fears that even a low incidence of cancers may claim a large number of lives.

---

93.   Foster D. Snell, Inc., Draft Final Report: Economic Impact Studies of the Effects of Proposed OSHA Standards for Vinyl Chloride, at III-3 (Sept. 13, 1974) [hereinafter cited as Snell Economic Impact Study].

94.   *Id*. at III-2; EPA EIS, *supra* note 85, at 3-31, -39.

95.   EPA SCIENTIFIC AND TECHNICAL REPORT, *supra* note 90, at 21-23.

96.   EPA Task Force Report, *supra* note 85, at 7.

97.   Snell Economic Impact Study, *supra* note 93, at III-4, -8.

98.   N. Ashford *et al.*, *supra* note 5, at 3i-41, -45 (appendix concerning VC regulation in the workplace). The number of cancers found in these workers, while not large in absolute terms, represents an extremely high incidence in the small population.

99.   EPA Task Force Report, *supra* note 85, at 11.

100.   *OSHA Permanent Standard for VC*, *supra* note 1, at 35,892-93.

, The VC and PVC workers are represented primarily by three unions: the United Rubber Workers, the United Steelworkers, and the Oil, Chemical and Atomic Workers. On their own and through the Industrial Union Department of the AFL-CIO, these unions were major participants in setting the VC occupational exposure standard. The fabrication workers are represented by a variety of unions, and some are not unionized at all.

The technological and economic capabilities of the VC, PVC, and fabrication industries to lower the release of VC—in plants, to the surrounding air, and through later-escaping residual in PVC—have been constantly at issue in the regulatory actions described in subsequent sections. The difficulty of predicting the future technological and economic limits to changes in these industries is discussed elsewhere,[101] but here it is useful to give some indication of their clearly demonstrated past and present capabilities.

Without need for any significant technological breakthroughs, in the four years since VC's carcinogenicity became clear, the VC, PVC, and fabrication industries have significantly reduced their releases of VC. In response the regulations or the threat of regulations, the VC and PVC industries have been shown to be able to reduce workplace airborne concentrations of VC from about 250 parts per million (ppm) to about one ppm,[102] to reduce VC emissions to the outside by about 95 percent,[103] and to reduce the VC residual content of food packaging by several orders of magnitude.[104] New plants face no difficulties meeting these lowered levels.[105] Furthermore, there is no sign that the limits of current technologies have been reached and the possibility remains that fundamental technological breakthroughs could occur.

These reductions have been achieved without any significant economic strain on the companies or damage to PVC's market position and future growth prospects. Throughout the 1960s and early 1970s, PVC consumption grew at a staggering rate as prices declined and the number of uses increased.[106] In 1973, the business analysts forecast uninterrupted growth; the major problem experienced at that time was the tight supply of petrochemical raw materials.[107]

---

101. See notes 61-72 *supra*.

102. See text accompanying notes 227, 325-383 *infra*.

103. EPA EIS, *supra* note 85, at 1-4; EPA SCIENTIFIC AND TECHNICAL REPORT, *supra* note 90, at 113-14.

104. See text accompanying note 535 *infra*.

105. *PVC Rolls Out of Jeopardy, Into Jubilation*, CHEMICAL WEEK, Sept. 15, 1976, at 34, 36.

106. *See* Snell Economic Impact Study, *supra* note 93, at III-3, exhibit III-2; EPA EIS, *supra* note 85, at 2-1.

107. *Tight Monomer Supply Plagues PVC Producers*, CHEM. & ENG'R NEWS, May 28, 1973, at 6.

In 1974 and 1975, VC and PVC consumption dropped sharply, marking the first break in the trend of phenomenal growth. The slump, however, was not caused by a consumer response to the revelation of VC's carcinogenicity and to the costs of complying with subsequently-imposed standards. Rather, the slump had two extrinsic causes: (1) attempts in the early 1970s to pass on to consumers the rising costs of petrochemical feedstocks; and (2) the general economic recession in 1974 and 1975, which was particularly severe in the building construction industry, a major user of plastics.[108] The slump was shared equally by all the major plastics.

With the end of the recession and the revival of the housing industry, plastics generally and PVC in particular returned to the prior trend of profitable growth. Presently, new plants are being built to meet anticipated demand, without any apparent hindrance from current and proposed regulations.[109] Hence, it appears that somewhat greater reductions in VC exposure could be demanded of the industries without rendering either current operations or expansion unprofitable.

As the following survey of VC's toxicity will show, there is no basis for thinking the VC hazard has been eliminated by the measures already taken, or that it will be eliminated by the additional measures conceded by the industries to be both technologically and economically within their reach. Further reductions are justified by the medical evidence. The point at which the industries would be seriously burdened economically is, however, impossible to predict reliably.

2.   Health Risks and Sources of Exposure to Vinyl Chloride

The toxic effects of VC are now known better than those of nearly any other industrial chemical. VC's carcinogenicity has been well established by human experience, animal experiments, and other laboratory tests. The bitter experience of occupational exposure has confirmed VC's ability to cause cancers and a host of lesser effects in humans. The risks extend beyond the workers; millions of other people are exposed to VC. This subsection surveys the evidence of VC's toxicity and the extent of human exposure to the chemical.

a.   Acute and chronic human toxicity

Before 1974, when VC had not yet been connected to human cancer, other dangers of the chemical were well known. VC is extremely flammable, and concentrations in air exceeding 40,000 ppm are explosive.[110]

---

108.   Taguchi, *1976 Outlook Brighter in U.S. and European Chemical Industries*, CHEM. ECON. & ENG'R REV., Apr., 1976, at 14; Greek, *Vinyl Chloride May Face Shortages By 1977*, CHEM. & ENG'R NEWS, Aug. 11, 1975, at 8.

109.   *PVC Rolls Out of Jeopardy, Into Jubilation, supra* note 105, at 34.

110.   Haley, *Vinyl Chloride: How Many Unknown Problems?*, 1 J. TOXICOLOGY & ENVT'L HEALTH 47, 49 (1975) [hereinafter cited as *VC: How Many Unknown Problems?*].

Several workers have died from inhaling extremely high concentrations.[111] Exposure to concentrations greater than 8,000 ppm VC causes one to become dizzy, drowsy, disoriented, and eventually unconscious.[112] Lower doses inhaled over a period of a work shift make one prone to deep, dreamless sleep.[113]

Before 1974, VC concentrations of 250 to 300 ppm were common for many job categories in the VC and PVC industries.[114] Among workers exposed to these concentrations for periods of months or years a number of effects had been identified. Many workers suffered enlargement and fibrosis of the liver and spleen.[115] Many exhibited Reynaud's syndrome, characterized by circulatory degeneration in the extremities and by a cold feeling or a feeling of pins and needles in the hands and feet.[116] Many developed sclerdoma, a skin condition, and acroosteolysis, a rare disease characterized by the shrinking of the last bones in the fingers and toes.[117] Although workers who suffered one of these effects did not always suffer the others, the effects were grouped under the name "vinyl chloride disease."[118]

When VC's capacity to cause cancer in humans became clear in 1974, close medical examination of VC and PVC workers identified numerous acute and chronic effects of VC that previously had gone unnoticed. Impaired arterial circulation and fibrosis of the liver and spleen were found to occur at a microscopic level long before they were clinically observable.[119]

---

111. Spirtas, McMichael, Gamble, & Van Ert, *The Association of Vinyl Chloride Exposures With Morbidity Symptoms*, 36 AM. INDUS. HYGIENE ASS'N J. 779 (1975).

112. EPA SCIENTIFIC AND TECHNICAL REPORT, *supra* note 90, at 85; *VC: How Many Unknown Problems?, supra* note 110, at 61.

113. *VC Hearings, supra* note 1, at 40 (testimony of Dr. Marcus Key, Director, National Institute for Occupational Safety and Health).

114. Kramer & Mutchler, *The Correlation of Clinical and Environmental Measurements For Workers Exposed to Vinyl Chloride*, 33 AM. INDUS. HYGIENE ASS'N J. 19 (1972) [hereinafter cited as *Worker Exposure to VC*]; EPA SCIENTIFIC AND TECHNICAL REPORT, *supra* note 90, at 43, 91-94.

115. Lilis, Anderson, Nicholson, Daum, Fischbein, & Selikoff, *Prevalence of Disease Among Vinyl Chloride and Polyvinyl Chloride Workers*, 246 ANNALS N.Y. ACAD. SCI. 22 (1975) [hereinafter cited as *Prevalence of Disease*]; Lange, Jühe, Stein, & Veltman, *Further Results in Polyvinyl Chloride Production Workers*, 246 ANNALS N.Y. ACAD. SCI. 18 (1975) [hereinafter cited as *Further Results*].

116. *Prevalence of Disease, supra* note 115, at 22; *Further Results, supra* note 115, at 18.

117. *Prevalence of Disease, supra* note 115, at 22; *Further Results, supra* note 115, at 18; Sakabe, *Bone Lesions Among Polyvinyl Chloride Production Workers in Japan*, 246 ANNALS N.Y. ACAD. SCI. 78 (1975); *VC: How Many Unknown Problems?, supra* note 110, at 62-63.

118. Veltman, Lange, Jühe, Stein, & Bachner, *Clinical Manifestations and Course of Vinyl Chloride Disease*, 246 ANNALS N.Y. ACAD. SCI. 6 (1975).

119. Maricq, Johnson, Whetstone, & LeRoy, *Capillary Abnormalities in Polyvinyl Chloride Production Workers: Examination By In Vivo Microscopy*, 236 J. AM. MED. ASS'N 1368 (1976); Popper & Thomas, *Alterations of Liver and Spleen Among Workers Exposed to Vinyl Chloride*, 246 ANNALS N.Y. ACAD. SCI. 172 (1975); Thomas & Popper, *Pathology of Angiosarcoma of the Liver Among Vinyl Chloride-Polyvinyl Chloride Workers*, 246 ANNALS

Microscopic examination revealed other changes in liver cells.[120] Some workers displayed a wide variety of abnormal liver function and blood tests.[121] Some suffered impairment of lung function.[122]

The medical researchers had hoped that these observable effects could be used to indicate who is at increased risk of developing cancer and how VC produces its carcinogenic effect. To their disappointment, however, none of these effects correlated well enough with observed cases of liver angiosarcoma or of other cancers to indicate clearly which workers are at increased risk, nor has the knowledge of these effects enabled researchers to explain how VC causes cancer.[123]

b. Human cancers

Throughout the spring of 1974, after the deaths of the four Goodrich workers became known, other companies reported additional angiosarcoma deaths among VC and PVC workers.[124] The toll has risen steadily since then. Thirteen cases of angiosarcoma of the liver had been counted among American workers by July 1974,[125] and a total of 25 cases were known

---

N.Y. ACAD. SCI. 268 (1975); Gedigk, Muller, & Bechtelscheimer, *Morphology of Liver Damage Among Polyvinyl Chloride Production Workers: A Report on 51 Cases*, 246 ANNALS N.Y. ACAD. SCI. 278 (1975).

120.   See sources cited in note 119 *supra.*

121.   Blood platelet count has been down in some, but not all, victims of liver angiosarcoma. Liver function tests show a wide variety of abnormalities. *Prevalence of Disease, supra* note 115; *Further Results, supra* note 115; Veltman, Lange, Jühe, Stein, & Bachner, *supra* note 118; Marsteller, Lelbach, Müller, & Gedigk, *Unusual Splenomegalic Liver Disease as Evidenced by Peritoneoscopy and Guided Liver Biopsy Among Polyvinyl Chloride Production Workers*, 246 ANNALS N.Y. ACAD. SCI. 95 (1975).

122.   Gamble, Liu, McMichael, & Waxweiler, *Effects of Occupational and Nonoccupational Factors on the Respiratory System of Vinyl Chloride and Other Workers*, 18 J. OCCUPATIONAL MED. 659 (1976).

123.   In promulgating the permanent standard for workplaces, OSHA noted the failure to find in blood tests, liver function tests, and certain other examinations a reliable indicator of increased cancer risk. *OSHA Permanent Standard For VC, supra* note 1, at 35,895. Since the fall of 1974, when OSHA's observation was made, there has been little change in the state of knowledge of VC's carcinogenesis. Some hope of identifying VC-induced changes at an early stage is promised by two recent techniques. The first is ultrasonography, a technique for "taking a picture" of internal organs such as the liver and spleen without surgery through a sort of "sonar." This technique can reveal fibrosis and other gross changes to these organs. Taylor, Barrett, Williams, Smith, & Duck, *Preliminary Results of Grey-scale Ultrasonography in the Detection of Vinyl Chloride Related Liver and Spleen Disease*, 69 PROC. ROYAL SOC'Y MED. 292 (1976). Another technique detects microscopic changes in the circulatory system in the fingers. It was reasoned that the Reynaud's syndrome and acroosteolysis would be preceded by subclinical changes, which, if they could be found, would be an indication of increased risk. Maricq, Johnson, Whetstone, LeRoy, *supra* note 119. Neither of these techniques, however, offers any assurance of detecting VC-induced changes before the changes at the cellular level which eventually lead to cancer have already occurred.

124.   Occupational Safety and Health Administration, *Vinyl Chloride: Proposed Standard*, 39 Fed. Reg. 16,896 (1974) [hereinafter cited as *OSHA Proposed Standard for VC*].

125.   *OSHA Permanent Standard for VC, supra* note 1, at 35,891.

worldwide one month later.[126] Although the majority of cases involved workers at PVC plants, other workers were also affected.[127] There were 38 cases worldwide by June 1975,[128] at least 51 cases by December 1976,[129] and at least 68 cases by the spring of 1978.[130]

Although in absolute terms these numbers are not large, the rate of liver angiosarcoma in various groups of PVC workers studied ranges from 400 to 3,000 times the expected incidence in the general population.[131] Since the latency period—the time between initial exposure to VC and the clinical appearance of liver cancer—has been averaging about 20 years, more cases can be expected as the result of high exposures in the 1950s, 1960s, and early 1970s.[132]

Many of the employees who have died of liver angiosarcoma worked as cleaners of the polymerization reactor (the chamber in which VC is converted to PVC) or worked in areas with similarly high VC exposures.[133] These workers probably were the most heavily exposed, in terms of both momentary peaks and sustained averages. The precise levels are not known but are estimated to have included peak exposures of several thousand ppm and an average of 250 to 300 ppm.[134] Other liver angiosarcoma victims presumably had lower, less sustained exposures to VC.[135]

---

126.   *VC Hearings, supra* note 1, at 60-62 (statement of Dr. Joseph K. Wagoner).

127.   Those affected included a worker at a VC plant, a worker who filled pesticide cans with VC propellant, and an accountant and a worker at PVC cloth fabricating plants. *Id*. These last two are assumed to have had very low exposures.

128.   *Id*. at 60; EPA SCIENTIFIC AND TECHNICAL REPORT, *supra* note 90, at 72, 82.

129.   Reported Cases of Angiosarcoma of the Liver Among Vinyl Chloride Polymerization Workers (Dec. 6, 1976) (typewritten tabular data enclosed with letter to the author from Rose Kaminski, Statistician (Health), Illness Effects Section, Division of Surveillance, Hazard Evaluations, and Field Studies, National Institute for Occupational Safety and Health (Dec. 6, 1976)).

130.   Personal communication with Rose M. Kaminski, Statistician (Health), Illness Effects Section, Division of Surveillance, Hazard Evaluations, and Field Studies, National Institute for Occupational Safety and Health, Apr. 18, 1978.

131.   The lower figure is from Heath, Falk, & Creech, *Characteristics of Cases of Angiosarcoma of the Liver Among Vinyl Chloride Workers in the United States*, 246 ANNALS N.Y. ACAD. SCI. 231, 233 (1975). The higher figure is from EPA. EPA, *National Emission Standards for Hazardous Air Pollutants, Proposed Standard for Vinyl Chloride*, 40 Fed. Reg. 59,532 (1975) [hereinafter cited as *EPA Proposed Standard for VC*]. These figures are the result of comparing the rates of angiosarcoma of the liver in workers with the rates in the general population, assuming that the general population cases are not caused by VC. But if, as the remainder of this section suggests, some of the cases in the general population may be caused by nonoccupational VC exposure, then these figures understate the potency of the chemical.

132.   *VC Hearings, supra* note 1, at 25 (statement of Dr. Irving J. Selikoff); Heath, Falk, & Creech, *supra* note 131, at 231.

133.   Nicholson, Hammond, Seidman, & Selikoff, *Mortality Experience of a Cohort of Vinyl Chloride-Polyvinyl Chloride Workers*, 246 ANNALS N.Y. ACAD. SCI. 225, 226-27 (1975). *See also* Fox & Collier, *Mortality Experience of Workers Exposed to Vinyl Chloride Monomer in the Manufacture of Polyvinyl Chloride in Great Britain*, 34 BRIT. J. INDUS. MED. 1 (1977).

134.   *Worker Exposure to VC, supra* note 114.

135.   EPA SCIENTIFIC AND TECHNICAL REPORT, *supra* note 90, at 72, 82.

The long-term risks of VC exposure may not be limited to liver angiosarcoma. One study of PVC workers identified a statistically significant excess incidence of cancers of the brain and the respiratory system.[136] A study of the causes of death among fabrication workers identified no liver angiosarcomas, but it did suggest an increased incidence of cancers of the digestive system among both men and women and the breast and the urinary system in women.[137] Evidence of other effects has appeared in populations other than workers. One study has shown a statistically significant excess of birth defects and central nervous system tumors among the children of families in three Ohio communities that have hosted PVC plants for as long as 28 years.[138]

c. Animal bioassays and other tests for carcinogenicity

VC's carcinogenicity has been confirmed by the results of experiments on animals and by other laboratory tests. VC has been shown to cause cancer in animals both when inhaled and when ingested. The first hint that the chemical causes cancer came from the publication in 1971 of the results of Italian experiments sponsored by the European and American VC and PVC producers. In these tests rats inhaling high concentrations of VC (30,000 ppm) developed cancerous tumors of the skin, lung, and bone.[139] Further tests sponsored by the producers were concluded and reported to the Occupational Safety and Health Administration (OSHA) in early 1974. As shall be seen in the case study of OSHA's standard setting, the data arrived at a crucial time. On February 15, at OSHA's fact-finding hearing on VC, the Italian researchers reported their then-unpublished findings that VC had induced angiosarcoma of the liver in rats inhaling concentrations as low as 250 ppm.[140] On April 15, OSHA received reports from tests conducted in

---

136.   Tabershaw & Gaffey, *Mortality Study of Workers in the Manufacture of Vinyl Chloride and its Polymers*, 16 J. OCCUPATIONAL MED. 509 (1974). *See also* Monson, Peters, & Johnson, *Proportional Mortality Among Vinyl-Chloride Workers*, THE LANCET, Aug. 17, 1974, at 397.

137.   Chaizze, Nichols, & Wong, *Mortality Among Employees of PVC Fabricators*, 19 J. OCCUPATIONAL MED. 623, 628 (1977) [hereinafter cited as *Mortality Among Fabrication Employees*]. The authors noted a number of flaws in the design and data for their study that precluded drawing firm conclusions from it. In particular, it would be useful to follow the population of fabrication workers for some years into the future, as a sufficient latency period may not yet have elapsed for some effects to manifest themselves.

138.   Infanté, *Oncogenic and Mutagenic Risk in Communities with Polyvinyl Chloride Production Facilities*, 271 ANNALS N.Y. ACAD. SCI. 49, 50 (1976). *Cf.* Infanté, McMichael, Wagoner, Waxweiler, & Falk, *Genetic Risks of Vinyl Chloride*, THE LANCET, Apr. 3, 1976, at 734 (finding increased fetal loss among wives of workers exposed to VC).

139.   Viola, Bigotti, & Caputo, *Oncogenic Response of Rat Skin, Lungs, and Bones to Vinyl Chloride*, 31 CANCER RESEARCH 516 (1971) [hereinafter cited as *Oncogenic Response of Rats to VC*].

140.   Occupational Safety and Health Administration, *Emergency Temporary Standard for Exposure to Vinyl Chloride*, 39 Fed. Reg. 12,342 (1974) [hereinafter cited as *OSHA Emergency Temporary Standard for VC*].

Illinois of similar results in mice at the lowest level of exposure then being tested, 50 ppm.[141]

Animal test results stood at this point until early 1975. It was reported then that *ingestion* by rats of as little as approximately 17 milligrams per kilogram of body weight produces liver angiosarcoma and other cancers.[142] Most recently, in September 1976, the results of another round of inhalation experiments demonstrated that VC causes liver angiosarcoma in rats at 25 ppm, and that it causes mammary tumors at one ppm, the lowest concentration yet tested.[143]

The animal experiments also support suspicions that VC causes human cancers other than angiosarcoma of the liver. The experiments have shown increased cancer incidence at many sites other than the liver, including the lungs, spleen, brain, and, as already noted, breast.[144] Experiments demonstrating the induction of cancer in two species other than rats—mice and hamsters—further confirm that VC is carcinogenic.[145] In the animal experiments the subjects were exposed to constant, prolonged doses of VC. The need was noted in mid-1974 for studies of the effects of single and sporadic doses, typical of many humans' exposure.[146] Such a study is now nearing completion, but the results are not yet available.[147]

d. Additional humans at risk

In addition to several hundred thousand workers in VC and PVC production and in PVC fabrication, millions of American have been, and continue to be, exposed to VC. First, about 4.6 million people live within

---

141. *OSHA Proposed Standard for VC, supra* note 124, at 16,896. The results of the Italian tests, also showing the induction of liver angiosarcoma at 50 ppm, were published in early 1975. Maltoni & Lefemine, *Carcinogenicity Bioassays of Vinyl Chloride: Current Results*, 246 ANNALS N.Y. ACAD. SCI. 195 (1975).

142. Maltoni, Ciliberti, Gianni, & Chieco, *Gli Effitti Oncongeni Del Cloruro Di Vinile Somministrato Per Via Orale Nel Ratto (Oncogenic Effects of VC Administered Orally to Rats: Preliminary Report)*, GLI OSPEDALI VITA, Dec., 1975 (unpaginated reprint on file in offices of the *Ecology Law Quarterly*).

143. Memorandum from Cesare Maltoni to the Members of the European Cooperative Group for the Experimental Bio-assays on Vinyl Chloride Carcinogenicity (undated) [hereinafter cited as Maltoni Memorandum].

144. See sources cited in notes 140-143 *supra*.

145. EPA SCIENTIFIC AND TECHNICAL REPORT, *supra* note 90, at 56. In addition, metabolites of VC have been shown to mutate bacteria and yeasts in the "quick tests" for mutagenicity. *See, e.g.*, Loprieno, Barale, Baroncelli, Bartsch, Bronzetti, Cammellini, Corsi, Frezza, Nieri, Leporini, Rosellini, & Rossi, *Induction of Gene Mutations and Gene Conversions by Vinyl Chloride Metabolites in Yeast*, 37 CANCER RESEARCH 253 (1977), and sources cited therein. Mutagenicity as revealed in these tests correlates well with carcinogenicity. *See* McCann & Ames, *supra* note 57; *From Microbes to Men, supra* note 57.

146. *VC Hearings, supra* note 1, at 80-81 (statement of Dr. Theodore R. Torkelson).

147. Telephone interview with Dr. Joseph McLaughlin, Director, Division of Toxicology and Medicine, Consumer Product Safety Commission, Feb. 27, 1978.

five miles of a VC or PVC plant.[148] In 1974, about 220 million pounds of VC escaped into the air surrounding such plants.[149] The plant neighbors appear to have been exposed to more than one ppm less than 10 percent of the time.[150] One air sample, however, measured 33 ppm near a plant,[151] suggesting that there may be short term, localized peak exposures.[152] In addition, VC is found in the sludge waste and water effluent of these plants. VC has been found in sludge at levels as high as 3,000 ppm,[153] and in water effluent as high as 20 ppm.[154] Most of this VC escapes into the air surrounding the plants;[155] some, however, makes its way into drinking water.[156] These VC emissions to the ambient air have been implicated as the cause of increased rates of cancer and birth defects in the surrounding communities.[157]

Another large group of persons is exposed to VC released in transportation. Only about one-third of VC production is polymerized at the site where it is produced. The rest must be shipped between VC and PVC factories under pressure as a liquified gas. About 95 percent of this is shipped in rail tank cars, and the rest in tank trucks, tank vessels, and barges.[158] These tanks may leak, puncture, or explode, sometimes in heavily populated areas.[159] Between 1971 and 1974, there were at least 24 accidental releases of VC from rail tank cars alone.[160] As VC diffuses from the site of a spill or an accident, transportation workers, nearby residents, travellers, and other bystanders can receive short-term exposures to VC concentrations ranging from a few parts per billion (ppb) to thousands of ppm. Transportation workers and emergency personnel such as firemen and police officers may

---

148.   EPA, *National Emission Standard for Hazardous Air Pollutants, Standard for Vinyl Chloride*, 41 Fed. Reg. 46,560 (1976) [hereinafter cited as *EPA Standard for VC*].
149.   EPA SCIENTIFIC AND TECHNICAL REPORT, *supra* note 90, at 18.
150.   *Id.*
151.   *Id.*
152.   *See id.*
153.   EPA Task Force Report, *supra* note 85, at 2.
154.   *Id.*
155.   *Id.*, apps., at 31-32.
156.   See note 89 *supra.*
157.   See sources cited in note 138 *supra.*
158.   EPA Task Force Report, *supra* note 85, at 7.
159.   See note 160 *infra.*
160.   Most of these accidents occurred in Texas and Louisiana, the states with the highest concentrations of VC and PVC facilities. There were several other accidents involving no release. Data on accidents and releases is derived from a computer file of the Department of Transportation which records incidents of hazardous materials leakage or accidents during this period, and from the appendix to H.R. REP. No. 1083, 93d Cong., 2d Sess. 30-34 (1974). One accident, in Fort Wayne, Indiana, necessitated the evacuation of 4,500 people. *Id.* at 32. When a rail tank car ruptures, as much as 30,000 gallons of VC escapes and returns to its gaseous state. The figure for the maximum tank size comes from an interview with Mary Williams, Chemical Engineer, Department of Transportation, Office of Hazardous Materials Operations, Oct. 28, 1976.

be subject to repeated exposures and, if accidents occur in the same places, so may residents and bystanders. These exposures are less sustained than those suffered by VC and PVC workers and plant neighbors, but peak concentrations may reach those experienced by PVC polymerization reactor cleaners, the most heavily exposed occupational group.

Third, people are exposed to VC through consumer products, food, and drinking water. Until late 1973 or early 1974, VC was used as an aerosol propellant in drug, cosmetic, pesticide, and other consumer products.[161] The user of a VC-propelled aerosol product such as a hair spray or a pesticide in a small, enclosed space such as a bathroom may have been exposed to short term concentrations approaching 400 ppm, and persons may have had an average exposure from all VC-propelled products in their homes equivalent to an average exposure of about 16 ppm in the factories.[162] VC has been detected in the air of rooms freshly painted with certain latex paints, but no VC emissions have been detected in a limited sampling of other new PVC products or from automobile interiors.[163] VC leaches into food and beverages from the more than 300 million pounds of PVC packaging and other PVC food-contact materials used annually.[164] VC also enters drinking water from raw water supplies and by leaching from increasingly common PVC pipe.[165] One study estimates average American daily human intake of VC through food, water, and air at 34 micrograms.[166]

The hazardousness of non-occupational exposures to VC is even less well understood than the risk to the workers. The danger from inhaling extremely low concentrations of VC, or from single or sporadic exposures to high VC concentrations, is unknown. Similarly, the relative risks of ingesting and inhaling VC are unknown.[167] Thus the urgency of reducing or eliminating these sources of exposure is impossible to assess.

---

161. See text accompanying notes 551-556 *infra.*

162. Gay, Lonneman, Bridbord, & Moran, *Measurement of Vinyl Chloride from Aerosol Sprays,* 246 ANNALS N.Y. ACAD. SCI. 286, 294-95 (1975).

163. Environmental Protection Agency, Office of Toxic Substances, Sampling and Analysis of Selected Toxic Substances: Task III—Vinyl Chloride, Secondary Sources, table 6, at 21 (Apr. 1976).

164. Food and Drug Administration, *Vinyl Chloride Polymers in Contact with Food, Notice of Proposed Rulemaking,* 40 Fed. Reg. 40,529, 40,530 (1975) [hereinafter cited as *FDA Proposed Rules for Food-Contact PVC*].

165. EPA SCIENTIFIC AND TECHNICAL REPORT, *supra* note 90, at 38-39; EPA PRELIMINARY REPORT ON DRINKING WATER CARCINOGENS, *supra* note 89, at 40-44; EPA Task Force Report, *supra* note 85, at 7, 19.

166. EPA SCIENTIFIC AND TECHNICAL REPORT, *supra* note 90, at 43.

167. *See* Withey & Collins, *A Statistical Assessment of the Quantitative Uptake of Vinyl Chloride Monomer from Aqueous Solution,* 2 J. TOXICOLOGY & ENVT'L HEALTH 311 (1976); Withey, *The Pharmacodynamics and Uptake of Vinyl Chloride Monomer Administered by Various Routes to Rats,* 1 J. TOXICOLOGY & ENVT'L HEALTH 381 (1976). In the former article, the authors estimate that for rats, 0.9 micrograms of VC in the daily intake of water is approximately equal to inhaling 6 ppm for eight hours. They caution against any direct extrapolation to human equivalences. Withey & Collins, *supra,* at 319-20.

B.   Vinyl Chloride in the Workplace—Occupational
Safety and Health Act

1.   The Key Issues for OSHA

As stated at the outset of this Article, the first evidence of VC's carcinogenicity in humans was a series of reports that PVC workers had developed angiosarcoma of the liver, an extremely rare form of cancer.[168] The relationship between VC and cancer and other health effects in workers has led to the regulation of the chemical by the Occupational Safety and Health Administration (OSHA). OSHA's regulation of VC was the earliest and most important of the agency responses to the VC hazard. The case study begins with a review of the history of OSHA's regulation and an analysis of the logic of the final VC workplace standard.

The protection of workers in VC, PVC, and fabrication plants is the responsibility of OSHA, part of the Department of Labor. In regulating a toxic substance under the 1970 Occupational Safety and Health Act (OSH Act)[169] the agency must set the most protective standard that is "feasible."[170] The feasibility requirement means that a standard must reflect at least a rough assessment and balancing of the health benefits it secures and the economic costs it imposes.[171]

In April 1974, about two months after the realization that VC causes human cancer, OSHA set an emergency temporary standard for worker exposure in VC and PVC plants.[172] This standard, in effect while a permanent standard was being prepared,[173] reduced the permissible VC exposure ceiling from 500 to 50 ppm. In October 1974, OSHA promulgated a permanent standard lowering the permissible exposure further, to a one ppm average, the level which the agency determined to be the lowest feasible.[174] In April 1975, after the Second Circuit Court of Appeals rejected industry objections,[175] the standard became effective.[176] Since then, VC and PVC plants have gradually approached full compliance with the one ppm limit. Despite industry claims that imposition of the standard would have disas-

---

168.   See text accompanying notes 124-130 *supra*.

169.   Pub. L. No. 91-596, 81 Stat. 1590, 29 U.S.C. §§ 651-678 (1970).

170.   OSH Act § 6(b)(5), 29 U.S.C. § 655(b)(5) (1970).

171.   *See generally* Currie, *OSHA*, 1 AM. BAR FOUNDATION RESEARCH J. 1107 (1976); Berger & Riskin, *Economic and Technological Feasibility in Regulating Toxic Substances Under the Occupational Safety and Health Act of 1970*, 7 ECOLOGY L. Q. 285 (1978).

172.   *OSHA Emergency Temporary Standard for VC, supra* note 140.

173.   *See* OSH Act § 6(c)(2), 29 U.S.C. § 655(c)(2) (1970).

174.   29 C.F.R. § 1910.1017 (1977). *See OSHA Permanent Standard for VC, supra* note 1.

175.   Society of the Plastics Indus., Inc. v. OSHA, 509 F.2d 1301 (2d Cir. 1975), *cert. denied sub nom.* Firestone Plastics Co. v. United States Dep't of Labor, 421 U.S. 992 (1975).

176.   Occupational Safety and Health Administration, *Occupational Safety and Health Standards, Standard for Exposure to Vinyl Chloride, Effective Date*, 40 Fed. Reg. 13,211 (1975) (promulgating the court-ordered April 1, 1975 effective date).

trous economic consequences, the standard has in fact been implemented with relative ease.

OSHA deserves credit for acting promptly to regulate VC, and the standard it set significantly reduces the workers' cancer risk. However, the evidence then available to OSHA and the policies of the statute would have supported a standard more stringent than the one set. This section concludes with the observation that OSHA's interpretation of what is a feasible standard under OSH Act was overly cautious and that more rigorous standards are required for the protection of workers from carcinogenic hazards.

2. The Statute: Substantive Criteria for Standard Setting

The primary purpose of OSH Act is "to assure so far as possible every working man and woman in the nation safe and healthful working conditions."[177] The statute divides responsibility for accomplishing this purpose between two agencies. The Secretary of Labor is authorized to set several kinds of safety and health standards,[178] to inspect workplaces,[179] cite violations,[180] and propose penalties and abatement periods.[181] The Secretary has delegated these powers to OSHA.[182] The statute gives a second agency, the Occupational Safety and Health Review Commission (OSHRC), the authority to adjudicate *de novo*, at the request of the cited employer or the affected employees, any violation OSHA alleges and any penalty or abatement period OSHA proposes.[183] OSHRC probably has the final say on a standard's meaning when the two agencies put forward conflicting but reasonable interpretations of its requirements.[184]

There have been three OSHA standards for VC. The most important is the "permanent standard," set in late 1974 and currently in effect.[185] There

---

177. OSH Act § 2, 29 U.S.C. § 651 (1970).
178. *Id.* §§ 4(b)(2), 6, 29 U.S.C. §§ 653(b)(2), 655 (1970).
179. *Id.* § 8(a), 29 U.S.C. § 657(a) (1970).
180. *Id.* § 9(a), 29 U.S.C. § 658(a) (1970).
181. *Id.* § 10(a), 29 U.S.C. § 659(a) (1970).
182. 29 C.F.R. § 1910.4(a) (1977), pursuant to OSH Act § 6(a), 29 U.S.C. § 655(a) (1970).
183. OSH Act §§ 8, 10, 29 U.S.C. §§ 659, 660 (1970).
184. This Article is concerned primarily with OSHA's responsibilities and performance in setting the VC standard. The implementation of an OSHA standard, however, sometimes raises problems of its interpretation. There is a dispute among the circuit courts as to whether OSHA or OSHRC has the power to interpret the meaning of words such as "feasible" when used in a standard itself. The predominant and better view is that, when OSHA and OSHRC both put forth reasonable interpretations, a court should defer to OSHRC's view. *See* Currie, *supra* note 171, at 1119-20. *But see* Berger & Riskin, *supra* note 171, at 310.
185. OSH Act § 6(b), 29 U.S.C. § 655(b) (1970). The statute does not call these standards "permanent," nor obviously are they impervious to amendment or repeal. However, the Conference Report and participants in OSHA standard setting refer to the § 6(b) standards as "permanent standards," to distinguish them from the two kinds of interim standards discussed in notes 186-187 *infra*. *See, e.g.*, H.R. REP. NO. 1765, 91st Cong., 2d Sess. 3-4 (1970), *reprinted in* [1970] U.S. CODE CONG. & AD. NEWS 5228, 5230 [hereinafter cited as OSHA CONFERENCE REPORT].

were two prior standards: a "national consensus standard" set in 1971 and directed only at VC's acute and chronic effects,[186] and an "emergency temporary standard" set in early 1974 to provide some immediate protection against VC's newly discovered carcinogenicity.[187] The following discussion examines the statute's substantive criteria for these standards, starting with the most complex and most important.

a. Permanent standards

Section 6(b) of the statute authorizes OSHA to set permanent standards for occupational exposure to toxic substances.[188] OSHA may set a standard on its own initiative,[189] in response to the petitions of employees or employers,[190] or in response to the recommendations of the National Institute for Occupational Safety and Health (NIOSH), which also was established by OSH Act.[191] Under section 6(b)(5) a standard for a toxic substance must be set at the level

> which most adequately assures, to the extent feasible, on the basis of the best available evidence, that no employee will suffer material impairment of health or functional capacity even if such employee has regular exposure to the hazard dealt with by such standard for the period of his working life. . . . In addition to the attainment of the highest degree of health and safety protection for the employee, other considerations shall be the latest available scientific data in the field, [and] the feasibility of the standards . . . .[192]

This passage and its legislative history express Congress's strong protective and precautionary purposes. The House Report states: "It is not

---

186. 29 C.F.R. § 1910.93, table G-1 (1973), *promulgated at* 36 Fed. Reg. 10,446. The national consensus standard for VC was superseded by the emergency temporary standard, and in turn, by the permanent standard, codified in 29 C.F.R. § 1910.1017 (1977). The 400-odd national consensus standards for air contaminants still in effect have been recodified in 29 C.F.R. § 1910.1000, table Z-1 (1977). These standards were promulgated pursuant to OSH Act § 6(a), 29 U.S.C. § 655(a) (1970).

187. *OSHA Emergency Temporary Standard for VC, supra* note 140 (then codified in 29 C.F.R. § 1910.93), replacing the national consensus standard in *id.* § 1910.93, table Z-1. In turn, the emergency temporary standard was replaced by the permanent standard, 29 C.F.R. § 1910.1017 (1977).

188. OSH Act § 6(b)(5), 29 U.S.C. § 655(b)(5) (1970).

189. *Id.* § 6(b)(1), 29 U.S.C. § 655(b)(1) (1970).

190. *Id.*

191. *Id.* OSH Act established NIOSH as an institute in the Department of Health, Education, and Welfare and gave it duties to aid OSHA in the development and implementation of occupational safety and health standards. *Id.* §§ 20-22, 29 U.S.C. §§ 669-671 (1970). One of NIOSH's duties is to develop "criteria documents" for toxic substances

> which will describe exposure levels that are safe for various periods of employment, including but not limited to the exposure levels at which no employee will suffer impaired health or functional capacities or diminished life expectancy as a result of his work experience.

Id. § 20(a)(3), 29 U.S.C. § 669(a)(3) (1970).

192. *Id.* § 6(b)(5), 29 U.S.C. § 655(b)(5) (1970).

intended that [OSHA] be paralyzed by debate surrounding diverse medical opinions."[193] In addition, the mandate to set the standard that "most adequately assures" lifelong health and to seek the "highest degree" of protection indicates OSHA's duty to resolve uncertainties about the existence of danger in the employees' favor, to some degree at least.

The courts have emphasized the precautionary nature of this section. The leading case is *Industrial Union Department, AFL-CIO v. Hodgson*,[194] in which the District of Columbia Circuit Court of Appeals reviewed challenges to the first permanent standard, for asbestos.[195] The court observed that the statute requires OSHA to base standards upon conclusions drawn both from well-established data and from uncertain information "on the frontiers of scientific knowledge."[196] The court stated that OSHA's decision making necessarily involves a mixture of conventional fact-finding and policy judgments that are essentially legislative in character.[197] Commenting on OSHA's determination to set the asbestos standard at a relatively low level, despite the objections of the industries, the court stated: "Inasmuch as the protection of the health of employees is the overriding concern of [the Act], this choice is doubtless sound, but it rests in the final analysis on an essentially legislative policy judgment, rather than a factual determination, concerning the relative risks of underprotection as compared to overprotection."[198] Two other circuits have adopted similar approaches to OSHA's treatment of uncertain health information.[199]

Only the requirement that a standard be "feasible" qualifies the employee's right to complete protection from harm.[200] The feasibility require-

---

193. H.R. REP. No. 1291, 91st Cong., 2d Sess. 18 (1970) [hereinafter cited as HOUSE REPORT].

194. 499 F.2d 467 (D.C. Cir. 1974). The case was decided while OSHA was preparing the VC standard.

195. 29 C.F.R. § 1910.1001 (1977).

196. 499 F.2d at 474.

197. *Id*. at 474-75.

198. *Id*. at 475.

199. Society of the Plastics Indus., Inc. v. OSHA, 509 F.2d 1301 (2d Cir. 1975) (vinyl chloride standard); Synthetic Organic Chem. Mfrs. Ass'n v. Brennan, 506 F.2d 385 (3d Cir. 1974), *cert. denied* 423 U.S. 830 (1975), *reh. denied* 423 U.S. 866 (1975) (14 carcinogens); American Iron and Steel Inst. v. OSHA, — F.2d —, 6 OSHC 1451 (3d Cir. 1978).

200. The use of the term "feasible" in a standard itself must not be confused with its use in the statute; the two uses have entirely different meanings. The meaning of the term when used in a standard is explored in Berger & Riskin, *supra* note 171, at 334-45. Here it is enough to say that the term "feasible" in a standard puts over until enforcement proceedings a determination of whether an employer must use engineering and work practice controls or whether it may rely on respirators to protect employees. At that stage, OSHRC, not OSHA, has the primary role in interpreting the term and in determining what control measures are required. See the cases interpreting the noise standard, 29 C.F.R. § 1910.95 (1977). The leading cases are Turner Co. v. Sec'y of Labor, 561 F.2d 82 (7th Cir. 1977), and two Commission decisions, Continental Can Co., 4 BNA OCC. SAF. & H. CASES 1451 (Rev. Comm. 1976); Castle & Cooke Foods, 5 BNA OCC. SAF. & H. CASES 1435 (Rev. Comm. 1977). From this point on, the use of the term

ment was added to section 6(b)(5) by the Senate Committee, on the suggestion of Senator Javits; the requirement appears explicitly nowhere else in the
statute. An explanatory comment by the Senator, in his individual views
attached to the Report, states:

> As a result of this amendment, the Secretary, in setting standards, is
> expressly required to consider feasibility of proposed standards.
> This is an improvement over [the section in the absence of the
> amendment], which might be interpreted to require absolute health
> and safety in all cases, regardless of feasibility . . . .[201]

In setting permanent standards for other toxic substances before the VC
hazard was recognized, OSHA took the position without discussion that it
must consider both the technological difficulty and the economic cost of
reducing a hazard in determining the stringency of a standard.[202] Several
unions have challenged OSHA's authority to consider economic factors, but
the courts have upheld OSHA's position.[203]

Industrial Union Department is the key case interpreting the feasibility
requirement.[204] The unions contended that in setting the permanent standard
for asbestos dust OSHA should not have considered the employers' cost of
compliance. The court rejected this claim, citing Senator Javits' commentary[205] and stating this doctrine:

> The thrust of these remarks would seem to be that practical con-
> siderations can temper protective requirements. Congress does not
> appear to have intended to protect employees by putting their em-
> ployers out of business—either by requiring protective devices un-
> available under existing technology or by making financial viability
> generally impossible.[206]

On the other hand, the court stated:

> Standards may be economically feasible even though, from the
> standpoint of employers, they are financially burdensome and affect
> profit margins adversely. Nor does the concept of economic feasibil-
> ity guarantee the continued existence of individual employers. It

---

"feasible" in a standard itself will be placed in quotation marks, to distinguish the use of the
term in the statutory sense.

201. S. REP. NO. 1282, 91st Cong., 2d Sess. 58 (1970) (Individual Views of Mr. Javits),
reprinted in [1970] U.S. CODE CONG. & AD. NEWS 5177, 5222 [hereinafter cited as SENATE
REPORT].

202. This view is correct, although the statute and the legislative history are by no means
explicit on the matter. See the discussion of the standards for asbestos and for the 14 carcinogens treated as a group in Berger & Riskin, *supra* note 171, at 311-18.

203. Industrial Union Dep't, AFL-CIO v. Hodgson, 499 F.2d 467 (D.C. Cir. 1974); AFL-
CIO v. Brennan, 530 F.2d 109 (3d Cir. 1975). The later case, on the standard for power presses,
was decided subsequent to the setting of the VC standard.

204. 499 F.2d 467 (D.C. Cir. 1974).

205. See text accompanying note 201 *supra*.

206. 499 F.2d at 477-78.

would appear to be consistent with the purposes of the Act to envisage the economic demise of an employer who has lagged behind the rest of the industry in protecting the health and safety of employees and is consequently financially unable to comply with the new standards as quickly as other employers.[207]

These statements envision a balancing of the value of reduced risk against the cost of controls, in which the acceptable severity of the burden on an industry depends on the severity of the health harms to be avoided. The stringency of the standard need not be limited by the technological or financial capabilities of the weakest employers in an industry. The statute explicitly provides means such as variances through which an individual employer may obtain some relief for its particular hardship.[208] The standard, however, must not impose technological or economic burdens that are unwarranted by the hazard to be avoided. Only in the relatively few situations where the danger is extreme and the economic value of the regulated activity is slight would a standard that closes a whole industry be justified.[209]

In *Industrial Union Department*, the unions had objected to OSHA's setting a single compliance date for the asbestos standard regardless of the possibility that some of the industries using the substance could feasibly comply earlier than the specified date. OSHA had stated only that "reasons of practical administration" precluded the setting of multiple compliance

---

207. *Id.* at 478 (footnote omitted).

208. A temporary variance called a "temporary extension order" is available if an employer establishes (1) that it cannot comply with a standard because of the unavailability of materials, equipment, or trained personnel, or because modifications to facilities require additional time, (2) that it is taking "all available" protective measures, and (3) that it has a plan to comply "as quickly as practicable." This extension may be granted for only one year at a time and for no more than a total of three years. OSH Act § 6(b)(6)(A), 29 U.S.C. § 655(b)(6)(A) (1970). It is available only for relief of technological hardship; the Conference Report states: "Economic hardship is not to be a consideration for qualification for a temporary extension order." CONFERENCE REPORT, *supra* note 185, at 35. *See* Industrial Union Dep't, AFL-CIO v. Hodgson, 499 F.2d at 478 n.23.

A "permanent variance" is also available, permitting an employer to use measures other than those specified in a standard, so long as those measures provide equivalent safety and health protection. OSH Act § 6(d), 29 U.S.C. § 655(d) (1970). This provision simply permits an employer to use the least costly means of providing a required level of protection. It does not authorize consideration of costs to lessen the level of protection itself.

A third means of relieving individual hardship is the requirement that an employer be allowed a "reasonable time" to abate a violation. *Id.* § 10(c), 29 U.S.C. § 659(c) (1970). To some extent this provision allows for consideration of an employer's economic difficulties.

209. *See* AFL-CIO v. Brennan, 530 F.2d 109 (3d Cir. 1975):

We do not question that there are industrial activities involving hazards so great and of such little social utility that the Secretary would be justified in concluding that their total prohibition is proper if there is no technologically feasible method of eliminating the operational hazard.

Id. at 121. The court's discussion of economic feasibility immediately following suggests that the above observations apply to that issue as well as to technological feasibility. *Id.* at 122-23. *See* Berger & Riskin, *supra* note 171, at 322-23.

dates. The court remanded the question to the agency, holding that compliance could be postponed no longer than feasibility requires, and that OSHA's statement was an inadequate explanation of the impracticability of determining the feasibility of earlier compliance dates for some industries.[210] The general formulation, and its application in this case, however, leave many questions about feasibility unanswered. *Industrial Union Department* does not indicate how OSHA should weigh incommensurable health and economic interests, except to say that feasibility considerations should not compromise health protection needlessly.[211] The case does not clarify how strongly standards may force the development of new technology nor how heavily they may burden an industry's economic position when lives are at stake. As shall be seen below, OSHA's regulation of VC does not greatly illuminate the appropriate terms of trade between health benefits and economic burdens. Although the Second Circuit Court of Appeals narrowed the agency's range of consideration somewhat in its review of the VC standard,[212] substantial doctrinal questions remain open today.

In addition, the *Industrial Union Department* formulation does not indicate how OSHA should decide questions of a standard's feasibility in the frequent case where there are gaps in the technological and economic data needed for a firm determination of the costs of control. This was one of the major issues in the regulation of VC. As shall be seen below, OSHA held, and the Second Circuit agreed, that the agency need not have certain knowledge that a particular level of control can be accomplished at a particular cost. Within limits, OSHA may base the conclusion that a standard is feasible, *i.e.*, that its requirements are warranted, on uncertain and suggestive evidence of an industry's technological and economic capabilities.[213] This view is consistent with the protective purposes of the

---

210. Industrial Union Dep't, AFL-CIO v. Hodgson, 499 F.2d at 480-81.

211. *See id*. at 479.

212. Society of the Plastics Indus., Inc. v. OSHA, 509 F.2d 1301 (2d Cir. 1975). See text accompanying notes 322-324 *infra*.

213. One case subsequent to the regulation of VC bears significantly on the limits to OSHA's power to force the development of new controls. In 1976, OSHA established a permanent standard for coke oven emissions. 29 C.F.R. § 1910.1029 (1977). The standard sets an exposure limit and specifies the use of particular equipment and work practices. Recognizing that the use of these control measures would not be sufficient to meet the exposure limit at all facilities, OSHA also required the employers to carry out a program to research, develop, and install new controls, until the limit was met. The Third Circuit Court of Appeals held that OSH Act did not empower the agency to impose such an "open-ended" requirement on the employers. The court reaffirmed that OSHA may force the development and use of new technology, but only to the extent that a new technique already "looms on today's horizon." American Iron & Steel Inst. v. OSHA, — F.2d —, 6 OSHC 1451, 1461 (3d Cir. 1978). The court did not attempt to define the rather vague concept contained in the quoted phrase. Thus, although OSHA cannot require open-ended commitments of the kind set in the coke oven emission standards (at least in the Third Circuit), the precise limits on the agency's power to force technological and economic change are still unclear.

statute and complements the rule for resolving medical uncertainties.[214] It encourages industries, which have better information than the government or the unions about their control capabilities, to come forward with all available data relevant to feasibility. The contrary rule would encourage industries to withhold such data.

As the discussion thus far indicates, OSHA has substantial discretion to base permanent standards on uncertain data and to resolve doubts in favor of greater protection, provided the agency adequately supports and explains its decisions. The statute also gives OSHA substantial discretion on the form of standards. OSHA may set standards that establish performance requirements, such as a particular concentration of a chemical in workplace air, standards that specify the use of particular means of emission control or personal protection, or standards that are combinations of the two types.[215] Most of the early standards for toxic substances establish permissible airborne concentrations, either as ceiling values not to be exceeded or as averages to be calculated over a workshift (time-weighted averages). Employers must meet the levels by using "feasible" engineering and work practice controls; where the level cannot be achieved by such controls, employers must have employees wear respirators.[216]

b. National consensus standards

Congress recognized that permanent standards could not be established immediately after the passage of OSH Act. In order to guarantee a minimum level of protection while the need for permanent standards was investigated, section 6(a) of the statute directed OSHA by 1972 to adopt as federal regulations, without any requirements for rulemaking proceedings, any existing "national consensus standards."[217] These are safety and health standards developed prior to the passage of OSH Act, generally by industry-funded trade associations or research organizations, and voluntarily agreed

---

214. See text accompanying notes 191-199 *supra*.

215. The statute defines an "occupational safety and health standard" as "a standard which requires conditions, or the adoption or use of one or more practices, means, methods, operations, or processes, reasonably necessary or appropriate to provide safe or healthful employment and places of employment." OSH Act § 3(8), 29 U.S.C. § 652(8) (1970). "Conditions" allows the promulgation of performance standards; the other phrases permit the promulgation of specifications standards.

The section addressed specifically to toxic substances control re-emphasizes this point. It states: "Whenever practicable, the standard promulgated shall be expressed in terms of objective criteria and of the performance desired." *Id.* § 6(b)(5), 29 U.S.C. § 655(b)(5) (1970).

There are several other pertinent characteristics of permanent standards. A standard may provide for warning signs and labels and may require employers to furnish periodic medical examinations for their employees. OSH Act § 6(b)(7), 29 U.S.C. § 655(b)(7) (1970). It may also require employers to keep records of exposure monitoring, medical examinations, and other information, and to make the records available to OSHA and the employees. *Id.* §§ 6(b)(7), 8(c)(1), 29 U.S.C. §§ 655(b)(7), 657(c)(1) (1970).

216. *See* 29 C.F.R. § 1910.1000(e) (1977) (national consensus standards for air contaminants). *See also id.* § 1910.1001(c) (permanent standard for asbestos).

217. OSH Act § 6(a), 29 U.S.C. § 655(a) (1970). A national consensus standard must meet

to by individual companies.[218] In 1971, OSHA adopted en masse some 400 such standards for air contaminants, including one for VC.[219] These standards merely codified contemporary industrial practice, dissatisfaction with which was the motive for passing OSH Act. The standards generally were set at levels necessary to prevent acute and chronic effects. They were not designed to protect against the long-term effects of lower doses, which largely had not been investigated. The Senate and House Committees made clear that national consensus standards were not substitutes for more stringent permanent standards when further research demonstrated the need for a higher level of protection.[220]

c. Emergency temporary standards

Section 6(c) empowers OSHA to set an "emergency temporary standard" (ETS) when it is "necessary" in order to "protect" employees from "grave danger" due to new or newly-discovered hazards.[221] An ETS may be promulgated without advance notice or opportunity for comment, although it must be accompanied by a statement explaining OSHA's reasons for concluding that it is needed.[222] It is effective immediately upon publication. It also serves as the proposal for a permanent standard, which must be promulgated within six months.[223]

It appears that an ETS, like a permanent standard, must be feasible, *i.e.*, that its requirements must be set with regard to a balancing of health benefits and control costs.[224] The focus of the analysis, however, is on the health effects of exposure and costs of regulation during the period needed

---

two requirements. First, it must have been "adopted and promulgated by a nationally recognized standards-producing organization under procedures whereby it can be determined by [OSHA] that persons interested and affected by the scope or provisions of the standard have reached substantial agreement on its adoption." Second, it must have been "formulated in a manner which afforded an opportunity for diverse views to be considered." *Id.* § 3(9), 29 U.S.C. § 652(9) (1970).

218. SENATE REPORT, *supra* note 201, at 5-6, [1970] U.S. CODE CONG. & AD. NEWS at 5181-82; HOUSE REPORT, *supra* note 193, at 16-17.

219. 36 Fed. Reg. 10,466 (1971). See note 186 *supra*.

220. SENATE REPORT, *supra* note 201, at 6; HOUSE REPORT, *supra* note 193, at 17.

221. OSH Act § 6(c)(1), 29 U.S.C. § 655(c)(1) (1970).

222. *Id.* § 6(e), 29 U.S.C. § 655(e) (1970). *See* Dry Color Mfrs. Ass'n v. Dep't of Labor, 486 F.2d 98, 104 (3d Cir. 1973).

223. OSH Act § 6(c)(2)-(3), 29 U.S.C. § 655(c)(2)-(3) (1970). The ETS expires if a permanent standard has not been promulgated within six months. If a permanent standard is set within this period, the ETS remains effective until the permanent standard goes into effect. Since OSHA may delay the effective date of the permanent standard by as long as 90 days, *id.* § 6(b)(4), 29 U.S.C. § 655(b)(4) (1970), the ETS may be in effect for as long as nine months. If the effectiveness of the permanent standard is delayed longer by a judicial stay pending review, *id.* § 6(f), 29 U.S.C. § 655(f) (1970), the ETS remains in effect for this period. *See id.* § 6(c)(2), 29 U.S.C. § 655(c)(2)(1970).

224. The statute and the legislative history are not explicit on this issue. However, there is no reason to believe that Congress intended to preclude OSHA from considering economic factors in setting an ETS and then to allow the agency to consider such factors immediately thereafter in establishing a permanent standard.

to prepare a permanent standard. In this balancing, the agency must not ignore the health effects of exposure in the regulatory interval, even though they may not manifest themselves for many years. On the other side of the ledger, a given level of control is more difficult and more expensive for an industry to achieve in the short run than in the long run. Thus an ETS generally will be less stringent than the permanent standard that follows.[225]

3. OSHA's Early Regulation of VC: The National Consensus Standard

Prior to the enactment of OSH Act, the VC and PVC industries had established their own standard for employees' exposure to VC, an exposure ceiling of 500 ppm. The standard had been developed by the American Conference of Government and Industrial Hygienists (ACGIH) in 1946 with only VC's acute effects on the liver in mind.[226] In the 1960s, the concentrations prevailing in these plants averaged between 200 and 300 ppm for the most highly exposed workers, although peak concentrations occurred that were more than an order of magnitude higher.[227] Self-enforcement was not sufficient to assure compliance with the 500 ppm ceiling.

In 1971, OSHA adopted the 500 ppm standard as a national consensus standard.[228] In 1972, ACGIH recommended that the standard be lowered to 200 ppm, in view of developing information on VC's chronic liver toxicity.[229] OSHA took no action on this recommendation, and the occupational standard remained at 500 ppm until the discovery of VC's human carcinogenicity in the spring of 1974.

4. Regulation of VC as a Carcinogen: The Emergency Temporary Standard

The preparation of a more stringent standard for exposure to VC began within days of the disclosure in January 1974 of liver cancers among the Goodrich workers. In April, just two months later, OSHA promulgated an ETS that reduced the exposure ceiling to 50 ppm.[230] This standard remained in effect until superseded by the permanent standard in April 1975.[231] The ETS deserves a close examination both in its own right and in light of its

---

225. There are two cases which have struck down emergency temporary standards, although on grounds other than feasibility. Florida Peach Growers Ass'n, Inc. v. United States Dep't of Labor, 489 F.2d 120 (5th Cir. 1974) (vacating the ETS for use of certain pesticides); Dry Color Mfrs. Ass'n, Inc. v. Dep't of Labor, 486 F.2d 98 (3d Cir. 1973) (vacating the ETS for two of 14 carcinogens).

226. *VC Hearings, supra* note 1, at 40 (statement of Dr. Marcus Key, Director, National Institute for Occupational Safety and Health). *See* AMERICAN CONFERENCE OF GOVERNMENTAL INDUSTRIAL HYGIENISTS, DOCUMENTATION OF THE THRESHOLD LIMIT VALUES 199 (rev. ed. 1966).

227. *Worker Exposure to VC, supra* note 114.

228. OSHA, *National Consensus Standards and Established Federal Health Standards*, 36 Fed. Reg. 10,466, 10,505 (1971) (adding former 29 C.F.R. § 1910.93).

229. *VC Hearings, supra* note 1, at 40 (statement of Dr. Marcus Key).

230. *OSHA Emergency Temporary Standard, supra* note 140.

231. See note 275 *supra.*

relationship to the permanent standard. Although the ETS provided employees with some immediate protection, it is questionable whether it was set low enough. There are weaknesses in OSHA's explanation of the medical, technological, and economic reasons for choosing the 50 ppm level.[232] OSHA carried these weaknesses over into the rationale for the permanent standard.

On February 15th, about three weeks after the Goodrich disclosure, OSHA and NIOSH jointly held a fact-finding hearing on the need for regulatory action. The scope of the government's concern widened beyond the PVC plants, where deaths had already been reported, to encompass other sources of occupational exposure to VC. Witnesses at the hearing addressed the safety of workers in VC and fabrication plants as well.[233]

At that time OSHA received reports of animal experiments confirming the carcinogenicity of VC. OSHA learned that in the Italian experiments VC had induced liver angiosarcomas in rats inhaling VC at concentrations as low as 250 ppm. No tumors had yet been found in rats exposed at 50 ppm, the next lower dose and the lowest dose then being tested. These experiments, however, were not yet complete.[234]

OSHA received conflicting advice from the unions and the industries. The major unions representing the VC, PVC, and fabrication workers petitioned OSHA to set an ETS applicable to these three industries, with an exposure ceiling as close to zero as possible.[235] The petitions requested restricting VC use to closed systems, monitoring exposure levels, and issuing respirators and protective clothing to employees exposed to detectable levels. As a means of enforcing compliance, the petitions requested that OSHA require each manufacturer to obtain a permit to handle VC.[236] In

---

232.   One month after the issuance of the ETS, the unions petitioned OSHA to amend the standard downward, citing deficiencies in the rationale for the choice of the 50 ppm exposure limit, and citing additional evidence that had become available since the ETS was issued. This data further undermined the rationale for the choice of 50 ppm. Industrial Union Dep't AFL-CIO, Petition to Amend the Emergency Temporary Standard for Exposure to Vinyl Chloride, (May 8, 1974) [hereinafter cited as Unions' Second Petition]. OSHA took this evidence into account when on May 10th it issued a revised proposal for the permanent standard. See text accompanying notes 257-258 *infra*. But OSHA did not change the ETS. The unions contemplated filing suit to challenge the ETS as too lenient. However, doubtful that they could obtain a decision before the ETS was superseded by a permanent standard, they instead directed their subsequent efforts at obtaining a more protective permanent standard. Personal communication from Sheldon Samuels, Director, Health, Safety, and Environment, Industrial Union Dep't, AFL-CIO (Apr. 21, 1977).

233.   The notice of the hearing called generally for information on "[e]mployee populations potentially or actually exposed to vinyl chloride or other chemicals, and involved in the production and/or use of vinyl chloride." Dep't of Labor, *Possible Hazards of Vinyl Chloride Manufacture and Use, Request for Information and Notice of Fact-Finding Hearing*, 39 Fed. Reg. 3874 (1974).

234.   *OSHA Emergency Temporary Standard for VC, supra* note 140, at 12,342.

235.   *Id.*

236.   The unions requested a standard for VC on the model of standards recommended for certain other substances in 1973 by an OSHA Advisory Committee. *See* OSHA, *Standards*

contrast, some manufacturers urged that any reduction of the existing 500 ppm ceiling await a permanent standard-setting proceeding.[237] Other industry representatives recommended allowing a "working level" of a 50 ppm *average* exposure.[238]

In March, NIOSH recommended that OSHA set a permanent standard prohibiting the exposure of employees to "measurable concentrations" of VC and requiring the use of respirators at higher levels.[239] NIOSH explicitly opposed the establishment of a "working level" of 50 ppm. The Institute warned that the absence to that date of tumors in the animals exposed at 50 ppm did not indicate the safety of that dose, taking the position that a safe level of exposure to a carcinogen probably does not exist. Citing the statutory requirement that it indicate a safe exposure level when recommending standards to OSHA,[240] NIOSH rejected the specification of a "threshold limit value," a permissible concentration of VC in workplace air.[241]

Although NIOSH eschewed the setting of a threshold limit value, it did recommend that OSHA implement a method of monitoring VC by which to determine if "measurable concentrations" were present. NIOSH stated that this method was sensitive to about one ppm.[242] The recommended standard therefore would have the effect of permitting VC concentrations up to a ceiling of one ppm.[243]

On April 5th, OSHA issued an ETS covering VC and PVC plants.[244] The agency declined to lower the exposure limit as far as NIOSH had recommended and imposed only a ceiling of 50 ppm. OSHA made the requisite finding that exposures above this level placed the workers in "grave danger" of cancer and that the standard was "necessary to protect" them from it. The standard required the employers to take steps to reduce emissions to the workplace air. When VC concentrations exceeded 50 ppm, employers were required to remove workers to safe areas or to provide them

---

Advisory Committee on Carcinogens, Notice of Receipt of Recommendations, 38 Fed. Reg. 24,375 (1973).

237.   *OSHA Emergency Temporary Standard for VC, supra* note 140, at 12,342.

238.   Memorandum from Dr. Marcus Key, Director, NIOSH, to Assistant Sec'y of Labor, OSHA: Recommended Occupational Health Standard for the Manufacture of Synthetic Polymer from Vinyl Chloride 2 (Mar. 11, 1974) [hereinafter cited as NIOSH Recommendation].

239.   *Id.* at 3. The NIOSH recommendation is for a permanent standard, pursuant to OSH Act § 20, 29 U.S.C. § 669 (1970). The recommendation does not comment on the need for an ETS.

240.   OSH Act § 20(a)(3), 29 U.S.C. § 669(a)(3) (1970).

241.   NIOSH Recommendation, *supra* note 238, at 2-3.

242.   *Id.* at 3.

243.   The NIOSH recommendation of one ppm as the "not detectable" level was the first mention of the level that OSHA later proposed for the permanent standard. After an interlude with the ETS set at a higher level, to be discussed in the text immediately following this note, the one ppm level completely dominated the proceedings. No lower level was ever considered, though the justification for stopping at one ppm was never sufficiently established. See text accompanying notes 258-262, 293-299 *infra*.

244.   *OSHA Emergency Temporary Standard for VC, supra* note 140, at 12,343.

with respirators.[245]

The statement of reasons supporting the ETS reveals the 50 ppm standard to be an unsteady compromise between the desires of the unions and of the industries. The statement opened with observations on which there was little room for doubt. The animal experiments and the deaths of employees of additional companies had put to rest uncertainty that VC, not some other chemical, had caused the deaths of the Goodrich workers.[246] At this point, however, agreement ended. OSHA justified the chosen level on two assertions, one resting on medical contentions and the other on technological and economic ones. OSHA contended first, that it lacked sufficient evidence that lower exposures were dangerous and second, that 50 ppm was the lowest level that VC and PVC plants could attain immediately. Examined closely, the first contention is unpersuasive, and the second, at the very least, was inadequately explained.

As the first basis for the chosen standard, OSHA asserted that the medical evidence would not support a finding of "grave danger" at 50 ppm or less.[247] OSHA noted that VC concentrations to which the human victims had been exposed were unknown. Current levels were better known; some employees were exposed to levels approaching 230 ppm. But the assessment of the human effects of such doses was precluded by the long latency period, which averaged nearly 20 years for the dead Goodrich workers. Consequently, the assessment of the human cancer risk from particular doses of VC depended on inferences from the results of animal tests. OSHA noted that liver angiosarcomas had been found at 250 ppm but, to that date, not at 50 ppm. OSHA referred to tests at 50 ppm on four species, reported in 1961, which had not shown the induction of cancer.[248] The agency reasoned that, in view of the ignorance of human sensitivity, "VC must be considered carcinogenic in man at the same level" as in animals, *i.e.*, at 250 ppm. But since cancer had not been shown to occur at 50 ppm, OSHA declined to find that "grave danger" existed at that level.[249]

The last conclusion was medically unsound for two reasons. First, a close look at the 1961 study shows that it could not be relied upon as an accurate test for carcinogenicity. The experiments had been concluded and the animals sacrificed too early to reveal any latent tumors that might have been generated. Thus the absence of tumors in this experiment had no

245. *Id.*

246. Since January, Union Carbide and Goodyear, as well as Goodrich, had reported the liver angiosarcoma deaths of PVC workers. The cancer had been induced in animals at 250 ppm, a level comparable to human exposure. Moreover, under microscopic examination the tumors from the livers of the animals and the dead employees were indistinguishable. *Id.* at 12,342.

247. *Id.*

248. Torkelson, Oyen, & Rowe, 22 AM. INDS. HYGIENE ASS'N J. 354 (1961), cited in *OSHA Emergency Temporary Standard for VC, supra* note 140, at 12,342.

249. *OSHA Emergency Temporary Standard for VC, supra* note 140, at 12,342-43.

probative value. Second, as the unions argued, since no safe levels of exposure to carcinogens can be identified, some employees are at risk of cancer from any dose, and they must therefore be considered in "grave danger."[250]

OSHA's second basis for setting the ETS at 50 ppm was that "in our practical judgment, [50 ppm] is the lowest level which can be complied with immediately."[251] This statement was not an adequate explanation for so important a conclusion. OSHA did not put forward a legal test either to define "immediately" or to determine how much an ETS may hinder normal plant operations.

In view of the need for speed, such a legal test need not require precise fact-finding, and such an explanation need not be long or detailed. However, unless the agency articulates some criteria to control its judgment concerning an industry's immediate capabilities to reduce exposure, and unless it makes some analysis of data and opinion to support the judgment in a particular case, it is impossible to know that an ETS is as protective as the statute intends.[252]

5. The Proposal for the Permanent Standard

New developments regarding VC's toxicity and consideration of the industries' long-term control capabilities convinced OSHA to issue a re-

---

250. Unions' Second Petition, *supra* note 232, at 3-5.

251. *OSHA Emergency Temporary Standard for VC, supra* note 140, at 12,342.

252. In their petition for amendment of the ETS, the unions argued that the determination of what control measures are feasible must be made with reference to "what can be achieved in well-managed plants on an operation-by-operation basis," *i.e.*, that OSHA must examine what exposure levels can be achieved by the best plants at each step of VC and PVC manufacture and handling. The unions noted that OSHA's own survey of VC and PVC plants showed that the 50 ppm level was seldom exceeded in most operations. They asserted that for "many, if not most" operations the industries could "easily achieve" a ten ppm ceiling, without the need for instituting engineering changes, but simply through work practice changes and better mainte-nance. Additional protection could come immediately from respirators and protective clothing. Thus the unions concluded that it was immediately feasible to approach the NIOSH-recom-mended level of one ppm. Unions' Second Petition, *supra* note 232, at 6-7. OSHA was not compelled to accept the unions' view, but it should have put forward criteria and factual analysis of its own.

The unions also cited evidence received subsequent to the issuance of the ETS that called for its revision. Ten days after setting the ETS, OSHA learned that VC had been shown to cause liver angiosarcomas in animals exposed to 50 ppm. This evidence made untenable OSHA's conclusion that "grave danger" did not exist at that level. *Id.* at 6. See note 232 *supra*.

Perhaps conceding the weakness of the choice of 50 ppm, in promulgating the ETS OSHA had noted that it would be effective for only a short time, and the agency had committed itself to re-evaluating "the whole question" of the existence of safe human exposure levels to VC in the permanent standard-setting process to follow. Meanwhile, OSHA was satisfied to have ordered "a substantial reduction" in the 500 ppm standard. *OSHA Emergency Temporary Standard for VC, supra* note 140, at 12,342.

Recently, OSHA has taken some steps to define the feasibility criteria that will govern the design of an ETS. *See* OSHA, *Identification, Classification, and Regulation of Toxic Substances Posing a Potential Carcinogenic Risk*, 42 Fed. Reg. 54,148, 54,176 (1977) [hereinafter cited as *OSHA Proposed Cancer Policy*].

vised, more stringent proposal in early May.[253] Although OSHA's treatment of medical and balancing issues improved in the proceeding to set the permanent standard, some of the same errors and shortcomings of explanation of the ETS also exist in the permanent standard.

The principal change from the ETS made in the proposed permanent standard was the reduction of the exposure ceiling to the so-called "undetectable level" recommended by NIOSH, approximately one ppm.[254] The standard would apply to the fabrication industry as well as to the VC and PVC industries, since exposures in fabrication plants could be expected to exceed one ppm.[255] Employers in all three industries would have to establish a program to institute "feasible" engineering and work practice changes designed to bring exposures below the limit "as soon as feasible." Until the standard could be met by the use of engineering and work practice controls alone, and thereafter in emergencies, employers would have to provide workers with respirators and would have to see that they were used.[256]

Since the issuance of the ETS, the danger of low doses of VC had become clearer. On April 15, 1974, ten days after setting the ETS, OSHA learned that the completed animal tests at 50 ppm had demonstrated the induction of liver angiosarcomas.[257] In light of this evidence OSHA concluded that the exposure level must be further reduced. The agency acknowledged the dim prospect that any threshold could be identified in the forseeable future,[258] and that no medically defensible exposure limit could be found. Consequently, the stopping point had to be founded on considerations of feasibility.

While this proposal improved on the ETS, it too had defects in its rationale. From a medical standpoint, the gap between the one ppm ceiling and the 50 ppm level then considered carcinogenic had to be viewed as precariously small. In the statement accompanying the proposal, OSHA did no more than state certain conclusions about what approaches, results, measures, and timing were feasible. This was not a convincing demonstration that the proposed standard was the most protective permitted by considerations of feasibility.

The weakest link in the agency's logic was the decision to set the exposure limit in terms of a fictional undetectable level. To explain the

---

253. *OSHA Proposed Standard for VC, supra* note 124.

254. *Id.* at 16,896, 16,897-98 (proposed 29 C.F.R. § 1910.93q(b)(6),(f),(g)).

255. *Id.* at 16,896; *id.* at 16,897 (proposed 29 C.F.R. § 1910.93q(d)(1)). This greatly enlarged the number of workers covered, from about 6,000 in the VC and PVC plants to more than 300,000. See text accompanying notes 98-99 *supra*.

256. *OSHA Proposed Standard for VC, supra* note 124, at 16,897; *id.* at 16,898 (proposed 29 C.F.R. § 1910.93q(f)-(g)). The proposed standard included detailed requirements for exposure monitoring medical surveillance, and record keeping. *Id.* at 16,897-900 (proposed 29 C.F.R. § 1910.93q(e),(o)-(q)).

257. *Id.* at 16,896.

258. *Id.*

choice of a detection technique sensitive to no less than one ppm, OSHA stated: "Although more sensitive methods may be available now or in the future, the methodological sensitivity proposed appears to be the most feasible and generally available."[259] Despite OSHA's apparent doubts, it is clear that at that time there existed detection techniques far more sensitive than the one OSHA designated. Some companies were already using monitoring equipment sensitive to 100 parts per billion (ppb) or less.[260] In March and early May, sampling air surrounding VC and PVC plants, EPA recorded many measurements in the range of only a few ppb.[261] OSHA did not state any general economic or technological criteria for determining which existing measurement techniques were feasible, nor in this instance did the agency explain why more sensitive techniques were not sufficiently "feasible and generally available." Moreover, OSHA should have expected the rapid development of more sensitive and less expensive techniques, since the regulation of VC would probably stimulate engineers to investigate a detection problem formerly of little interest. Most important, OSHA gave no reasons why the protectiveness of the standard should be restricted by purported limits to detection techniques, rather than by the difficulty and cost of controlling emissions.[262]

Another weakness in the proposal was the lack of specificity as to the conditions under which engineering and work practices would have to be used in lieu of respirators. OSHA stated only that such measures must be instituted "as soon as feasible."[263] The phrase does not indicate how forcefully the standard was to push more rapid technological and organizational innovations.

A proposal need not contain the fully articulated rationale for a rule. It must supply adequate notice of the agency's intended approach and of the issues to be addressed in the comment period or in a hearing; the complete rationale may await the promulgation of the final rule.[264] Without question,

259. *Id.*

260. Letter from Everett L. Smith, Manager, Safety and Training, Cities Service Co., to David R. Bell, Office of Standards Development, OSHA 3 (July 16, 1974), *reprinted in* OSHA, Final Environmental Impact Statement, Proposed Regulation, Vinyl Chloride, at app. C (Sept. 5, 1974) [hereinafter cited as OSHA EIS]. The letter states that the sensitivity could probably be increased another order of magnitude.

261. EPA SCIENTIFIC AND TECHNICAL REPORT, *supra* note 90, at 18-28.

262. There is no indication that OSHA considered specifying particular control measures that must be taken. The specification of the use of particular equipment, such as valves or seals, and particular operating procedures, such as methods of cleaning the polymerization reactors, might have led to VC concentrations in the workplace air lower than one ppm. Such specifications could have been limited by an explicitly articulated criterion of what costs it was feasible to impose on each industry. Compare the 1976 standard for coke oven emissions, 29 C.F.R. § 1910.1029 (1977), which makes more extensive use of specifications. Compare also OSHA's standard for VC to EPA's, which sets out detailed specifications. 40 C.F.R. §§ 61.60-.71 (1977), discussed in text accompanying notes 416-419 *infra*.

263. *OSHA Proposed Standard for VC, supra* note 124, at 16,897.

264. *See generally* Portland Cement Ass'n v. Ruckelshaus, 486 F.2d 375, 5 ERC 1593 (D.C. Cir. 1973). *See also* the discussion of judicial review in text accompanying notes 950-998 *infra*.

this proposal satisfied the notice function. It was, however, the only occasion on which OSHA addressed the issue of why the standard should not be more stringent; the statement accompanying the final promulgation of the permanent standard essentially addressed only the issue of why the standard should not be more *lenient*. As indicated above, there are several key points at which OSHA's rationale for stopping at the one ppm ceiling was inadequately supported and explained.

6. Comments on the Proposal

During the summer of 1974, OSHA collected comments and held extensive hearings on the VC proposal.[265] The major issues of dispute were whether the proposed exposure limit was supported on medical grounds and whether it was technologically and economically feasible.[266] The VC, PVC, and fabrication industries opposed the standard as too stringent. With some reluctance the unions decided to support OSHA rather than to press for a more stringent standard.[267]

The industries' representatives argued that the medical evidence did not support a one ppm exposure ceiling. They did not dispute the conclusion that VC is a carcinogen, but they contended that OSHA lacked sufficient evidence of its harmfulness at low doses to support the chosen exposure limit. The Society of the Plastics Industries (SPI), a trade association, noted that the employees who had developed cancer had been exposed to high

---

265. *OSHA Permanent Standard for VC, supra* note 1, at 35,890. The agency commissioned a consultant to prepare an economic impact study. Snell Economic Impact Study, *supra* note 93. OSHA itself prepared an environmental impact statement. OSHA EIS, *supra* note 260.

266. The respirator requirement was also at issue. *See* Society of the Plastics Industries, Inc. v. OSHA, 509 F.2d 1301, 1310 (2d Cir. 1975).

267. Despite their doubts about the safety of exposure to one ppm VC and despite their belief that a more stringent standard was feasible, the unions decided to embrace the proposal and help OSHA rebut the objections of the VC, PVC, and fabrication industries. The Industrial Union Department stated that although at one ppm "[s]ubstantial risks will still prevail," the unions could "do no less than to support the proposal." Industrial Union Dep't, AFL-CIO, Testimony on a Vinyl Chloride Standard 14 (June 25, 1974) [hereinafter cited as Industrial Union Dep't Testimony]. The Oil, Chemical, and Atomic Workers (OCAW) called the proposed limit "reasonable" and stated that any less protection would "continue the subsidy being given by the American workers of years of their lives to produce vinyl chloride." Statement of Anthony Mazzocchi, Citizenship-Legislative Director, Oil, Chemical, and Atomic Workers International Union, on Proposed Permanent Standard on Vinyl Chloride 1 (July 9, 1974) [hereinafter cited as OCAW Testimony].

There were strong practical reasons for the unions' decision. An effort to force OSHA to lower the exposure limit further might have delayed the issuance of a standard. If the delay extended beyond October 5, the ETS would expire. Once that had happened, with no firm date to aim at, OSHA might delay substantially longer before completing the rulemaking, and the eventual standard might be the same, or even weaker than one the unions would obtain by supporting the agency. If the unions were able to convince OSHA to issue a more stringent standard, the nearly inevitable judicial review at the behest of the industries would be harder to win. Personal communication with Sheldon Samuels, Director, Health, Safety, & Environment, Industrial Union Dep't, AFL-CIO (Apr. 21, 1977).

concentrations for long periods. SPI pointed to a number of VC and PVC plants at which to that date no cancer had been found. SPI also asserted that no conclusions about VC's potency in humans could be drawn from the animal tests, as the relative sensitivity of rodents and humans was unknown. On the basis of preliminary evidence about how VC is metabolized in the human body, SPI suggested that a threshold exists for human carcinogenesis at about 220 ppm VC.[268]

In contrast, cancer specialists from NIOSH and the National Cancer Institute, as well as persons appearing on behalf of the unions, contended that safe human doses of carcinogens could not be determined.[269] They stated that properly designed animal tests would be expected to show that VC causes cancer at doses lower than 50 ppm. In addition, they noted that there was evidence that VC causes cancers besides liver angiosarcoma, and that it might cause cancer in the children of women exposed during pregnancy.[270] These experts and the unions argued that any exposure to VC should be considered to present some risk.[271]

Although these disagreements on the medical evidence were substantial, most of the debate concerned the feasibility of the proposal. The industries represented that it was technologically impossible for VC and PVC plants to meet the one ppm ceiling, and that the cost of approaching it would force these companies out of business.[272] The economic impact study, which was based almost entirely on industry sources of information, supported this view.[273] The industries contended that the unavailability of PVC would have serious economic repercussions beyond the effects on them, as PVC users would be forced to make costly and time-consuming substitutions of other materials.[274]

---

268. The industry comments in this paragraph are summarized in Post-Hearing Memorandum of the Society of the Plastics Industry, Inc., Proposed Findings of Fact and Conclusions Supported by the Record 2-24 (Aug. 23, 1974) [hereinafter cited as SPI Post-Hearing Memo].

269. *OSHA Permanent Standard for VC, supra* note 1, at 35,802. *See also* Industrial Union Dep't Testimony, *supra* note 267, at 6; Statement of Bertram Cottine and Andrea Hricko, Health Research Group, on Proposed Permanent Standard on Vinyl Chloride 4-5 (July 9, 1974) [hereinafter cited as HRG Testimony]. They were joined in this view even by some medical witnesses employed by the industries. *OSHA Permanent Standard for VC, supra* note 1, at 35,892.

270. Industrial Union Dep't Testimony, *supra* note 267, at 9-10, 14. See text accompanying notes 136-138 *supra*.

271. *Id. See also* OCAW Testimony, *supra* note 267, at 1 (stating OCAW's ratification of the Industrial Union Dep't testimony).

272. SPI Post-Hearing Memo, *supra* note 268, at 3-18.

273. The study asserted that the technology did not exist to meet the proposed standard at any VC or PVC plant, even if they were given as long as four years to comply. Snell Economic Impact study, *supra* note 93, at VI-1 to -2. The study projected that the cost of the futile attempt to reach one ppm would cause a PVC price increase of about 80 percent, assuming that the companies would make the effort rather than close. *Id.* at exhibit V-12. For various exposure limits between 50 and one ppm, the study estimated that compliance times would range between six months and two and a half years, that PVC costs would increase between four and 15 percent, and that the companies would consider closing as much as one fourth of PVC production capacity rather than bringing it into compliance. *Id.* at exhibits V-12 to -14.

274. General Motors Corp., which uses PVC in many car parts, claimed that the sub-

The industries also contended that fabrication plants should not be subject to the standard. They claimed that VC levels in those plants already were below or close to the proposed ceiling. Because the only source of VC in those plants was the residue in PVC resins, high exposure levels were impossible. The residue level itself would decline as control measures were instituted at PVC plants. In light of their view that the danger from low doses had not been shown, the industries argued that the extensive requirements for exposure monitoring, health testing, and record keeping would be an unjustifiable burden on fabrication firms, especially on small companies.[275]

SPI recommended less stringent alternative standards. The trade association urged that fabrication facilities be excluded and the OSHA set higher exposure limits, in terms of averages rather than ceilings,[276] for VC and PVC plants. For VC plants SPI recommended a standard declining in steps by October 1975 to a five ppm average, with a ten ppm ceiling for short-term exposures. For PVC plants, the association suggested a standard declining to a ten ppm average by October 1976, with a 25 ppm short-term ceiling.[277]

The unions and the Health Research Group disputed the industries' contentions. The unions believed that the means already existed or could be found shortly to maintain exposure levels below one ppm. They contended that the proposed limit could be met through engineering and work practice controls alone, without the need for extensive use of respirators. The unions accused the industries of attempting to "blackmail" OSHA into setting a more lenient standard by exaggerating the difficulty and cost of compliance and falsely predicting massive economic dislocations. The unions contended that, with a few possible exceptions, the costs were fully within each company's reach.[278] They demanded that the companies be given the choice either to make the necessary changes at existing plants "as quickly as possible" or, if they found the changes too expensive, to close the plants down.[279] The unions also noted that variances were available for those plants "genuinely" unable to comply.[280] The unions opposed the exclusion

---

stance's unavailability might force the layoff of 450,000 General Motors workers, with a ripple through the economy affecting 1.8 million other jobs. SPI Post-Hearing Memo, *supra* note 268, at 18 n.8. Arthur D. Little, Inc., an economic consultant, suggested that a loss of between 1.7 and 2.2 million jobs and a loss of $65 to 90 billion in GNP might result. *Id.* at 18. Among other weaknesses, these estimates do not seem to account for any substitutions of other products for PVC.

275. *Id.* at 10-12.

276. A number of industry representatives indicated confusion over setting of the exposure limit in terms of equipment of a particular detection sensitivity. They expressed their preference that the limit, whatever its level, be stated directly as a permissible concentration. *See, e.g.*, letter from Everett L. Smith, *supra* note 260.

277. SPI Post-Hearing Memo., *supra* note 268, at 6.

278. OCAW Testimony, *supra* note 267, at 1, 5; Industrial Union Dep't Testimony, *supra* note 267, at 2, 13.

279. Industrial Union Dep't Testimony, supra note 267, at 13, 22.

280. OCAW Testimony, *supra* note 267, at 2-4.

of the fabrication industry from the standard.[281] They recommended only one major change in the proposal; to reduce the possibility of economically motivated delay in instituting available controls, the unions urged OSHA to adopt a compliance deadline more specific than "as soon as feasible."[282]

The Health Research Group criticized the economic impact study. The Group noted that the study was based almost entirely on the pessimistic representations of the affected companies, accepted by the consultant at face value without any significant independent research into the difficulty and cost of compliance. The study failed to consider any impacts beyond the asserted immediate costs to the VC and PVC industries, or to consider whether the costs were justified by the health threat.[283]

OSHA did little in response to these criticisms. The agency's only apparent consideration of the feasibility of setting the exposure limit lower than one ppm is found in the environmental impact statement, completed in September. OSHA stated:

> At any level of exposure except zero (which in effect would ban vinyl chloride manufacture), there may be a risk that a worker will contact [sic] liver angiosarcoma. However, a complete ban, causing a total shutdown of vinyl chloride or PVC plants, would severely disrupt the economy and worsen the employment situation. In all likelihood a shutdown of VC and PVC plants would reverberate throughout the economy by effecting work stoppages in important sectors of the economy.[284]

The agency seems to have given no serious consideration to exposure limits between one ppm and zero.

7. The Permanent Standard

On October 4, 1974, OSHA promulgated the permanent standard.[285] The agency made two major changes, which made the standard more lenient than the proposal. First, instead of limiting VC concentrations to a one ppm ceiling, the permanent standard allows an *average* concentration of one ppm calculated over an eight-hour work shift, and it permits excursions up to five ppm averaged over any 15 minute period.[286] Second, the standard released fabrication plants from exposure monitoring, health testing, and record keeping if a prescribed sequence of monitoring showed VC levels to be less

281. The unions supported their inclusion for two reasons. First, if the PVC industry's reductions in the levels of VC residual were insufficient to bring the airborne VC concentration in fabrication plants below the proposed limit, the fabrication plants would be required to take steps to bring VC levels below the limit. Second, the employees would have the benefit of mandatory medical surveillance and record keeping. *Id.* at 2.

282. Industrial Union Dep't Testimony, *supra* note 267, at 13, 22.

283. Health Research Group, Comments, In the Matter of the Economic Impact Statement on the Proposed Permanent Standard on Occupational Exposure to Vinyl Chloride (Sept. 9, 1974).

284. OSHA EIS, *supra* note 260, at 84.

285. 29 C.F.R. § 1910.1017 (1977).

286. *Id.* § 1910.1017(c).

than 500 parts per billion (ppb), half the allowable level.[287]

OSHA did not base these changes on any retreat from its prior medical conclusions. The seriousness of the human health hazard was emphasized by the deaths of more employees during the comment period. For several reasons OSHA declined to accept industries' studies that purported to show the absence of a cancer risk to employees exposed to low concentrations.[288] OSHA reiterated that the uncertainties involved in assessing cancer risks precluded the establishment of a safe dose of VC and made prudent the assumption that humans are at least as susceptible as the most sensitive animal species.[289] The agency rejected again the proposition that cancer must have been shown to occur in humans at a particular dose before that level may be held to be a cancer hazard.[290]

OSHA's reasons for relaxing the standard must be found in considerations other than medical concerns. While abandoning its proposal to set the exposure limit in terms of a fictional "no detectable level,"[291] OSHA conceded the VC and PVC industries' claims of infeasibility. Noting the differences of opinion between the industries and the unions on the feasibility of meeting the one ppm ceiling, and granting the uncertainty about the level attainable with currently available controls, OSHA stated:

> [A]ny estimate as to the lowest feasible level attainable must necessarily involve subjective judgment. Likewise, the projections of industry, labor, and others concerning feasibility are essentially conjectural. . . .[292]
>
> . . . .
>
> [T]his limit is based on an evaluation of the best available evidence and on a judgment that the health and safety of employees must be protected to the fullest extent feasible. In view of the fact that release of VC in the VC and PVC manufacturing processes are [sic] variable, the 1 ppm ceiling level provided in the proposal would require maintenance of an average level significantly more difficult

---

287. *Id.* § 1910.1017(b)(1), (d).

288. The agency stated that since the latency period for low exposures could exceed that for high doses, a sufficient time had not elapsed to evaluate the effects of low doses. In addition, the number of employees in the plants asserted to be safe was too small to support statistically significant conclusions. Finally, some studies were skewed by the failure to include former employees in the samples. *OSHA Permanent Standard for VC, supra* note 1, at 35,891-92. See text accompanying note 268 *supra.*

289. *Id.* The agency concluded that the induction of tumors in mice at 50 ppm outweighed the suggestion of a human threshold at 220 ppm. See text accompanying note 268 *supra.* OSHA also noted the evidence that VC causes tumors at many sites in the animals: lungs, kidneys, brain, skin, and other organs. In addition, one study suggested that workers exposed to VC suffer an increased rate of many types of cancer other than liver angiosarcoma. Thus liver angiosarcoma might not be the sole important human effect, but only the most obvious. *Id.* at 35,891-92.

290. *Id.* at 35,891.

291. 29 C.F.R. § 1910.1017(c) (1977). The monitoring technique specified in the standard is four times more sensitive than that in the proposal. *Id.* § 1910.1017(d)(4).

292. *OSHA Permanent Standard for VC, supra* note 1, at 35,892.

to attain through feasible engineering controls. Therefore, the exposure limit prescribed in the proposal has been rejected.[293]

The agency believed that an average, rather than a ceiling, of one ppm was feasible through a combination of engineering and work practice controls and respirators. OSHA conceded that with currently available technology the VC and PVC industries could not achieve the one ppm average in all portions of all plants "in the near future," but the agency concluded that "in time," through the use of new technology and practices, they could meet the required limit without respirators "for most job classifications most of the time."[294] The agency believed that the PVC industry would require as long as "several years" before respirators were needed only "occasionally."[295] OSHA declined to specify either particular control measures or deadlines for full compliance without respirators.

While OSHA stood firmly behind the feasibility of the standard finally adopted, the agency did not present adequate evidence and reasoning for concluding that no standard below the one ppm average was feasible. Like the proposal, the permanent standard lacks criteria defining feasibility in terms of the technological and economic consequences warranted by a particular health threat.

The second major change in the proposal was the exemption of fabrication plants from exposure monitoring, health testing, and record keeping requirements once two consecutive sequences of monitoring showed VC concentrations to be below an "action level" of an average concentration of 500 ppb, half the exposure limit. Monitoring would not have to be repeated

---

293. *Id.* at 35,893.

294. *Id.* at 35,892.

295. *Id.* at 35,894. The standard still sets no firmer deadline for compliance without the need for respirators than that it must be achieved "as soon as feasible." 29 C.F.R. § 1910.1017(f) (1977). OSHA attempted to portray this open-ended deadline as a spur to more rapid attainment of the exposure limit than would be possible if particular dates were fixed; each firm would comply as rapidly as it could. *Id.* at 35,893-94. But the use of the term "feasible" in the standard itself puts the determination of what is required over until the enforcement stage, where the determination is ultimately made not by OSHA but by OSHRC. If anything, this encourages delay. See note 184 *supra*.

OSHA made another change regarding the respirator requirement. For the first year of the standard, each employee had the option to forego the use of a respirator when exposures were between the one ppm average and a 25 ppm ceiling. OSHA stated that this option was needed to "mitigate" problems of training and fitting employees for respirators and to provide for "other adjustments which may be required." OSHA stipulated that employers notify, at least quarterly, workers about their exposure, have respirators available for them, and inform them of the dangers of VC and "the purpose, proper use, and limitations" of respirators. *Id.* at 35,894; 29 C.F.R. § 1910.1017(g)(1) (1977).

It is difficult to see the justification for this change. It would appear to be for the employees' benefit, but the unions had not sought it. OSHA had emphasized that it would be in the initial period, while engineering changes were made, that the respirators would be most needed. There are good reasons why the unions sought to make respirator use mandatory. OSHA could not effectively assure that in putting the choice to the employees an employer would not downplay the risks of these exposure levels or the effectiveness of the respirators, or otherwise pressure the employees in their decision.

unless the employer made major changes in operations or unless OSHA had reason to believe that exposures exceeded the action level. Since it was generally agreed that most fabrication plants could meet the 500 ppb level, OSHA argued that they need be subject only to these "minimal burdens."[296]

The change appears at first to be only a small adjustment in the requirements of the proposal. However, once OSHA abandoned the fiction of setting the exposure limit in terms of the "no detectable level," the agency gave up the primary justification for not examining whether a lower exposure limit was feasible for the fabrication industry than for the VC and PVC industries. This approach is contrary to the meaning of the statute. *Industrial Union Department* stands for the proposition that when regulating substances with no known safe dose, OSHA must set the most protective standard that is feasible for each readily distinguishable industry using the substance.[297] In that case the subject of dispute was whether there should be multiple compliance dates; the doctrine applies equally to the selection of multiple exposure limits. The fact that there was near unanimity that "most if not all," fabrication plants could meet the one ppm *ceiling* with engineering controls alone[298] should have suggested to OSHA that a lower exposure limit for this industry was feasible. Yet OSHA did not address this question.[299]

OSHA scheduled the standard to become effective on January 1, 1975.[300] Shortly after its promulgation, the industries sought judicial review.

8. Judicial Review of the Permanent Standard

The industries' petitions for review were consolidated in the Second Circuit Court of Appeals under the name *Society of the Plastics Industries, Inc. v. OSHA*.[301] Not satisfied by the relaxation of the proposal, the industries contended that OSHA lacked the evidence to set so low an exposure limit and that the limit was technologically infeasible.[302] Although

---

296. *OSHA Permanent Standard for VC, supra* note 1, at 35,892-93.

297. Industrial Union Dep't, AFL-CIO v. Hodgson, 499 F.2d 467 (D.C. Cir. 1974). See text accompanying notes 210-211 *supra*.

298. *OSHA Permanent Standard for VC, supra* note 1, at 35,892.

299. The cancer risk of the fabrication workers is not trivial, even when exposures are below one ppm. Although an individual worker's risk may be low, there are more than thirty times as many fabrication workers as VC and PVC workers. See text accompanying notes 97-99 *supra*. Thus the absolute number of cancers occurring among the fabrication employees could be comparable to the number among VC and PVC workers exposed at higher levels.

300. *OSHA Permanent Standard for VC, supra* note 1, at 35,898 (former 29 C.F.R. § 1910.93q(o)). The date was later amended to April 1, 1975, pursuant to the order of the court in Society of the Plastics Indus., Inc. v. OSHA, 509 F.2d 1301 (2d Cir. 1975), and the standard recodified in 29 C.F.R. § 1910.1017(o) (1977).

301. 509 F.2d 1301 (2d Cir. 1975), *cert. denied sub nom.* Firestone Plastics Co. v. United States Dep't of Labor, 421 U.S. 992 (1975).

302. 509 F.2d at 1303, 1310. The petitioners raised other, less important issues as well. *See id.* at 1303.

initially the unions were expected to challenge the standard as being too high,[303] the Industrial Union Department intervened in support of OSHA.[304] The court stayed the standard's effective date while it expedited the consideration of the case.[305] At the end of January 1975, the court rejected the industries' claims and directed that the standard become effective on April 1.[306]

Following the District of Columbia Circuit's approach in *Industrial Union Dep't, AFL-CIO v. Hodgson*,[307] the Second Circuit held that OSHA may make policy judgments to resolve uncertainty and to decide between conflicting interests, provided the agency identifies the considerations it relies on and sets out its reasoning.[308]

The VC cases presented medical issues similar to those discussed in the asbestos case.[309] The Second Circuit rejected the industries' contention that OSHA lacked sufficient evidence to set the exposure limit at the one ppm average. The industries argued that an exposure limit must be supported by evidence of human effects at that level.[310] The court acknowledged that the issue of VC's harmfulness at one ppm was (using the phrase from the asbestos case) "on the frontiers of scientific knowledge" and that (in its own phrase) "though the factual finger points, it does not conclude."[311] The court stated, however: "Under the command of [OSH Act], it remains the duty of [OSHA] to act to protect the workingman, and to act even in circumstances where existing methodology or research is deficient."[312] The court then recounted the evidence it found sufficient to support OSHA's medical conclusions.[313]

---

303. *OSHA's Rules Spur Suits*, CHEMICAL WEEK, Oct. 9, 1974, at 14.

304. Brief for Intervenor Industrial Union Dep't, Society of the Plastics Industries v. OSHA, 590 F.2d 1301 (2d Cir. 1975).

305. 509 F.2d at 1307 n.3.

306. *Id.* at 1311.

307. 499 F.2d 467 (D.C. Cir. 1974).

308. 509 F.2d at 1303-04.

309. See text accompanying note 210 *supra*.

310. Brief of Petitioners Tenneco *et al.* 25-29, Society of the Plastics Indus. v. OSHA, 509 F.2d 1301 (2d Cir. 1975) [hereinafter cited as Tenneco Brief]; Brief for Petitioner Society of the Plastics Industry 10, Society of the Plastics Indus. v. OSHA, 509 F.2d 1301 (2d Cir. 1975) [hereinafter cited as SPI Brief]. The SPI Brief complains that OSHA has attempted to use an "alleged evidentiary void" to support its standard, when it must affirmatively support it. *Id.*

311. Society of the Plastics Indus., Inc. v. OSHA, 509 F.2d 1301, 1308 (2d Cir. 1975). Note that the court mischaracterized the final standard as the "lowest detectable level." Apparently no party brought squarely to the court's attention the abandonment of this approach.

312. *Id.*

313. *Id.* at 1306-08. The court stated several key points. First, at least 13 workers exposed to VC already had died of liver angiosarcoma, a rate far higher than that at which the disease occurs in the general population. Second, the same cancer had been induced in animals at 50 ppm, the lowest level tested. Third, none of the medical expert witnesses at the hearing had identified a safe level for humans, and many had testified that safe levels for carcinogens could not presently be found and might not exist at all. Even assuming that 50 ppm was the lowest level that would cause cancer in animals, the one ppm standard left a safety margin of only 50-to-one. This was a narrow margin in view of expert testimony that when determining safe human doses to non-carcinogens with well-defined no-effect levels in animals, "toxicological

The court next addressed the industries' infeasibility claims. The industries claimed that OSHA lacked sufficient evidence for concluding that the one ppm average could be met in VC and PVC plants through engineering and work practice controls.[314] They cited the unanimous testimony by industry representatives that the necessary techniques did not exist, and pointed to the similar conclusions of the economic impact study. They argued that the mere "suggestion" by the unions and the Health Research Group that the limit could be achieved, unsupported by any technical evidence, could not outweigh the industries' representations. Thus, they concluded, OSHA's determination was based only on an unsupported "belief" and should not stand.[315]

The court recounted OSHA's statement of reasons[316] and concluded that the standard was not "clearly impossible" to achieve.[317] The court noted that many "useful" available control techniques had not yet been instituted, and that may sources of emissions "can be easily pinpointed and largely corrected." The court emphasized that OSHA may set standards that exceed the technological "status quo" and that force the development of new control methods: "[OSHA] may raise standards which require improvements in existing technologies or which require the development of new technology, and [the agency] is not limited to issuing standards based on devices already developed."[318] Noting that time had not borne out the industries' prior predictions of the impossibility of meeting the ETS, the court stated: "It appears that they simply need more faith in their own technological potentialities."[319] Moreover, even if engineering and work practice controls failed to bring exposures within the limit, the court noted that the standard could be satisfied by the use of respirators.[320] In sum, the court found the standard "entirely feasible."[321]

---

principles" call for a safety margin of 100-to-one. The vast majority of these experts supported reducing VC exposure to the lowest level possible. The court specifically approved OSHA's reliance on the animal tests to support its conclusion that humans are in danger from exposure to low doses. *Id.* at 1308.

314. Whereas in the hearings the industries had emphasized about equally their technological and economic problems, before the court they concentrated almost exclusively on the former. *See* SPI Brief, *supra* note 310, at 10-11. Taking the position that meeting the exposure limit was technologically impossible, they appear to have concluded that detailed discussion of the economic issues was unnecessary. Consequently, although the court noted the industries' economic allegations, it too never squarely addressed the question of economic feasibility.

315. *Id.* at 17-21; Tenneco Brief, *supra* note 310, at 15-24.

316. See text accompanying notes 292-295 *supra*.

317. 509 F.2d at 1309.

318. *Id.*

319. *Id.*

320. *Id.* at 1310. The industries had argued that the respirators themselves were also infeasible. They insisted that the respirators would be needed nearly full-time because of the shortfall of technological and operational controls. They asserted that the respirators caused a variety of safety hazards more immediate than the danger of cancer from VC. SPI Brief, *supra* note 310, at 17-27; Tenneco Brief, *supra* note 310, at 29-34. The court disagreed that they would be needed full-time, and characterized the industries claims of "dire consequences" as "exaggerated." 509 F.2d at 1310.

321. *Id.* Disposing of the industries' last major challenge, the court affirmed the inclusion

Pervading the opinion is a strong sense of disbelief in the industries' protestations of impossibility and economic catastrophe. Perhaps because of this disbelief, the court did not address extensively to what degree doubts about feasibility may be resolved in a standard's favor, or how heavy an economic burden a standard may impose. Nevertheless, one can extract from *Society of Plastics* some partial answers to the questions left unanswered by *Industrial Union Department*.

As noted above, *Industrial Union Department* requires OSHA to take into account a standard's economic impact on a regulated industry. However, the case does not preclude a standard addressed to a severe health hazard from requiring control measures too expensive for some companies in the industry to bear. When the health risks so warrant, a standard is not invalid if it forces some companies to close and imposes on others price increases, profit losses, and a consequent loss of competitive position in their product or capital markets.[322]

Society of Plastics adds to this doctrine. First, in concluding that the statute authorizes technology-forcing, the court implicitly endorsed the imposition of significant economic burdens on the industries. Within as yet ill-defined limits, OSHA may make the industries invest considerably in research and development of new controls and the agency may require expensive modifications of equipment and work routines. Some of the phrases quoted above suggest that, at least when lives are at stake, these economic burdens may be very heavy.[323]

Second, the concept of technology-forcing itself implies an approach to the resolution of uncertainties. Critical to the concept is the assumption that more often than not the control results sought actually can be achieved, and that an industry's protestations to the contrary are motivated by financial considerations or institutional conservatism. Thus a technology-forcing stat-

---

of the fabrication plants within the standard. The court found that the deaths of two fabrication workers from liver angiosarcoma and the presence of VC residual in PVC resins were ample reasons to include the fabrication industry. *Id.* at 1310. The court ordered OSHA to reschedule the effective date of the permanent standard, which had passed while the case was under consideration. *Id.* at 1311. *See* OSHA, *Standard for Exposure to Vinyl Chloride; Effective Date*, 40 Fed. Reg. 13,211 (1975) (moving effective date to April 1). The one year period for optional use of respirators was also moved back accordingly. The Supreme Court refused to stay the effective date on March 31, and denied certiorari in late May. Firestone Plastics Co. v. United States Dep't of Labor, 420 U.S. 1002, 421 U.S. 992 (1975).

322. See text accompanying notes 204-209 *supra*.

323. *See* AFL-CIO v. Brennan, 530 F.2d 109, 121 (3d Cir. 1975), quoted and discussed in note 209 *supra*. In *Society of Plastics*, the court might have used more guarded language had it been reviewing a more stringent standard that posed more credible issues of impossibility and crushing cost, or if it had been addressing a challenge from the unions asking it to order OSHA to consider setting a lower exposure limit. Nevertheless, the case stands for the proposition that a standard is not infeasible solely because compliance will be difficult and expensive and may significantly alter the market position or structure of an industry. *But see* American Iron & Steel Inst. v. OSHA, — F.2d —, 6 OSHC 1451 (3d Cir. 1978), discussed in note 213 *supra*.

ute such as OSH Act directs the agency to resolve doubts in favor of feasibility. The industries, then, bear the burden of showing clearly that the task is not possible or that the cost is not justified by the health benefits.[324]

9. Industry Compliance With the Permanent Standard

It became apparent very soon after the VC and PVC industries had lost their legal challenge that meeting the permanent standard would not be so difficult or costly as they had predicted. Even before the standard was promulgated, new "stripping" devices were being designed and built to remove VC from exhaust air and newly-formed PVC, and new processes were being developed to combine formerly separate steps in PVC manufacture, thereby eliminating some movement of the material in the open air.[325] Even as the major companies filed their lawsuits, Robintech, a smaller company, announced that it expected its plants to meet the one ppm limit without the need for respirators.[326]

By April 1975, when the standard became effective, even the major companies admitted that they could operate without curtailing production.[327] Improvements continued throughout 1975. By August, the standard appeared to the VC and PVC industries "not to be a serious operating or cost problem," and the use of respirators had been found not to hamper production significantly.[328] None of the threatened shutdowns had occurred, and it was stated that any future closings of PVC plants "will be for other, economic reasons."[329] Soon Goodrich, Tenneco, Diamond Shamrock, and

---

324. Unless the court's disbelief in these industries' particular case renders the opinion's tone unreliable, *Society of Plastics* establishes that when the health threat is severe, even unanimous industry assertions of impossibility and ruin will not suffice to make the showing of technological impossibility or disproportionate cost. An industry probably would have to show that all currently available control measures either have been installed or have been rejected for well-defined reasons of ineffectiveness or cost, and that all avenues of research and development have been explored and do not promise to change the outlook in the near future. Since lives may rest on small increments of exposure reduction, and since industries are in the best position to develop and produce evidence regarding difficulty and cost, this is a fair and appropriate rule.

325. *Putting VCM Emissions on Skids*, CHEMICAL WEEK, Sept. 18, 1974, at 66-67. Progress was being made even though the industries were giving up interest in increased use of ventilation, an early control measure, in light of indications that EPA would soon curb emissions to the outside air.

For a discussion of "stripping," see text accompanying notes 522-523 *infra*.

326. *OSHA's Rules Spur Suits, supra* note 303, at 14.

327. Goodrich and Dow reported average exposures of six and ten ppm, respectively. Diamond Shamrock estimated that the price of PVC would need to rise only about five percent to cover the costs of compliance. *Vinyl Chloride Makers Meet OSHA Standard*, CHEM. & ENG'R NEWS, Apr. 7, 1975, at 4.

328. Greek, *Vinyl Chloride May Face Shortages by 1977*, CHEM. & ENG'R NEWS, Aug. 11, 1975, at 8, 9.

329. *Id. See also Goodrich Cuts Cost of Meeting VCM Limits*, CHEMICAL WEEK, Dec. 10, 1975 at 59; Brody, *Goodrich Curbs Chloride Hazard*, New York Times, § 2, at 57, col. 1 (Dec. 7, 1975).

other companies were licensing a wide variety of new emission control devices.[330]

OSHA's inspections and air samplings during the first year of the standard's enforcement generally confirmed the industries' reported progress, although the results showed a significant number of readings greatly exceeding the five ppm ceiling.[331] In the spring of 1976, SPI reported that at most plants, while VC levels were much reduced, exposures still averaged more than one ppm.[332] OSHA's inspection data for 1976 and 1977 show continued progress towards meeting both the average and short-term ceiling limits. More than 90 percent of the samples taken were in compliance with the standard, although several peak exposures of 25 ppm were recorded.[333]

Obviously, the industries' forecasts of economic ruin did not come true. Furthermore, it seems that compliance with the OSHA standard has not seriously strained the financial capacity of these companies. As discussed earlier, the PVC market suffered a severe slump in 1974 and 1975. This slump cannot be attributed either to consumers' fears of cancer or to the costs of compliance with environmental regulations.[334] Now that the construction industry and the general economy have largely recovered from the recession of the early 1970s, the historical boom in plastics sales has resumed, and PVC does not seem to have lost any significant share of the market.[335] As the plastics market has improved, VC and PVC prices have

---

330. *See* Brody, *supra* note 329; *Patents Show Way To Remove Residual VCM,* CHEMICAL WEEK, June 16, 1976, at 32; *Getting Out the Last Traces of VCM,* CHEMICAL WEEK, Aug. 11, 1976, at 35.

331. Occupational Safety & Health Admin., National Detailed Test/Sample Inspection, Analysis of Test/Sample Data Reported During Period July 1974 - June 1975, at 18 (Mar. 25, 1976); During Period July 1975 - June 1976, at 20 (July 26, 1976) [hereinafter cited as OSHA Inspection Data].

332. Personal communication with John Lawrence, Technical Director, Society of the Plastics Industry (Mar. 8, 1976). No information has been compiled on the extent to which in the first year of the standard the employees elected not to use respirators in the one-to-25 ppm range. The option must have been exercised often enough to make an extension of the option economically attractive, for when the period expired, four companies sought variances to permit the continuation of the option. OSHA, *Firestone Plastics Co., Application for Temporary Variance and Interim Order; Denial of Interim Order,* 41 Fed. Reg. 9,634 (1976); OSHA, *Air Products and Chemicals, Inc., Borden Chemical Co., and Union Carbide Co., Applications for Temporary Variances and Interim Orders; Denial of Interim Orders,* 41 Fed. Reg. 18,943-46 (1976). OSHA denied the variances on the ground that the extra time was sought not because of the unavailability of necessary materials or personnel, but solely for economic reasons, which may not be the basis for a temporary variance. Personal communication with Dorothy Pohlman, OSHA Office of Variance Determination, May 5, 1977. *See also* note 208 *supra*.

333. OSHA Inspection Data, *supra* note 331, Sample Data Reported During Period July 1976 - Sept. 1976, at 13 (undated); During Period Oct. 1976 - Mar. 1977, at 265 (Apr. 15, 1977). From time to time, violations of the standard are still reported. *See, e.g., Plastics Plant Inspectors: Five Exposed to Cancer-Causing Gas,* S.F. Chronicle, Apr. 14, 1978, at 21, col. 1.

334. Greek, *supra* note 328, at 8. See text accompanying note 108 *supra*.

335. *Key Chemicals: Vinyl Chloride,* CHEM. & ENG'R NEWS, Aug. 23, 1976, at 13; *Plastics*

risen apace with prices for other plastics.[336] New plants are being built to meet anticipated growth in demand; they are not expected to have any difficulty complying with the standard, nor do their construction costs seem to have been significantly elevated by it.[337] The industries' current view of the effects of the OSHA standard is best summarized in the headline of a September 1976 article in a chemical trade publication: "PVC Rolls Out Of Jeopardy, Into Jubilation."[338]

10. Evaluating OSHA's Actions

At the outset, this discussion of OSHA's actions pointed out that under OSH Act the agency must set standards that reflect at least a rough balancing of the health benefits of a standard against its economic costs. The process for developing standards involves a separate assessment of the health risks and of the technological difficulty and economic costs of controls, followed by a weighing of one against the other. The quantities are too uncertain to state precisely and the interests are too different to compare directly. Nevertheless, it is not enough to make general, conclusory findings in lieu of articulating to some degree the quantities and interests at stake and the terms of trade between them.[339]

Except for a short lapse in the explanation of the medical basis for the ETS, throughout its regulation of VC OSHA approached the issue of the safety of carcinogens in a basically sound manner. That is, OSHA adopted the prevailing scientific consensus that no-effect levels for carcinogens cannot presently be identified, and it concluded that no exposure to VC could be considered safe. However, the agency apparently made no attempt to estimate even roughly the ranges of risk that might be associated with doses at one ppm and less.[340]

OSHA's performance on the assessment of the costs of control and the weighing of benefits and costs was weaker. OSHA never articulated its basic principles for interpreting the meaning of feasibility. The agency never

---

Maintain Momentum, CHEMICAL WEEK, Nov. 24, 1976, at 32; *Thermoplastics Poised for a Good Five Years*, CHEM. & ENG'R NEWS, Nov. 8, 1976, at 14. There is some indication that PVC has lost some of the packaging market; however, this is due not to the OSHA regulations but to the prospect of regulations by the Food and Drug Administration on food packaging. *See Second Thoughts on Using PVC*, CHEMICAL WEEK, July 31, 1974, at 19; *PVC Makers Confident on Food-Contact Uses*, CHEM. & ENG'R NEWS, Sept. 15, 1975, at 11.

336. *PVC Rolls Out of Jeopardy, Into Jubilation*, CHEMICAL WEEK, Sept. 15, 1976, at 34.

337. *See id.* at 34, 36. Plant construction cost increases are expected, but are not attributed to OSHA regulation. *Id.* at 36.

338. *Id.* at 34.

339. OSHA does deserve credit for acting rapidly in response to the VC hazard. It promulgated a permanent standard only nine months after the human cancer hazard became apparent.

340. Some preliminary estimates by statisticians at the National Cancer Institute were available. *See From Mouse To Man, supra* note 37, at 239-40.

addressed the feasibility of imposing a lower exposure limit for fabrication plants than for VC and PVC plants. OSHA repeatedly failed to offer empirical support for its assertion that exposure levels below the one ppm average would be infeasible for VC and PVC plants. Viewed both at the time and in retrospect, the standard was technologically and economically easy for the industries to meet.

OSHA's statements and actions suggest that it was following an unarticulated principle that a standard is not feasible if it would cause more than slight changes in the number of firms in an industry, or in an industry's profit and growth rates, its output, or competitive position. The feasibility requirement should not be taken to give an industry such complete protection·when lives are at stake. OSHA never considered whether there are substitutes for the uses of PVC, whether some uses are too frivolous to justify putting workers at any risk, or whether the size of the industry and the number of workers exposed should be kept from growing. The long-term effect of a toxic substance standard should be to channel growth away from industries hazardous to health and towards safer forms of employment. The proper balance between health protection and the protection of economic interests is ill-defined, but it is clear that in regulating VC, OSHA did not address it adequately.

There is now ample medical, technological, and economic evidence to support a reduction in the permanent standard for VC. Cancer has been induced in animals at one ppm, the level of the current standard.[341] A recent study has shown an elevated rate of many cancers among the fabrication workers.[342] This is not to say that OSHA should immediately reopen the VC proceedings. There are 1,500 to 2,000 chemicals that are known or suspected carcinogens that OSHA has yet to regulate.[343] Since VC is already controlled to a great degree, many of these substances have a higher call on OSHA's limited resources. The lesson to draw from the regulation of VC is that OSHA must take a more aggressive approach to defining and determining feasibility.[344]

Two other observations may be made. First, OSHA's standard does not apply to all workers significantly exposed to VC. Uncovered are workers in the transportation of VC between VC and PVC plants and in the transportation of PVC resin between PVC and fabrication plants. As shall be discussed below, the debilitating consequences of poorly-defined jurisdictional lines

---

341. *See* Maltoni Memorandum, *supra* note 143.

342. *See Mortality Among Fabrication Workers, supra* note 137.

343. *OSHA Proposed Cancer Policy supra* note 252, at 54,148. Of these, OSHA has presently completed the process of promulgating regulations for only 20 substances.

344. *See* the 1976 coke oven emissions standard, 29 C.F.R. § 1910.1029 (1977), and the statement of reasons for its promulgation at 41 Fed. Reg. 46,784 (1976). In this standard OSHA seems to have taken some of these lessons to heart. The standard contains both an exposure limit to be achieved by "feasible" measures and a set of minimum specified controls. The

are nowhere more evident in hazardous substances regulation than in transportation. Three agencies in the Department of Transportation have primary jurisdiction over this area, but so long as these agencies do not act, OSHA has the authority to protect transportation workers.[345] At no point in its proceedings did OSHA address the hazard to these workers. They are still largely unprotected.[346]

A second problem with the OSHA standard is also a product of divided jurisdiction. As shall be shown in the next section, many of the emission sources to the air *outside* the plants, affecting the health of plant neighbors, are the same as sources to the air inside. The control efforts required by OSHA and EPA largely overlap, and the two agencies have had difficulty allocating the costs of compliance to one standard or the other.[347] More important is that OSHA and EPA each weighed essentially *all* of the costs of controlling VC exposure against only *part* of the risks. As a result, each agency underweighted the risks. Each set a less stringent standard than would have been set by a single agency considering the emissions to both the inside and outside of the plants.[348]

The focus of discussion now shifts to the second major regulatory action regarding VC, EPA's hazardous air pollutant standard. It will be seen that while the Clean Air Act required EPA to approach the setting of its standard somewhat differently than OSH Act had required of OSHA, EPA and OSHA experienced similar difficulties.

C. Vinyl Chloride Emissions from Factories—The Clean Air Act

1. The Key Issues for EPA

Under the Clean Air Act,[349] EPA has the responsibility for regulating emissions of "hazardous air pollutants" from factories and other stationary sources, and for reducing emissions to the extent required to provide "an

---

exposure limit was developed with reference to the performance of the cleanest plant in the industry. The standard was upheld in American Iron & Steel Inst. v. OSHA, — F.2d —, 6 OSHC 1451 (3d Cir. 1978).

345. OSH Act § 4(b)(3), 29 U.S.C. § 653(b)(3) (1970).

346. See text accompanying notes 613-678 *infra*.

347. OSHA apparently did not even try to make such an estimate. *See* OSHA EIS, *supra* note 260, at 74-77. For EPA's handling of this problem, see text accompanying notes 470-472 *infra*.

348. See text accompanying notes 470-472 *infra*. For a discussion of how the Toxic Substances Control Act might be used to resolve this problem in the future, see text accompanying notes 796-806 *infra*.

349. 42 U.S.C.A. §§ 7401-7642 (West Supp. 1978). The term "Clean Air Act" formerly referred to the Clean Air Amendments of 1970, Pub. L. No. 91-604, 84 Stat. 1676 (1970), which so drastically changed the 1967 Air Quality Act, Pub. L. No. 90-148, 81 Stat. 485 (1967), as to constitute virtually new legislation. Certain sections of the 1970 Clean Air Act were, in turn, amended by the Energy Supply and Environmental Coordination Act of 1974. Pub. L. No. 93-319, 88 Stat. 246 (1974). Subsequently, Congress amended the Act still another time. Clean Air

ample margin of safety" for public health.[350] The release of VC to the ambient atmosphere presented to EPA medical, technical, and economic problems very similar to those which the releases to workplace air presented to OSHA. Many of the same control measures reduce emissions to the air both inside and outside the factories. As in the OSHA proceeding, any regulatory action has distributional consequences; the reduction of emissions reduces the risk to persons living and working near VC and PVC plants and increases the difficulty and cost of production. Regulation of emissions to the general atmosphere, like regulation of emissions into workplace air, would seem to pose difficult balancing problems.

There is, however, a major difference between OSHA's responsibilities under OSH Act and EPA's apparent responsibilities under the Clean Air Act. The relevant provision of the Clean Air Act is section 112, the hazardous air pollutant section, originally enacted in 1970 and amended in 1977.[351] Whereas the term "feasible" in section 6 of OSH Act mandates the balancing of health and economic interests, on its face section 112—enacted in the same week as OSH Act—seems to require the complete elimination of risk from VC emissions, regardless of cost.[352]

Hesitant either to flout the literal meaning of section 112 or to set a standard effectively closing the VC, PVC, and related industries, EPA delayed setting any standard for VC emissions until October 1976,[353] more than two and a half years after the discovery of VC's human carcinogenicity. The standard sets a limit on the VC content of exhausts from certain processes, and it specifies the use of certain equipment and operational techniques.[354] The agency explicitly based the standard on a consideration of economic costs as well as health risks; EPA was determined to interpret section 112 to allow this result, apparently preferring a strained reading of the section to the imposition of a standard with what it viewed as unacceptably severe economic consequences.

Shortly after the promulgation of the standard, the Environmental Defense Fund (EDF) sought review in the courts to establish that section 112 requires more complete control of VC emissions than EPA had decided to require.[355] Significantly, EDF as well as EPA declined to insist on the literal reading of the section and a complete elimination of VC emissions. In

Amendments of 1977, Pub. L. No. 95-95, 91 Stat. 685 (1977). The 1977 amendments, among other things, recodified the Act from 42 U.S.C. §§ 1857-1857l to its present location in the Code, and officially designated the recodification as the "Clean Air Act."

350. Clean Air Act § 112, 42 U.S.C.A. § 7412 (West Supp. 1978).
351. *Id.* The 1977 amendments do not bear directly on this discussion.
352. See text accompanying notes 364-376 *infra*.
353. 40 C.F.R. §§ 61.60-.71 (1977).
354. *Id.* § 61.65.
355. Environmental Defense Fund v. Train, No. 76-2045, 7 ELR 20,547 (D.C. Cir., filed Nov. 19, 1976, settled and dismissed June 24, 1977).

February 1977, EDF and the agency reached a settlement under the terms of which EPA agreed to amend the standard so as to establish a "goal" of eliminating emissions and to set a schedule of emission reductions over the subsequent years calculated to approach that goal.[356]

Such amendments were proposed in June 1977[357] but have not yet been promulgated. Currently, the revision of the VC standard, as well as the promulgation of additional hazardous air pollutant standards, is being delayed while EPA develops its response to another EDF petition, filed in November 1977, to establish the terms of the VC settlement as general principles for the regulation of the hundreds of airborne carcinogens that are candidates for control under section 112.[358]

The recent Supreme Court decision in *Adamo Wrecking Co. v. United States*[359] has temporarily derailed EPA's hazardous air pollutant control efforts. In January 1978, the Court overturned a criminal indictment for violation of work practice requirements in the 1973 standard for asbestos. The Court held that hazardous air pollutant standards promulgated prior to the 1977 Clean Air Act Amendments were void unless expressed in terms of numerical limits on emissions, and that standards specifying the use of particular work practices, equipment, or operational methods were not authorized until the passage of those Amendments.[360] The decision renders

---

356. The negotiations and settlement are described in Environmental Defense Fund, Petition for the Initiation of Rulemaking Proceedings to Establish a Policy Governing the Classification and Regulation of Carcinogenic Air Pollutants Under the Clean Air Act 18-19 (undated; accompanied by press release dated Nov. 7, 1977) [hereinafter cited as EDF Petition for a General Policy on Carcinogenic Air Pollutants].

357. Environmental Protection Agency, *Vinyl Chloride, National Emission Standards for Hazardous Air Pollutants, Proposed Amendments*, 42 Fed. Reg. 28,154 (1977) [hereinafter cited as *EPA Proposed Amendments to VC Standard*].

358. EDF Petition for a General Policy on Carcinogenic Air Pollutants, *supra* note 356, at 19-20.

359. 98 S. Ct. 566 (1978).

360. The defendant, a demolition contractor, was indicted under § 113(c)(1)(C) of the Clean Air Act, 42 U.S.C.A. § 7413(c)(1)(C) (West Supp. 1978), for failing to comply with the requirement in the asbestos standard to wet down asbestos before engaging in wrecking activities that could result in the substance's being released to the general atmosphere. 40 C.F.R. § 61.22(d)(2)(i) (1977). The Court held that the portion of the asbestos standard that includes "work practice" requirements is not an "emission standard" within the meaning of § 112. 96 S. Ct. at 570.

The Court noted that in 1977, after a number of lower courts had split on the permissibility of work practice requirements, Congress added § 112(e) authorizing such requirements. Whereas § 112(b)(1)(B), as enacted in 1970, Pub. L. No. 91-604, 84 Stat. 1676 § 112(b)(1)(B) (1970), authorized the setting of "emission standards," the 1977 amendment permits EPA to set a standard in terms of "a design, equipment, work practice, or operational standard, or combination thereof," instead of an "emission standard," in certain specified circumstances. Clean Air Act § 112(e), 42 U.S.C.A. § 7412(e) (West Supp. 1978). The apparent purpose of this amendment was to remove ambiguity over the issue by clarifying EPA's authority to set these types of standards. *See* H.R. REP. NO. 95-564, 95th Cong., 1st Sess. 131-32 (1977) (Conference Report on 1977 Amendments).

The Court, however, took the amendment as an affirmation that in 1970 Congress had *not* intended to authorize such standards. 98 S. Ct. at 570.

both the VC standard and the asbestos standard invalid. The decision is likely to be overcome either by the repromulgation of the standard, or by another congressional amendment of the Act.[361]

The VC proceedings and, more recently, the consideration of a generic

---

Justice Stevens argued persuasively in dissent that the majority had read the provisions and their 1970 and 1977 legislative histories incorrectly. He showed that there is no evidence that in 1970 Congress intended the term "emission standard" to have the restrictive meaning that the majority of the Court gave it. He showed also that there is no evidence that the 1977 Amendment was meant to signal the current Congress's belief that the1970 version of § 112 meant what the majority now asserted. He viewed the 1977 Amendment as ratifying and giving an explicit statutory foundation to EPA's interpretation that in appropriate circumstances a work practice standard was authorized under § 112. 98 S.Ct. at 583. Justice Stevens concluded:

> There is only one relevant lesson that may be learned from [the history of the asbestos standard and the 1977 Amendment]: As soon as someone challenged the Administrator's power to promulgate work practice rules of this sort, Congress made it unambiguously clear that the Administrator had that power. . . . In short, what Congress *said* in 1977 sheds no light on its understanding of the original meaning of the 1970 Act. But what Congress *did* when it expressly authorized work practice rules persuasively indicates that, if Congress in 1970 had focused on the latent ambiguity in the term "emission standard," it would have expressly granted the authority that the Administrator regarded as implicit in the statute as written.

98 S.Ct. at 583.

361. It might not be sufficient to repromulgate the asbestos and VC standards under the 1977 Amendments. As Justice Stevens pointed out, under the majority's reading of § 112, an "emission standard" and a "design, equipment, work practice, or operational standard" are distinct even under the 1977 Amendments. 98 S. Ct. at 583. Stevens demonstrated that although § 112(e) allows EPA to *set* a work practice or equipment standard, the standard may not be enforced. This absurd result comes about because § 112(c), which establishes what conduct is a violation of the Act and is punishable under § 113(c)(1)(C), 42 U.S.C.A. § 7413(c)(1)(C) (West Supp. 1978), speaks only of "emission standards." Nothing in § 112(c) forbids violations of a standard set in the forms authorized by § 112(e).

The majority might not go so far as to hold a standard set under § 112(e) unenforceable. While the logic of the distinction between "emission standards" and the other types does apply with equal force to § 112(c), another section of the Act makes clear that Congress desired the standards set under § 112(e) to be enforceable. Section 304(a)(3) authorizes citizen suits to enforce any "emission standard or limitation under this Act." 42 U.S.C.A. § 7604(a)(3) (West Supp. 1978). This phrase, in turn, was defined in 1977 by § 304(f)(3) to include "any requirement under section 111 or 112 (without regard to whether such requirement is expressed as an emission standard or otherwise)." Pub. L. No. 95-190, § 14a, 95th Cong., 1st Sess., 91 Stat. 1404, 42 U.S.C.A. § 7604(f)(3) (West Supp. 1978). It would be anomalous to hold that a work practice or equipment standard could be enforced by any member of the public, but not by EPA.

There is another possible means of finding the work practice or equipment standards enforceable. Under § 304(a)(1) (relating to "persons" *against* whom an action may be brought), the United States is included in the definition of "persons." Any "person" can *bring* a suit under § 304(a). Thus EPA may be able to bring a citizen suit to enforce these standards, despite problems with enforcing the standards through § 113, 42 U.S.C.A. § 7413 (West Supp. 1978).

As a practical matter, an amendment overruling *Adamo* might be preferable to taking either of the above routes towards an enforceable standard. Such an amendment would obviate the need for new rulemaking hearings, which would consume agency resources that could be used more profitably elsewhere, and which would offer opportunities for industries to delay the imposition of binding standards for these substances. An amendment also would avoid the need for taking the devious approach to enforcement through the citizen suit provision.

Adamo obviously affects the hazardous air pollutant control effort, but since the issues that it raises are largely peripheral to this discussion, the case will not be discussed further in the text.

approach to the regulation of carcinogenic air pollutants have raised several key issues for EPA. First, EPA must determine what section 112 requires. On its face the section precludes the balancing of risk and benefit that the agency believes desirable. The question arises whether the agency should bend the provision as it has, or whether it should enforce the statute as written and leave Congress the task of revising it if Congress dislikes the result.[362] Second, assuming that EPA's course is acceptable, or assuming Congress were to change section 112 to permit economic balancing, EPA, like OSHA, must address the appropriate terms on which health and economic interests should be balanced.

2. The Hazardous Pollutant Section and its Early Use

The hazardous pollutant section of the Clean Air Act,[363] was designed specifically to permit stringent, uniform, and relatively quick federal regulation of substances that pose risks of the most severe effect, even at relatively low concentrations.[364] The statute defines a hazardous air pollutant as a substance emitted by a stationary source[365] which, in the judgment of the EPA Administrator, "causes, or contributes to, air pollution which may reasonably be anticipated to result in an increase in mortality or an increase in serious irreversible, or incapacitating reversible, illness."[366] Within 180 days of designating a substance a hazardous air pollutant, EPA must propose an emission standard, and within 180 days of the proposal, after holding a public hearing, the agency must promulgate the standard, unless the Administrator "finds, on the basis of information presented at such hearings, that such pollutant clearly is not a hazardous air pollutant."[367] The standard becomes effective for new plants immediately, and for existing plants 90 days later.[368]

EPA must set the standard at the level that in the Administrator's judgment "provides an ample margin of safety to protect the public health . . . ."[369] Significantly, the section does not direct EPA to consider the

---

362. Although Congress enacted a significant amendment to § 112 in 1977, see note 360 *supra*, Congress declined then to address the balancing issue. See note 386 *infra*.
363. Clean Air Act § 112, 42 U.S.C.A. § 7412 (West Supp. 1978).
364. *See* H.R. REP. NO. 1783, 91st Cong., 2d Sess. 45-47 (1970) (Conference Report on the Clean Air Act), *reprinted in* [1970] U.S. CODE CONG. & AD. NEWS 5374, 5379-80.
365. Clean Air Act § 112(a)(2), (3), 42 U.S.C.A. § 7412(a)(2), (3) (West Supp. 1978).
366. *Id.* § 112(a)(1), 42 U.S.C.A. § 7412(a)(1) (West Supp. 1978). Until 1977, the language of this section was slightly different. However, there never was any serious contention that VC did not satisfy the original language, and the change has no practical significance for the present discussion.
367. *Id.* § 112(b)(1)(B), 42 U.S.C.A. § 7412(b)(1)(B) (West Supp. 1978).
368. *Id.* § 112(b)(1)(C), (c)(1)(B)(i), 42 U.S.C.A. § 7412(b)(1)(C), (c)(1)(B)(i) (West Supp. 1978). In general terms, thereafter § 112(c) makes it a violation of the Act for a person to construct or operate a source with emissions of a kind or amount not permitted by a standard adopted under § 112(b)(1)(B). Section 113(b)(3), 42 U.S.C.A. § 7413(b)(3) (West Supp. 1978), authorizes EPA to enforce violations of § 112(c). See note 361 *supra* regarding a possible restrictive interpretation of § 112(c) in Adamo Wrecking Co. v. United States, 98 S. Ct. 566 (1978).
369. Clean Air Act § 112(b)(1)(B), 42 U.S.C.A. § 7412(b)(1)(B) (West Supp. 1978). The Supreme Court's decision in Adamo Wrecking Co. v. United States, 98 S.Ct. 566 (1978), that

costs associated with control in choosing the requirements that provide an "ample" safety margin. The legislative history of the Clean Air Act makes clear that where language regarding the costs of control was omitted, its absence was purposeful, reflecting congressional intent that EPA should consider only health-related information.[370] In addition, section 112 establishes a relatively low standard of proof that a substance is harmful; the evidence need only show possible causation or contribution to the enumerated serious health effects. Combining these two factors, once EPA concludes that a substance is a hazardous air pollutant, the statute directs the agency to set a highly protective standard that eliminates possible serious risks without regard to cost.[371]

The only provision under which some flexibility conceivably exists for consideration of the difficulty and cost of compliance is the availability to individual stationary sources of waivers of compliance for up to two years, if the Administrator "finds that such period is *necessary* for the installation of controls and that steps will be taken during the period of waiver to assure that the health of persons will be protected from imminent endangerment."[372] Neither the agency nor the courts have addressed this provision to

---

hazardous air pollutant standards set before 1977 (including the VC standard) must specify numerical emission limits, is discussed in notes 359-361 *supra* and accompanying text.

370. *See* Union Electric Co. v. EPA, 427 U.S. 246, 8 ERC 2143 (1976), in which the Court took this view regarding § 110(a) of the Act, 42 U.S.C.A. § 7410(a) (West Supp. 1978). Compare the section on new source performance standards, § 111(b)(1)(A), which explicitly requires EPA to take costs into account, with § 112(b)(1)(B). 42 U.S.C.A. §§ 7411(b)(1)(A), 7412(b)(1)(B) (West Supp. 1978). This difference in the otherwise closely parallel sections is persuasive that the silence on costs in § 112 was purposeful. *See generally* Kramer, *Economics, Technology, and The Clean Air Act of 1970: The First Six Years*, 6 ECOLOGY L.Q. 161, 194-196 (1976).

371. The legislative history of § 112 does not speak to the meaning of an "ample margin of safety." Some help interpreting § 112 comes from commentary on another section. Section 109, 42 U.S.C.A. § 7409(b)(1) (West Supp. 1978), requires that a primary ambient air quality standard be set at the level necessary to protect public health with an "adequate" margin of safety. The 1970 Senate Report defines "adequate" protection of "public health" as something less than protection of the most sensitive *individual* from adverse effects. It is defined as follows:

> In requiring that national ambient air quality standards be established at a level necessary to protect the health of persons the Committee recognizes that such standards will not necessarily provide for the quality of air required to protect those individuals who are otherwise dependent on a controlled internal environment such as patients in intensive care units or newborn infants in nurseries. However, the Committee emphasizes that included among those persons whose health should be protected by the ambient standard are particularly sensitive citizens such as bronchial asthmatics and emphysematics who in the normal course of daily activity are exposed to the ambient environment. *In establishing an ambient standard necessary to protect the health of these persons, reference should be made to a representative sample of persons comprising the sensitive group rather than to a single person in such a group.*
>
> *Ambient air quality is sufficient to protect the health of such persons whenever there is an absence of adverse effect of the health of a statistically related sample of persons in sensitive groups from exposure to the ambient air.*

S. REP. NO. 1196, 91st Cong., 2d Sess. 10 (1970) (emphasis added). Assuming that "public health" has the same meaning in the hazardous air pollutant section as above, and that "ample" means at least as much as "adequate," a standard set under § 112 must be at least as protective as this. It must be aimed at protecting the group of those most sensitive to the regulated substance.

372. Clean Air Act § 112(c)(1)(B)(ii), 42 U.S.C.A. § 7412(c)(1)(B)(ii) (West Supp. 1978)

date.[373]

With regard to carcinogenic substances, a straightforward, literal reading of the statute seems to require that EPA set standards that completely eliminate emissions. Since thresholds for the carcinogenic effect of such substances presently cannot be identified, no level of exposure to a carcinogen may be considered entirely safe.[374] Any safety margin for public health can be achieved only by entirely eliminating human exposure to the substance.[375] Since the technology to produce VC and PVC without releasing any VC emissions does not now exist, and since its development is not foreseeable at a cost that would permit any but perhaps the most valuable uses of the chemical to compete with substitutes, a "zero emissions" standard would force these industries to close.[376]

There is some evidence from the legislative history of the 1970 Act that Congress considered and approved of this result. A summary of the Conference Report, presented to the Senate by Senator Muskie, stated with regard to section 112:

> The standards must be set to provide an ample margin of safety to protect the public health. This could mean, effectively, that a plant would be required to close because of the absence of control techniques. It could include emission standards which allowed for no measurable emissions.[377]

EPA, however, has never been comfortable with the apparent policy of section 112 to minimize the risk of death or serious illness from air pollutants regardless of cost. The agency has been reluctant to act under the hazardous air pollutant section since its enactment in 1970. Prior to regulating VC, EPA had set only three other hazardous air pollutant standards, for asbestos, beryllium, and mercury.[378] The agency proposed these standards

---

(emphasis added). "Necessary" may be limited to claims of technological, rather than economic necessity.

In addition, the President may exempt a source from compliance with hazardous air pollutant standards for up to two years "if he finds that the technology to implement such standards is not available and the operation of such source is required for reasons of national security." *Id.* § 112(c)(2), 42 U.S.C.A. § 7412(c)(2) (West Supp. 1978).

373. Unlike other sections of the statute, discussed in text accompanying notes 393-399 *infra*, § 112 contemplates that the federal government rather than the states will have the primary role in enforcing hazardous air pollutant standards. However, states are delegated responsibility for enforcement of even these standards if they develop an implementation and enforcement procedure that the EPA Administrator finds to be "adequate." Clean Air Act § 112(d), 42 U.S.C.A. § 7412(d) (West Supp. 1978). Even if enforcement has been delegated to a state, EPA retains the power to take enforcement action as well. *Id.*

374. See text accompanying notes 34-57 *supra*.

375. *Id.*

376. *EPA Proposed Standard for VC, supra* note 131, at 59,534.

377. SENATE COMM. ON PUB. WORKS, SUMMARY OF THE PROVISIONS OF CONFERENCE AGREEMENT ON THE CLEAN AIR AMENDMENTS OF 1970, *reprinted* in A LEGISLATIVE HISTORY OF THE CLEAN AIR AMENDMENTS OF 1970, SER. NO. 93-18, 93d Cong., 2d Sess. 133 (1974).

378. 40 C.F.R. §§ 61.01-.55 (1977), *promulgated at* 38 Fed. Reg. 8820 (1973). See notes 359-361 *supra* and accompanying text (discussion of Adamo Wrecking Co. v. United States, 98 S.Ct. 566 (1978), which partially invalidated the asbestos standard).

together in late 1971[379] and promulgated them only in 1973.[380] This was long after the expiration of the 180-day statutory deadline, and EPA acted then only under the compulsion of a court order.[381]

The preambles accompanying the proposal and promulgation of these three standards reveal that EPA took economic considerations into account, despite the absence of statutory authority to do so. In the proposal the agency stated: "These standards are based on information derived from many sources, including health effects levels, meteorology, technical analysis of control capability, and consideration of economic impact. The overriding considerations are health effects."[382] The preamble to the final standard contains the averments that each standard "was not based on economic considerations,"[383] but at least in the case of asbestos there is evidence to the contrary. Asbestos is a carcinogen, and no safe dose of the substance has been identified. Yet the EPA standard permits some emissions of asbestos to the ambient air. The agency asserted that it was not "necessary" to prohibit all emissions in order to provide an "ample margin of safety to protect the public health," but this conclusion was based on questionable inferences from the available medical evidence.[384] The preamble reveals that EPA had economic considerations in mind as well as health considerations. The agency stated:

> EPA considered the possibility of banning production, processing, and use of asbestos or banning all emissions . . . into the atmosphere, but rejected these approaches . . . . Either approach would result in the prohibition of many activities which are extremely important; moreover, the available evidence relating to the health hazards of asbestos does not suggest that such prohibition is necessary to protect public health.[385]

---

379. EPA, *National Emission Standards For Hazardous Air Pollutants, Proposed Standard for Asbestos, Beryllium, Mercury*, 36 Fed. Reg. 23,239 (1971) [hereinafter cited as *EPA Proposed Rules for Asbestos, Beryllium, and Mercury*].

380. EPA, *National Emission Standards for Hazardous Air Pollutants, Asbestos, Beryllium, and Mercury*, 38 Fed. Reg. 8820 (1973) [hereinafter cited as *EPA Standards for Asbestos, Beryllium, and Mercury*].

381. Environmental Defense Fund v. Ruckelshaus, Civil No. 2399-72, 3 ELR 20,173 (D.D.C. 1973). This was a citizen suit under § 304 of the Clean Air Act, 42 U.S.C.A. § 7604 (West Supp. 1978), for an order requiring EPA to promulgate standards proposed more than 180 days before. The court ordered EPA to promulgate the standard within 60 days of its decision.

382. *EPA Proposed Rules for Asbestos, Beryllium, and Mercury, supra* note 379, at 23,239.

383. *EPA Standards for Asbestos, Beryllium, and Mercury, supra* note 380, at 8822, 8824-25.

384. *EPA Standards for Asbestos, Beryllium, and Mercury, supra* note 380, at 8820. EPA alluded to the evidence of cancer hazards at low doses of asbestos, but then stated: "On the other hand, the available evidence does not indicate that levels of asbestos in most community air cause asbestotic disease." *Id.* The agency went on to infer the absence of a hazard, or at least a failure to have demonstrated one to exist, from the absence of positive evidence of harmfulness. The point is that in view of the methodological problems that render epidemiological studies relatively "insensitive" to events occurring at a low rate, it would not be surprising if some effect actually were taking place. For these reasons, the absence of data cannot be taken as persuasive evidence of the absence of a carcinogenic risk.

385. *EPA Standards for Asbestos, Beryllium, and Mercury, supra* note 380, at 8820.

No environmental group or other interest group challenged the failure to prohibit asbestos emissions entirely, and the issues regarding the consideration of economic factors remained dormant until the VC proceedings.[386]

3. EPA's Search For Alternatives to the Use of Section 112

Early in its consideration of VC, EPA concluded that the hazard did not warrant the severe action that section 112 calls for on its face. As early as September 1974, an EPA Task Force on VC concluded that a major reduction in emissions was needed, but that the economic consequences of completely closing the VC and PVC industries were not warranted by the added safety that would be gained thereby.[387]

As alternatives to the use of section 112, between early 1974 and the issuance of the proposed standard in December 1976, EPA considered using at least four other sections of the Clean Air Act to regulate VC emissions: abatement conferences (section 115),[388] imminent hazard emergency powers (section 303).[389] a primary ambient air quality standard (section 109),[390] and a new source performance standard (section 111), which also may be applied to existing sources.[391] In September 1974, the agency rejected the former two alternatives;[392] EPA noted that abatement conferences are cumbersome and ineffectual,[393] and it concluded that there was no evidence that

---

386.   This was *not* an issue in Adamo Wrecking Co. v. United States, 98 S.Ct. 566 (1978), or in any of the lower court litigation over § 112 and the meaning of the term "emission standard." See notes 359-361 *supra* and accompanying text. However, all parties and the Court operated under the assumption, contended here to be faulty, that § 112 does not require the setting of an asbestos standard at zero emissions. Justice Stevens, for example, accepted at face value EPA's statement that the elimination of asbestos exposure was not "necessary" in order to provide "an ample margin of safety to protect the public health." 98 S.Ct. at 580 (dissenting opinion).

The dissent holds that the statute would permit EPA to prohibit asbestos emissions entirely, even if this would preclude building demolition. 98 S.Ct. at 580-81 (dissenting opinion). But there is no holding or any dicta in either the majority or the dissenting opinion to indicate reliably how the Court would view the application of the "ample margin of safety" requirement to carcinogens if a case posed this issue squarely. The decision in Union Electric Co. v. EPA, 427 U.S. 246, 8 ERC 2143 (1976), suggests, but does not compel, the conclusion that the Court would enforce the law literally, and leave to Congress the responsibility to change it, should Congress see fit. *See id.* at 272, 8 ERC at 2152 (concurring opinion); note 370 *supra*; Kramer, *supra* note 370, at 194-96.

387.   This view was expressed repeatedly throughout EPA's investigation. *See* EPA Task Force Report, *supra* note 85, at 16-17 (Sept. 1974); U.S. Environmental Protection Agency, Office of Air Quality Planning and Standards, Analysis of Air Pollution Regulatory Alternatives for Vinyl Chloride (Draft) 37-42 (Sept. 30, 1974) [hereinafter cited as EPA VC Air Pollution Alternatives]; EPA EIS, *supra* note 85, at 2-19 to -25 (Oct. 1975); *EPA Proposed Standard for VC, supra* note 131, at 59,534 (Dec. 1975); *EPA Standard for VC, supra* note 148, at 46,561 (Oct. 1976).

388.   42 U.S.C.A. § 7415 (West Supp. 1978).

389.   *Id.* § 7603.

390.   *Id.* § 7409.

391.   *Id.* § 7411.

392.   EPA VC Air Pollution Alternatives, *supra* note 387, at ES-9.

393.   *Id.* at 35-36. The abatement conference is a holdover from the 1967 Air Quality Act,

would support a district court's finding that an imminent hazard existed from VC emissions.[394]

EPA later rejected the other two alternatives to section 112 as well.[395] While a primary standard could be set under section 109 for ambient concentration of VC, the agency noted that ambient standards were not intended for, nor are they well suited to, regulating a discretely localized pollutant.[396] Under section 109, the states are responsible for developing and enforcing implementation plans for attaining compliance with ambient standards; this procedure would raise additional problems for the control of VC. The state process would take far longer than federal development and enforcement of a hazardous pollutant standard; moreover, there could be great variation in and dispute over the means and timetables that the states

Pub. L. No. 90-148, § 108(d), 81 Stat. 485 (1967), as amended in Clean Air Act § 115, 42 U.S.C.A. § 7415 (West Supp. 1978). It is an ineffectual tool for cleaning up the air, relying on EPA's limited persuasive powers as mediator between the states and the polluters and presuming the states' eagerness to control the emissions in question. For further discussion of the conference's inadequacy for dealing with VC, see EPA VC Air Pollution Alternatives, *supra* note 387, at 35-36.

394. *Id.* at 36-37; EPA Task Force Report, *supra* note 85, at 16. The Administrator may seek an injunction from a district court against emissions if they constitute an "imminent and substantial endangerment" to health. Clean Air Act § 303, 42 U.S.C.A. § 7603 (West Supp. 1978). The section was designed to deal with short-term severe situations in which the various state and federal rulemaking and enforcement alternatives would take too long to give adequate protection. EPA VC Air Pollution Alternatives, *supra* note 387, at 36. However, the injunction would have to be sought in the court for each district where VC or PVC plants are found, *id.* at 37, and serious danger would have to be proved by a preponderance of evidence, under ordinary rules of civil procedure.

The Task Force concluded that there is "no scientific evidence" to indicate that VC emissions pose an imminent hazard to people living near plants. EPA Task Force Report, *supra* note 85, at 16. Much depends, however, on the meaning of "imminent hazard," a subject that currently is unsettled. An attempt to obtain an immediate injunction by proving the existence of an imminent hazard based on the threat of future harm was rejected by the Eighth Circuit Court of Appeals in 1975. Reserve Mining Co. v. United States, 514 F.2d 492, 534, 7 ERC 1618, 1648-49 (8th Cir. 1975). On the other hand, the District of Columbia Circuit Court of Appeals has held that under the Federal Insecticide, Fungicide, and Rodenticide Act, an imminent hazard may be created immediately by exposure to a toxic substance, even though the effects of that exposure will not become apparent until long into the future, so long as the exposure creates an irrevocable risk. Environmental Defense Fund v. Ruckelshaus, 439 F.2d 584, 595-96, 2 ERC 1114, 1121-22 (D.C. Cir. 1971).

395. *EPA Proposed Standard for VC, supra* note 131, at 59,534.

396. *Id.* Ambient air quality standards are specifically designed to deal with widely dispersed pollutants, or reactive products of pollutants, from "numerous or diverse mobile or stationary sources" that EPA judges "may reasonably be anticipated to endanger public health or welfare." Clean Air Act § 108(a)(1), 42 U.S.C.A. § 7408(a)(1) (West Supp. 1978). Since the ambient air quality is determined by averaging samples taken at many points, there may be significant variation in localized exposures, such as in the immediate vicinity of a facility emitting VC. A major advantage of the ambient standards approach is that it avoids the immediate need to attribute particular ambient pollution to a specific source, something which was beyond the state of the art of air pollution diffusion modeling in 1970 and which remains largely so today. *See generally* Mandelker & Sherry, *Emission Quota Strategies as an Air Pollution Control Technique*, 5 ECOLOGY L.Q. 401, 403-04 (1976); Roberts, Croke, & Booras, *A Critical Review of the Effects of Air Pollution Control Regulations on Land Use Planning*, 25 J. AIR POLL. CONT. A. 500 (1975). *See also* EPA EIS, *supra* note 85, at 2-9 to -10.

chose in order to meet the standard.[397] Alternatively, a new source performance standard might have been set for VC, but this procedure also has the
drawbacks of state responsibility for its achievement and of a lengthy
development period.[398] Moreover, section 111 explicitly requires that EPA
take into account the costs of control.[399] The agency felt that it might have to
give economic considerations more weight under section 111 than it intended to give them under section 112.[400]

4. EPA's Reinterpretation of The Hazardous Pollutant Section

EPA eventually decided to regulate VC under section 112, but the
agency determined not to apply the section literally to an "apparent non-
threshold pollutant" such as VC.[401] In its proposed standard the agency
pointed out that Congress had never considered explicitly the consequences
of applying section 112 to such pollutants and concluded: "Congress did not
intend to impose the costs associated with complete emission prohibition in
every case involving such a pollutant."[402] EPA was correct that Congress
did not specifically address the problem of carcinogens and other substances
lacking identifiable thresholds. However, the agency made no mention at all
of the statement in the summary of the Conference Report presented to the

---

397.   The Administrator must set a primary standard at a level that he judges, "allowing an
adequate margin of safety, [is] requisite to protect the public health." Clean Air Act § 109(b)(1),
42 U.S.C.A. § 7409(b)(1) (West Supp. 1978). See the discussion of what is an adequate safety
margin to protect public health in note 371 *supra*. Section 110, 42 U.S.C.A. § 7410 (West Supp.
1978), creates a complex joint federal-state implementation process in which many years can
pass before enforceable emission limits or requirements are established for individual sources.
On the drawbacks of this approach for control of VC, see EPA EIS, *supra* note 85, at 2-9 to -10;
EPA Proposed Standard for VC, supra note 131, at 59,534.

398.   *EPA Proposed Standard for VC, supra* note 131, at 59,534. The Administrator may
set standards of performance for emissions from new stationary sources if he judges that a
category of sources "causes, or contributes significantly to, air pollution which may reasonably
be anticipated to endanger public health or welfare." Clean Air Act § 111(b)(1), 42 U.S.C.A. §
7411(b)(1) (West Supp. 1978). EPA is authorized to enforce directly new source performance
standards, although states may develop and seek approval of their own enforcement plans. *Id.*
§ 111(c), 42 U.S.C.A. § 7411(c) (West Supp. 1978). EPA may apply a new source performance
standard to existing sources as well, through a state plan preparation and enforcement process
similar to that for a primary ambient air quality standard. *Id.* § 111(d), 42 U.S.C.A. § 7411(d)
(West Supp. 1978). *See* EPA EIS, *supra* note 2-4, at 2-11 to -13; *EPA Proposed Standard for
VC, supra* note 131, at 59,534.

399.   A new source performance standard must prescribe the best "adequately demonstrated" control technology, "taking into consideration the cost of achieving such [standard]."
Clean Air Act § 111(a)(1)(C). 42 U.S.C.A. § 7411(a)(1)(C) (West Supp. 1978).

400.   Personal communication with Marcia Gelpe, Assistant Professor of Law, University
of Minnesota, formerly an attorney in the General Counsel's Office in EPA (Jan. 5, 1977). *See
also* EPA EIS, *supra* note 85, at 2-11 to -13; *EPA Proposed Standard for VC, supra* note 131, at
59,534.

401.   *EPA Proposed Standard for VC, supra* note 131, at 59,534.

402.   *Id.* Note the phrase "in every case." EPA appears to be holding open the possibility
that in the case of a substance of very high risk or very low benefit, a complete prohibition of
emissions would be appropriate.

Senate by Senator Muskie, which apparently accepts the possibility that some standards will require some plants to close.[403]

In lieu of zero emissions standards for "apparent non-threshold" pollutants, EPA interpreted the section to require "emission reduction to the lowest level achievable by the use of the best available control technology."[404] In determining the best[405] available measures, EPA declined to undertake "a fine balancing of costs against benefits" regarding each particular control measure under consideration.[406] Instead, the agency defined a control measure to be "available" if: (1) it was in use at one or more plants in the broader chemical industry and was "generally adaptable" to VC or PVC plants within the time allowed for achieving the standard; and (2) it did not impose costs that were "grossly disproportionate to the emission reduction achieved."[407] EPA characterized this last criterion as a "limited" consideration of costs.[408] So interpreted, section 112 resembles the section regulating new sources (section 111), except that the consideration of economic factors is solely in federal hands and purportedly is more restricted.

EPA stated that the best available control technology approach, qualified by the "grossly disporportionate" costs criterion, "will produce the most stringent regulation of hazardous air pollutants short of requiring a complete prohibition in all cases."[409] Whether this statement is true depends on the test EPA uses to define "grossly disproportionate" costs and the rigor with which it sifts economic evidence.

5. The Designation of VC as a Hazardous Pollutant and the Proposed Standard

In December 1975, after almost two years of delay, EPA designated VC a hazardous pollutant and proposed detailed control requirements for the VC and PVC industries.[410] The designation was based on data strongly suggesting that VC posed serious risks to the general public living near these

---

403. See text accompanying note 377 *supra*.

404. *EPA Proposed Standard for VC, supra* note 131, at 59,534.

405. The regulations state that the purpose of the "best available technology" standard is to "minimize risk to public health by establishing an emission standard which will reduce emissions to the level attainable with the best available control systems." *Id.* at 59,534. EPA did not define the term "best," and the term might be considered self-explanatory. Although the agency's use of the term appears tautological, the clear purpose of the standard is to force use of the control technology which will most effectively reduce emissions so long as this is consistent with the definition of availability as discussed in the text.

407. *Id.*

408. *Id.*

409. *Id.* at 59,534. Note again that with the phrase "in all cases," EPA reserves the right to designate some situations where a zero emission standard is appropriate. See note 402 *supra*.

410. *EPA Proposed Standard for VC, supra* note 131.

facilities. EPA estimated that approximately 4.6 million people lived within five miles of a VC or PVC plant, and that they were exposed to more than one ppm VC approximately 10 percent of the time. Moreover, from sampling in 1974 and 1975, the agency had found occasional higher concentrations in the air near those plants, including one reading at 33 ppm.[411] While there were no data at that time on the human or animal toxicity of exposures near VC and PVC plants, EPA concluded that these exposures posed risks that brought VC within the definition of a hazardous air pollutant. The major items of evidence supporting this conclusion were: (1) the recording as of June 1975 of as many as 38 cases of liver angiosarcoma in workers exposed to VC; (2) the incidence of that disease in at least four workers thought to have been exposed to relatively low levels of VC; (3) indications that VC workers suffered excess rates of cancer in many organs other than the liver; and (4) the induction of liver angiosarcoma and other cancers in animals exposed to VC at 50 ppm, the lowest level then tested.[412] EPA concluded, paraphrasing the hazardous pollutant definition: "Reasonable extrapolations from these findings cause concern that present ambient levels of vinyl chloride may cause or contribute to the same or similar disorders."[413] EPA concluded that regulating on the basis of this uncertain but highly suggestive evidence of danger was preferable to waiting for the development of epidemiological data proving the occurrence of cancers among the populations surrounding the plants. To develop information on the human effects of low-level exposures would take a very long time, as the latency period for the effects of such exposures might exceed 30 years. In the meantime, an additional generation would have been put at an irreversible risk.[414]

In the environmental impact statement accompanying the proposed VC standard, EPA defined the meaning of "grossly disproportionate" costs for the purpose of designating control measures required for the VC and PVC industries. The agency judged that the industry could absorb a price increase of as much as 10 percent for PVC resins "without significant ill effects," but that greater price rises would lead to "appreciable substitution" of alternative materials by PVC users.[415]

EPA proposed a detailed set of control measures to reduce emissions from VC and PVC plants by about 95 percent, and estimated that these

411. *Id.* at 59,533-34; EPA SCIENTIFIC AND TECHNICAL REPORT, *supra* note 90, at 18.
412. *EPA Proposed Standard for VC, supra* note 131, at 59,532; EPA SCIENTIFIC AND TECHNICAL REPORT, *supra* note 90, at 1-3.
413. *EPA Proposed Standard for VC, supra* note 131, at 59,533.
414. *Id.*
415. EPA EIS, *supra* note 85, at 7-20. This was admittedly a rough estimate. The EIS added:

> No attempt has been made to test the assumption that a 10 percent price increase would have minimal impact. It is extremely doubtful that such a determination could

measures would necessitate raising the prices of PVC resins by an average 7.3 percent in order to maintain profit rates.[416] The major requirements were to be: (1) a 10 ppm limit on the concentration of VC in the emissions from equipment used in VC and PVC manufacture; (2) work practice changes to reduce VC releases from the opening of polymerization reactors and other process equipment; (3) more effective "stripping" (the removal of residual VC from newly formed PVC by applying heat and vacuum); (4) better seals to prevent leakage from valves, pumps, pipe joints, and other equipment; (5) the use of valves and vacuum pressure to limit VC releases from disconnected hoses and other couplings; and (6) control devices to remove most VC from process water.[417] EPA also proposed to require that each plant have a regular program of leak detection and equipment maintenance and that operators periodically file detailed reports about exposure incidents and about compliance with the specified requirements.[418] The proposal also included a provision under which a manufacturer could obtain permission to use other control measures—essentially a variance—upon demonstrating to EPA that the alternatives were as effective as the measures the agency proposed.[419]

EPA rejected the imposition of more stringent controls, arguing that a complete ban on VC emissions would force the industries to close, and that this would have unacceptable economic consequences. The agency predicted that the VC and PVC companies, especially those not highly diversified into other industries, would be severely impacted and might fail; unemployment would increase, at least temporarily; although substitutes existed for most PVC uses, they would not be available for at least two years; and substitutes would be more costly, and might not have certain desirable features of PVC, such as its resistance to fire.[420]

EPA, however, stopped far short of proposing all the controls that the industries could afford to bear; the predicted impact of the prescribed measures did not even reach the agency's own cut-off point of a 10 percent price increase. The proposal would not impose the use of any measures that

ever be made on a before-the-fact basis with any degree of accuracy. It would appear that the use of a 10 percent price increase is a reasonable one, but the exact point at which substitutions or increased imports become a significant problem is a matter of conjecture.

Id. at 7-20 to -21.

416. *EPA Proposed Standard for VC, supra* note 131, at 59,544. *See also* EPA EIS, *supra* note 85, at 7-54 to -62.

417. *EPA Proposed Standard for VC, supra* note 131, at 59,535-40. With the exception of the 10 ppm limit on process exhausts, these are design and operational requirements that, under the holding of Adamo Wrecking Co. v. United States, 98 S.Ct. 566 (1978), were not authorized before 1977. See notes 360-361 *supra*.

418. *EPA Proposed Standard for VC, supra* note 131, at 59,542-43.

419. *Id.* at 59,547 (proposed 40 C.F.R. § 61.66).

420. *Id.* at 59,534.

could significantly alter the economic status quo, *i.e.*, that would significantly threaten the profitability of the VC and PVC industries, decrease the
amounts produced, change the industries' growth prospects, or alter their
shares of the wider plastics market. The agency declined to propose the use
of certain clearly available control measures that would have reduced emissions by approximately three percent more than the proposed 95 percent
reduction, stating that these controls would entail "grossly disproportionate" costs for equipment or energy, apparently meaning that they would
force price hikes of more than 10 percent.[421] Although EPA refused to
guarantee that the proposed requirements would not make the operation of
some small PVC plants uneconomical,[422] the agency emphasized that the
proposal would cause no serious changes in the industries.[423]

EPA proposed no regulations for the fabrication plants because their
already low emissions appear to come only from VC residual in PVC stock.
EPA's sampling had found "almost negligible" amounts of VC in air near
fabrication plants; the highest level found was six ppb.[424] The agency
determined that compliance with OSHA and EPA requirements by the VC
and PVC manufacturers would decrease the residual content of PVC stock to
the point that emissions from fabricators would be several orders of magnitude below the level of post-control emissions from VC and PVC
plants.[425] EPA decided that this level of emissions required no controls.

6. Promulgation of the Standard

After accepting comments and holding a public hearing in early 1976,
EPA promulgated the VC standard in October, four months after the statutory deadline.[426] EPA cited new research results that bolstered the designation of the substance as hazardous. On the basis of statistical extrapolations
from data on the chemical's toxicity to humans and animals, this report

---

421. *Id.* at 59,536-38. For example, the VC-laden emissions from the oxychlorination
reactor at VC plants might be incinerated, but the concentration of VC in this gas is too low to
burn without supplemental natural gas. This is not the case for VC-laden emissions from most
other steps of the process. *Id.* at 59,536-37. Similarly, equipment could be placed on the slurry
bend tanks and inprocess wastewater at PVC plants to reduce pre-control emissions by 0.1
percent. *Id.* at 59,538. EPA estimated that the costs of these devices would force PVC prices to
rise more than the 10 percent cut-off. See the cost analysis in EPA EIS, supra note 85, at 7-18
to -64, especially the tables at 7-54 to -62. Certain other measures were easier for the agency to
reject. As an example EPA gave the possibility of "placing a bubble around an industrial
complex and venting all air from the complex through an enormous control device." Another
example given was the use of incinerators in series. *EPA Proposed Standard for VC, supra* note
131, at 59,536.
422. *EPA Proposed Standard for VC, supra* note 131, at 59,536.
423. *Id.*
424. *Id.* at 59,534-35. EPA SCIENTIFIC AND TECHNICAL REPORT, *supra* note 90, at 18.
425. *EPA Proposed Standard for VC, supra* note 131, at 59,534-35.
426. *EPA Standard for VC, supra* note 148. Under § 112(b)(1)(B) of the Clean Air Act, 42
U.S.C.A. § 7412(b)(1)(B) (West Supp. 1978), an emissions standard must be promulgated
within 180 days after it is proposed.

estimated that uncontrolled emissions of VC could cause up to 20 extra cases of cancer per year among the 4.6 million plant neighbors, which would be diagnosed starting in the 1990s.[427] The report estimated that the standard's 95 percent emission reduction would lead to a proportionate decrease in cancer cases, resulting in a maximum of about one case per year.[428]

The standard differs from the proposal only in minor ways. In general, commentators on behalf of the industries accepted the proposal, arguing mainly as to the merits of details of the prescribed control technology. EPA accepted some such criticisms and rejected others.[429]

Some industry commentators took the view that EPA's consideration of costs was not generous enough. They argued that EPA should evaluate the costs and benefits of each available emission control measure and require only those with greater benefits than costs. EPA restated its view that the discretion to consider economic factors under section 112 was limited to determining only whether the costs of particular controls were "grossly disproportionate" to their benefits, and not to closely balancing the costs and benefits of each measure.[430]

In its comments EDF took the position that section 112 requires a standard more stringent than EPA's proposal.[431] Significantly, however, EDF did not press for the literal interpretation of the section. The environmental group criticized the agency for limiting its steps to prevent cancer to measures that would not significantly diminish the industry's profitability, growth rate, or market position. EDF urged the agency to ban all uses of PVC for which substitutes currently existed, and to ban other uses in the future as substitutes for them were developed.[432] Since substitutes exist or can be readily imagined for nearly all PVC uses,[433] this approach would

427. *EPA Standard for VC, supra* note 148, at 46,560; A. Kuzmack & R. McGaughy, Quantitative Risk Assessment for Community Exposure of Vinyl Chloride 1-8 (Dec. 5, 1975) [hereinafter cited as EPA Risk Assessment]. Although this report is dated shortly before the issuance of the proposed standard, the proposal did not mention it or rely on it. Realistically, the report was completed too late to be considered in the proposal.

428. EPA Risk Assessment, *supra* note 427, at ii-iii. Several commentators argued that the health effects of low-level exposures to VC were too uncertain to support designating VC a hazardous air pollutant. Essentially they argued that the doubts about the chemical's safety be resolved in favor of its uncontrolled use. EPA responded that the known effects of high doses on humans and animals and the absence of known thresholds for carcinogens were sufficient reason to place the substance on the list of hazardous pollutants, and that opponents of this action had not met their burden (imposed by § 112(b)(a)(B), 42 U.S.C.A. § 7412(b)(1)(B) (West Supp. 1978)) of presenting evidence showing clearly the existence of safe exposure levels. *EPA Standard for VC, supra* note 148, at 46,561.

429. *Id.* at 46,562-64.

430. *Id.* at 46,562.

431. Environmental Defense Fund, Statement to the U.S. Environmental Protection Agency on the Proposed National Emission Standard for Vinyl Chloride 14-16 (Feb..3, 1976) [hereinafter cited as EDF Comments].

432. *Id.*

433. The EIS indicates that substitutes exist for "approximately 85 percent (by weight)"

result shortly in a nearly complete ban of the substance. EDF acknowledged that some substitutes might themselves be dangerous but insisted that most potential substitutes were safer than PVC.[434]

EPA rejected EDF's recommendations. The agency emphasized that some untested and unregulated substitutes might endanger health and the environment more than the levels of VC emissions that would remain under the standard. In addition, EPA reiterated that PVC has desirable characteristics that substitutes lack, and that some workers would be unemployed, at least temporarily. The agency emphasized that the standard would reduce emissions and the corresponding risks "substantially."[435]

Foreseeing that some plants could not be in compliance with the new standard by its effective date 90 days later, EPA indicated that it would grant up to two-year waivers of compliance for plants needing to purchase and install control equipment.[436] The agency did not explain the criteria by which it would judge whether a waiver was "necessary."[437]

7. *The EDF Settlement and the Proposed Revision of the Standard*

Shortly after the promulgation, EDF petitioned the District of Columbia Circuit Court of Appeals for review, pressing its contention that the standard was too lax.[438] The environmental group's first contention was that the agency had failed to consider all the relevant health information available by the time of the promulgation. EDF cited a September 1976 report that in Italian experiments VC had been found to cause cancer in rats inhaling as little as *one* ppm, the lowest level that has been tested to date.[439] EDF contended that EPA may have underestimated the health risks from low exposures to VC.[440]

---

of PVC's uses. EPA EIS, *supra* note 85, at 2-23. The EIS also contains a list of PVC uses and indicates that substitutes presently are available for most. *Id.* at 7-69 to -70.

434. EDF Comments, *supra* note 431, at 15-16.

435. *EPA Standard for VC, supra* note 148, at 46,561.

436. *Id.* at 46,563. 40 C.F.R. § 61.66 (1977), promulgated in *id.* at 46,567, provides for waiver of compliance upon application by the operator of the source, if EPA finds the operator's proposed alternate control measures to be equal in effectiveness to those required by the standard. EPA suggested, however, that such applications be accompanied by requests for waivers of compliance under § 112(c) in anticipation of a finding that the proposed alternate measures were inadequate. *EPA Standard for VC, supra* note 148, at 46,563. The § 112(c) waiver provision is discussed in text accompanying notes 372-373 *supra*.

437. See text accompanying notes 372-373 *supra*.

438. Environmental Defense Fund v. Train, No. 76-2045 (D.C. Cir., filed Nov. 19, 1976; settled and dismissed June 24, 1977).

439. Personal communication with Robert Rauch, Staff Attorney, Environmental Defense Fund (Nov. 30, 1976). *See also* Memorandum from Ms. Verne Lesho, Secretary to Dr. N.M. Johnson, B.F. Goodrich Co., Akron, Ohio, to Dr. Peter Infante, National Institute for Occupational Safety and Health (Nov. 11, 1976) (reporting the Italian results). A later memorandum reports the results of Bulgarian studies on animals exposed to VC at one ppm which confirm the Italian tests. Memorandum from Edward J. Fairchild, II, Associate Institute Director, Cincinnati Operations, National Institute for Occupational Safety and Health, to Chief, Technical Evaluation and Review Branch, Office of Extramural Coordination and Special Projects, Re: Update Information on Vinyl Chloride (Jan. 3, 1977).

440. Personal communication with Robert Rauch, *supra* note 439. It may be, however,

EDF also argued that EPA had given too much weight to the economic interests of the VC and PVC industries. The group contended that the agency knew of, but ignored certain available control devices and techniques that would permit greater emission reductions at less cost than the controls EPA explicitly rejected. At the very least, EDF contended that section 112 requires a standard that will force the development of new control technology, with an eventual goal of eliminating carcinogenic emissions entirely.[441] The group argued that the section does not authorize EPA to hold industrial profit and growth rates and market position unharmed, and that only very limited consideration of costs can be permitted to qualify the technology-forcing character of the standard.[442]

In February 1977, EDF and EPA settled the case with an agreement along the lines EDF advocated.[443] In June 1977, EPA officially proposed to revise the VC standard as required by the settlement agreement.[444] The proposal embodies a significantly stronger approach to regulating airborne carcinogens than EPA had taken in the 1976 VC standard or in the asbestos standard. EPA stated that its objective was "to insure that the standard continues to approach the only level of emissions which is known to be absolutely protective of health, namely zero emissions . . . ."[445] To this end the agency proposed to tighten the requirements of the standard so as to force the best use of existing control measures and the development of new technology.[446]

Unlike the 1976 standard, the revised standard would differentiate between existing and new plants. Existing plants, currently subject to a 10 ppm limit on the concentration of VC in process exhausts, would have to reduce the concentration to five ppm within three years of the amendments' promulgation date. EPA stated its goal of "forc[ing] owners and operators to maximize the effectiveness of existing control systems" installed to meet the OSHA and EPA standards already in effect.[447] Existing plants would not be required to install major devices in addition to or in replacement of controls they had already implemented to meet these standards.[448] If the owner or operator could demonstrate that a particular plant was "unable" to meet the new limit in the three-year period, the plant could obtain more time under an "interim emission limit" fixed between five and 10 ppm at the

---

that the development of cancer by animals inhaling one ppm VC is consistent with EPA's estimate of the human risks. *See* EPA Risk Assessment, *supra* note 427, at D6-D7.

441. Personal communication with Robert Rauch, *supra* note 439.

442. *Id.*

443. The settlement is described in EDF Petition for a General Policy on Carcinogenic Air Pollutants, *supra* note 356, at 19.

444. *Id.*; *EPA Proposed Amendments to VC Standard, supra* note 357. As of June 1978 this proposal has not yet been finally adopted.

445. *EPA Proposed Amendments to VC Standard, supra* note 357, at 28,154.

446. *Id.*

447. *Id.* at 28,155.

448. *Id.* at 28,154-55.

lowest level the plant could attain.[449] EPA would review each interim limit every three years to determine if the plant were able to do better.[450]

New plants, those begun after the promulgation of the amendments, would have to meet the five ppm limit immediately.[451] EPA reasoned that new and existing plants should be treated differently because it is easier and less expensive to design a new facility with emission controls in mind from the outset than to "retrofit" them into existing plants. EPA determined that it would be "feasible" to install in new plants some devices that in 1976, when the agency was lumping new and existing plants together, were considered to impose "grossly disproportionate" costs.[452] EPA also proposed to reduce by 75 percent the amounts of VC residual permitted in "new" PVC resins, *i.e.*, resin of a grade not produced at a particular plant before the date of the proposal.[453]

A new feature of the proposal is an "emission offset" requirement. While EPA still declined to prohibit the construction of additional VC and PVC production capacity, the agency determined to prevent an increase in the emissions of VC in any particular area. No company could build a VC or PVC plant within eight kilometers (five miles) of another such facility, unless the company had secured a reduction in the other facility's emissions equal to those to come from the new plant.[454] This requirement gives companies an economic incentive to develop control technology. The incentive approach may secure more results than the traditional threat of penalties. Whether the offset policy would encourage companies to spread out the location of new plants is unknown; whether there is an incentive to spread locations depends on whether the economic advantages of clustering VC and PVC facilities exceed the cost of making further emission reductions in one's own existing plants or paying another company to do so.[455]

Absent from this proposal is the heavy emphasis on the costs of compliance found in the 1976 standard. The phrase "grossly disproportionate" costs does not appear in the proposal at all. Although the agency maintains its position against completely closing the VC and PVC industries, in this proposal it sets the balance of health and economic interests more in favor of the former than it had before. Even so, the proposal does not offer any criteria for making the trade-off between risk and benefit; indeed, it contains little discussion of the balancing issue.

449. *Id.* at 28,154, 28,158-59 (proposed rule 40 C.F.R. § 61.72).

450. *Id.* at 28,154, 28,159.

451. *Id.* at 28,155, 28,157-58 (proposed rules 40 C.F.R. §§ 61.62-.65).

452. *See id.* at 28,155. Note the discussion of modifications to the oxychlorination reactor at VC plants, *id.*

453. *Id.*

454. *Id.* at 28,156, 28,159 (proposed rule 40 C.F.R. § 61.73).

455. On the use of economic incentives in lieu of or as supplements to traditional standard-and-penalty approaches, see, *e.g.*, C. SCHULTZE & A. KNEESE, POLLUTION, PRICES, AND PUBLIC POLICY (1976). For a discussion of the application of the emission offset policy in the implementation of the Clean Air Act generally, see Comment, *The Tradeoff Policy: Solution to the Dilemma of the Clean Air Act?*, 1 HARV. ENVT'L L. REV. 352 (1976).

In this proposal, EPA appears to be edging toward the position that the economic growth of the industries is not sacrosanct. The agency noted that for certain kinds of PVC resins that are difficult to strip of their VC residual, it might not be possible to meet the new VC residual limits with existing technology. In this case, as EPA stated, "the manufacturer would have the option of developing [new] technology or not producing the resin."[456] EPA would set more stringent requirements for new production capacity than for existing capacity. The agency reasoned that the economic impact of banning an increase in the production of such a resin would be less than the impact of forbidding some current production of it; in the former case there would be no dislocation costs.[457] Possibly these remarks foreshadow an abandonment of the unsound and generally unstated tenet that health hazards, unless approaching the status of an imminent catastrophe, do not warrant the imposition of significant changes in an industry.

EPA has not yet determined whether to promulgate the amendments. Although the changes are supported by EDF,[458] they have been criticized by the VC and PVC industries, principally on the grounds that they will increase control costs.[459] There are differences of opinion on how great the increases will be.[460]

EPA appears to be delaying final action regarding the amendments primarily in order to reach a decision on an EDF petition filed in November 1977, requesting that the agency establish the terms of the VC settlement as a generic approach to the regulation of all airborne carcinogens.[461] It appears that the agency wants to resolve the controversy over its general policy before promulgating any additional standards.[462] This is a sensible position, as it would be unfortunate to promulgate one or two standards that could

---

456. *EPA Proposed Amendments to VC Standard, supra* note 357, at 28,155. By way of contrast, the agency noted that the 1976 standard had not considered the non-production of a particular resin to be a viable alternative for manufacturers. *Id.*

457. EPA put this point, somewhat obscurely, as follows:

It is EPA's judgment that the owner or operator making a new product has more freedom of choice than the owner or operator already making a particular product in selecting those resins which are to be produced. EPA's standard would be included in the variables under consideration when decisions are being made as to which resins are to be produced.

Id.

458. Comments of the Environmental Defense Fund on the Proposed Amendments to the Final Emission Standard for Vinyl Chloride (undated) [hereinafter cited as EDF Comments on Proposed Amendments].

459. *See Vinyl Chloride: MCA Recommends that EPA Withdraw Proposed Change in Emissions Standard*, 1 BNA CHEM. REG. REP.—CURR. REP. 1153 [hereinafter cited as *MCA Comments*].

460. *See* EDF Comments on Proposed Amendments, *supra* note 458, at 12-13 (summarizing the dispute over the costs of the amendments).

461. EDF Petition for a General Policy on Carcinogenic Air Pollutants, *supra* note 356. Another carcinogen, benzene, has been designated a hazardous air pollutant, but regulations for its control have not yet been promulgated. EPA, *Addition of Benzene to List of Hazardous Air Pollutants*, 42 Fed. Reg. 29,332 (1977).

462. *See MCA Comments, supra* note 459.

soon be inconsistent with a general policy applying to all airborne carcinogens. It is to be hoped, however, that the development of the policy does not excessively delay the issuance of the amendments to the VC standard.

8.   Evaluating EPA's Action

There is no question but that VC was a proper subject of regulation under section 112 of the Clean Air Act. That section was intended to control pollutants, such as VC, that pose serious health risks at low concentrations. It might be argued that setting a new source performance standard under section 111 (which, like section 112, allows regulation of existing sources) would have been been acceptable as well. *A fortiori*, a substance that is dangerous enough to satisfy the definition of a hazardous air pollutant also satisfies the definition of pollutants subject to section 111.[463] If EPA had used section 111, it would not have needed to interpret section 112 so tortuously in order to avoid what it perceived to be the section's undesirable stringency. However, to regulate substances such as VC under section 111 would make section 112 a useless appendage to the Act. Since Congress has established the latter section specifically for such pollutants, EPA may not ignore it.

The propriety of EPA's rejecting the literal meaning of the section's requirement that a hazardous air pollutant standard provide "an ample margin of safety" is more difficult to determine. EPA is correct that Congress did not explicitly consider the regulation of carcinogens, for which no safe level of exposure can be identified. But, as noted above, Congress did consider the general case in which the measures necessary to protect people from the risks of such substances might force the emission sources to close. In 1970, at least, Congress apparently found this an acceptable price to pay for safety.[464] It is possible that if Congress were confronted with the fact that the literal interpretation of section 112 would require the closing of all the industries that release carcinogens to the open air, it would change the rule to allow the balancing of risks and benefits in the same manner as is done in setting occupational health standards. However, whether EPA should bend the rule or whether Congress should change it is as important a question as what the rule should be. There is some value in forcing Congress to face the responsibility of deciding whether or not safety considerations should be balanced against economic ones.[465]

Even if one were to assume that under section 112 health and economic considerations should be balanced, it appears that EPA gave the latter too much weight in designing the standard currently in effect. While the "gross-

---

463.   Clean Air Act § 111, 42 U.S.C.A. § 7411 (West Supp. 1978)). See notes 398-400 *supra* and accompanying text.

464.   See text accompanying note 377 *supra*.

465.   It bears noting, however, that neither EPA nor the Environmental Defense Fund has incentives to use its limited resources to uphold these "governmental process" values.

ly disproportionate'' costs criterion sounded quite stringent, in practice it was quite lenient. As noted above, the 1976 standard will not significantly alter the VC or PVC industries' profits, size, growth rates, or shares of the plastics market.[466] While it may be reasonable to conclude that hazardous air pollutant standards need not completely eliminate emissions of ''non-threshold'' substances, it is also reasonable to conclude that section 112 is not satisfied by regulations for ''non-threshold'' substances that hold an industry essentially free from economic harm and significant change.[467] When air pollutants are known carcinogens the economic status quo does not deserve such complete protection.

EPA's decision not to regulate fabrication plants is defensible. If one accepts the view that section 112 does not require a zero emissions standard for VC, then the minimal emissions coming from fabrication facilities probably are acceptable. Their emissions already are low and will diminish further as the PVC manufacturers reduce the VC residual level in their product. Of course, if section 112 requires a zero emissions standard, the fabrication emissions problem will take care of itself; the closing of the VC and PVC plants would end the fabrication of PVC altogether.[468]

The shortcomings of EPA's original application of the ''grossly dispro-portionate'' costs test have already been discussed.[469] The unwarranted leniency of the standard would be largely rectified if the proposed reduction of the 10 ppm emission limit is promulgated. Regardless of EPA's final determination on the issue of adopting the ''zero emissions goal'' the agency should adopt the proposed five ppm emissions limit for the VC and PVC plants.

The EPA standard also provides another example of the double-counting problem alluded to in the discussion of the OSHA standard.[470] Like

---

466. See text accompanying notes 420-423 *supra*.

467. Similar considerations apply in the OSHA context. See text accompanying notes 340-345 *supra*.

468. The standard also does not cover certain specified ''miscellaneous'' sources that account for about three percent of VC emissions. *EPA Proposed Standard for VC, supra* note 131, at 59,535. The rationale for exempting them may rest too heavily on administrative convenience. Even though these ''miscellaneous'' facilities account for only small portion of total VC emissions, persons in the locales of these facilities are likely to remain exposed to the same risks that EPA determined needed to be reduced elsewhere.

The standard also fails to include other sources of air emissions, such as dumps for PVC sludge and solid waste. *See* EPA Task Force Report, *supra* note 85, at 20. Although EPA now has authority to regulate hazardous waste disposal directly under Title III of the 1976 Resource Conservation and Recovery Act, 42 U.S.C.A. §§ 6921-6931 (West Supp. 1978), the agency might have treated dumps as ''stationary sources'' for the purpose of regulating their air emissions. A stationary source for which a hazardous pollutant standard may be set is defined as: ''any building, structure, facility, or installation which emits or may emit any air pollut-ants.'' Clean Air Act § 111(a)(3), 42 U.S.C.A. § 7411(a)(3) (West Supp. 1978). This definition applies in the section governing new and existing source performance standards. *Id.* § 112(a)(3), 42 U.S.C.A. § 7412(a)(3) (West Supp. 1978).

469. See text accompanying notes 420-423 *supra*.

470. See text accompanying notes 347-348 *supra*.

OSHA, EPA failed to separate the emissions control costs allocable to reducing exposures *outside* the plants from the costs allocable to reducing exposures *inside* the plant.[471] As a result, EPA balanced all the control costs against only the risks to the persons outside the plant. Consequently, EPA, like OSHA, underweighted the hazards associated with VC. Like OSHA, EPA set a more lenient standard than it would have if it had conducted a symmetrical risk-benefit analysis.[472]

The most serious shortcoming in EPA's actions was the unjustifiable delay in setting the original VC standard. The agency was petitioned to set the standard as early as May 1974,[473] shortly after the human cancer hazard became known. In January 1975, EPA admitted that it had not yet designated VC a hazardous air pollutant precisely in order to avoid activating the statutory timetable for proposing and promulgating a standard.[474] At that time, EPA set June 1975 as the target date for proposing a standard.[475] Without explaining its failure to meet this target, EPA delayed the designation and the proposal until December of that year. Although the public hearing was completed and all the comments were filed by early 1976, and although EPA made no major changes in the proposal, the agency failed to promulgate the standard until October 1976.

At every step of the standard development process after the report of the VC Task Force in September 1974, EPA delayed. At that time the agency had most of the information on which it acted more than two years later.[476] The animal experiments and human data available in the fall of 1974 were sufficient to support the designation of VC as a hazardous air

---

471. The EPA environmental impact statement states:

> With regard to OSHA costs, it has been assumed that no significant incremental costs over and above the EPA air emission control costs would be necessitated by the current OSHA regulations. It has been assumed that the cost of OSHA regulations could be generally approximated by the cost of the fugitive control package that has been included in the air emission control cost totals for both ethylene dichloride-vinyl chloride plants and polyvinyl chloride plants. Costs for control of vinyl chloride emissions to the air that are presented in this section, then, include the costs that are believed to be required by the OSHA standards.

EPA EIS, *supra* note 85, at 7-19.

472. For discussion of how the Toxic Substances Control Act could be used to resolve this problem, see text accompanying notes 796-804 *infra*.

473. On May 31, 1974, Barry I. Castleman, an Environmental Engineer (then with the Maryland Public Interest Research group, now a consultant to EDF), and Albert J. Fritsch, of the Center for Science in the Public Interest, wrote the Administrator of EPA to request that EPA regulate VC emissions "promptly," ideally in concert with OSHA's standard, then expected to be promulgated in the following few months. EPA regarded this as a formal petition for the regulation of VC. Letter to Russell E. Train, Administrator, Environmental Protection Agency, from Barry I. Castleman & Albert J. Fritsch (May 31, 1974); Letter to Barry I. Castleman & Albert J. Fritsch from Russell E. Train (Aug. 8, 1974), *reprinted in Hearings on S. 776 before the Subcomm. on the Environment of the Senate Comm. on Commerce*, 94th Cong., 1st Sess. 181-82 (1975) [hereinafter cited as *Senate Hearings*].

474. Letter to Albert J. Fritsch, Center for Science in the Public Interest, from B.J. Steigerwald, Director, Office of Air Quality Planning and Standards, Environmental Protection Agency (Jan. 15, 1975), *reprinted in Senate Hearings, supra* note 473, at 185.

475. Letter to Albert J. Fritsch, *supra* note 474.

476. *See* EPA TASK FORCE REPORT, *supra* note 85 at 8-12. In addition, *compare id.* at 17

pollutant. EPA's position on the question of carcinogenic thresholds did not change significantly in the interim. If information available in the fall of 1974 were not enough, by the spring of 1975 EPA had learned that persons living near PVC plants might be suffering high rates of birth defects and other disorders besides cancer.[477] Finally, EPA's data collection effort virtually stopped after June 1975; no new toxicological or epidemiological information was collected after this point and most of the technological and economic analysis was complete by this time as well.

The delay seems to have been the result of EPA's reluctance to take the responsibility either for applying section 112 literally or for interpreting it in some other manner.[478] This is an aspect of the accountability problem; ideally, Congress, not the agency, should bear the responsibility for making this basic policy decision. Nonetheless, EPA should not have waited so long; the dilemma grew no easier with age, and in the meantime, the people who live and work near sources of VC emissions have needlessly been subjected to unacceptable risks.

D.   Vinyl Chloride in Food—The Food, Drug, and Cosmetic Act

1.   The Key Issues for FDA

The regulation of PVC food packaging and other food contact mate-

---

(estimating that emissions could be reduced by 90% at VC plants and 75% at PVC plants) *with EPA Standard for VC, supra* note 148, at 46,560 (estimating that emissions could be reduced by 95%).

    477.   EPA SCIENTIFIC AND TECHNICAL REPORT, *supra* note 90, at 84 (published in June 1975 and referring to the study reported in Infanté, *supra* note 138).

    478.   It has also been suggested that

> with the economy steadily worsening and Congress not passing toxic substances control legislation in the [1973-74] session, the EPA Administrator has been inclined to be overly cautious in regulating vinyl chloride.

Statement of Barry I. Castleman, in *Senate Hearings, supra* note 473, at 178.

    In replying to the May 1974 request of Mr. Castleman and Dr. Fritsch that VC be regulated as a hazardous pollutant "promptly" (discussed in note 473 *supra*), EPA stated that since there was "no imminent hazard" there was time for "a number of activities that will provide us with the information base to develop an optimum regulatory program," and that an assessment of "air quality data, emission control techniques and the health basis or criteria for possible standards" was taking place. Letter to Barry I. Castleman & Albert J. Fritsch from Russell E. Train, Administrator, Environmental Protection Agency (Aug. 8, 1974), *reprinted in Senate Hearings, supra* note 473, at 182. Although that assessment was completed in September 1974 with the publication of the Task Force Report, the Administrator wrote:

> The agency is doing everything possible to expedite the process of data collection and validation, public hearings and other procedural actions required by the Clean Air Act prior to a formal proposal.

Letter to Mr. Barry I. Castleman from Russell E. Train (Oct. 31, 1974), *reprinted in Senate Hearings, supra* note 473, at 184. Replying in April, 1975 to questions of Senator Philip Hart, the agency said:

> [I]n our view there is no basis to the assertion that the Agency is "stalling" with regard to vinyl chloride. We consider the approach sound, deliberate, and quite complicated.'

Letter to Senator Philip A. Hart from Robert G. Ryan, Director, Office of Legislation, Environmental Protection Agency (Apr. 10, 1975), *reprinted in Senate Hearings, supra* note 473, at 319. Yet the long delay undercuts the assertion that action was expeditious and leads to the conclusion that EPA's approach was quite conservative.

rials has involved issues different from those in the OSHA and EPA proceedings discussed thus far. The focus of those proceedings was the conventional problem of determining an acceptable balance of risks and benefits. The two relevant sections of the Food, Drug, and Cosmetic Act (FDCA),[479] however, do not permit the Food and Drug Administration (FDA) to engage in such balancing. Instead, one section explicitly prohibits intentionally adding to food any amount of a substance that causes cancer when ingested by animals or humans,[480] and FDA has interpreted the other section to have the same effect.[481] Whether packaging and other food-contact materials are subject to this prohibition turns on whether a carcinogenic substance—in this case residual VC in the PVC material—migrates, or "may reasonably be expected" to migrate, from the materials into foods.[482]

The meaning of this reasonable expectation requirement is the key issue in FDA's regulation of PVC. Tests of certain materials have failed to detect migrated VC, but available techniques for detecting the presence of VC in foods or in PVC itself have limited sensitivity. The question is whether VC migration must actually be detected in order to be reasonably expected, or whether it should be presumed to occur at concentrations lower than the sensitivity limits of available techniques.

In September 1975, FDA proposed to take the former view, and to prohibit the use of only those PVC materials from which migration had been detected.[483] As is discussed below, this was an unsound and improperly lenient interpretation of the reasonable expectation requirement. Moreover, although more than two years have elapsed since the proposal, FDA has never concluded its proceeding on the problem and even materials from which migration has been detected remain on the market.

Although FDA has not regulated PVC satisfactorily, the agency has rectified its interpretation of the reasonable expectation requirement. In a recent proceeding to end the use of bottles made from acrylonitrile copolymer, a plastic similar to PVC, FDA held that migration should be presumed to occur even below the detectable level.[484] Consistent application of the principles of the acrylonitrile decision would require FDA to end the food contact uses of PVC as well. It is to be hoped that such an application will occur soon.

---

479. FDCA §§ 1-902, 21 U.S.C. §§ 301-392 (1970 & West Supp. 1978). The amendments in 21 U.S.C.A. §§ 301-392 (West Supp. 1978) are not relevant to the present discussion.

480. FDCA § 409(c)(3)(A), 21 U.S.C. § 348(c)(3)(A) (1970).

481. *Id.* § 402(a)(1), 21 U.S.C. § 342(a)(1) (1970) (as interpreted in *FDA Proposed Rules for Food-Contact PVC, supra* note 164, at 40,533).

482. *See* FDCA § 201(s), 21 U.S.C. § 321(s) (1970).

483. *FDA Proposed Rules for Food-Contact PVC, supra* note 164. The proposal also covered PVC water pipe, from which VC leaches into drinking water. This aspect of the proposal is discussed together with EPA's authority under the Safe Drinking Water Act, 42 U.S.C. §§ 300f-300j-9 (Supp. V, 1975), in text accompanying notes 753-771 *infra*.

484. FDA, *Acrylonitrile Copolymers Used To Fabricate Beverage Containers; Final Decision*, 42 Fed. Reg. 48,528 (1977) [hereinafter cited as *FDA Acrylonitrile Decision*].

2. The Statute: Classification of VC as a Food Additive

The FDCA establishes a complex legal structure for the regulation of foods and substances added to foods.[485] The requirements that a food or a substance in food must meet depend on threshold definitions. Most PVC packaging and other food-contact materials are subject to regulation, if at all, under the 1958 Food Additives Amendment, codified primarily in section 409 of FDCA.[486] Other such materials, use of which was sanctioned by FDA before 1958, are subject to regulation, if at all, only under the older statutory prohibition against the addition of poisonous or deleterious substances to food, now codified in section 402(a)(1).[487]

Under section 409, substances that meet the definition of "food additive" are subject to premarket safety screening by FDA. An additive may not be used unless FDA has issued a regulation permitting the use.[488] The proponent of use, rather than the government, bears the burden of proof in the screening procedure.[489] To obtain a food additive regulation the proponent must demonstrate that upon a "fair evaluation" of the evidence[490] the

---

485. Important sections of the statute bearing on the regulation of food and substances added to food are: FDCA § 201(s) (food additive definition), § 402 (generally addressing adulteration of food), § 406 (tolerances for pesticides), and § 409 (food additives), 21 U.S.C. §§ 321(s), 342, 346, 348 (1970).

486. *Id.* § 409, 21 U.S.C. § 348 (1970).

487. *Id.* § 402(a)(1), 21 U.S.C. § 342(a)(1) (1970).

488. *Id.* § 402(a)(2)(C), 21 U.S.C. § 342(a)(2)(C) (1970). This section declares any additive that has not been issued a food additive regulation under § 409, 21 U.S.C. § 348 (1970), or any food containing such an additive, to be an "adulterated" substance, the sale of which is subject to injunction and which itself is subject to seizure. *Id.* §§ 301-304, 21 U.S.C. §§ 331-334 (1970).

489. *Id.* § 409(b)-(c), 21 U.S.C. § 348(b)-(c) (1970).

490. *Id.* § 409(c)(3)-(4), 21 U.S.C. § 348(c)(3)-(4) (1970). The statute also establishes the "fair evaluation" standard as the test to be applied by a court of appeals reviewing a food additive decision. *Id.* § 409(g)(2), 21 U.S.C. § 348(g)(2) (1970). The House and Senate Committees that drafted the 1958 Food Additives Amendment envisioned the "fair evaluation" standard as a new test, a test meant to require more support for a decision than the traditional substantial evidence test. Precisely how the test would function is unclear, for it has never been employed. The Senate Report states:

Your committee agrees with the House that the Secretary's findings of fact and orders should not be based on isolated evidence in the record, which evidence in and of itself may be considered substantial without taking account of contradictory evidence of possibly equal or even greater substance.

Following the appearance before it of a panel of outstanding scientists, the House subcommittee expressed itself as impressed with the wide range of scientific judgment factors which are involved in determining the safety of a food additive. Considering the eminent qualifications of all the scientists and experts who participated in these panel hearings, the scientific testimony of any one of the participants must be considered "substantial evidence." Nevertheless, any conclusions based solely on the scientific judgment of any one of the participants without taking account of contradictory scientific views expressed by other participants cannot be considered conclusions based upon a fair evaluation of the entire record.

Thus, under this legislation, the Secretary's findings of fact and orders based thereon must be based upon a fair evaluation of the entire record. The committee adopted the language "fair evaluation of the entire record" because it seemed to express most clearly the standard of judicial review of administrative findings of fact and orders based thereon which the committee feels should prevail.

additive is "safe" for its intended uses.[491] If a substantial question of the additive's safety arises thereafter, the proponent must rebut it and re-establish that the additive is "safe." Although the statute itself gives no definition of the term "safe" for the general rule of toxic effects,[492] a special provision addresses the meaning of the term when the effect in question is cancer.

This provision is the so-called Delaney Clause, which states that an additive may not be considered safe and may not be used in any amount "if it is found to induce cancer when ingested by man or animal, or if it is found, after tests which are appropriate for the evaluation of the safety of food additives, to induce cancer in man or animal."[493] In passing the Delaney Clause, Congress adopted two important policies. First, Congress accepted the prevailing medical theory that animal experiments are good predictors of a chemical's human carcinogenicity, and that no level of exposure to a carcinogen can be shown to be safe. Second, Congress made the judgment that the benefits of food additives are not great enough to outweigh even a minute risk of cancer. The Delaney Clause prohibits the intentional addition of cancer-inducing substances to food, without any administrative inquiry into their economic value.[494]

Thus, for regulations under section 409, much turns on whether PVC materials are food additives. A food additive is defined as

---

S. REP. NO. 85-2422, 85th Cong., 2d Sess. 7-8 (1958). See the nearly identical language in H.R. REP. NO. 85-2284, 85th Cong., 2d Sess. 6 (1958).

    491.   FDCA § 409(c)(3), 21 U.S.C. § 348(c)(3) (1970).

    492.   In identical language, the House and Senate Reports on the Food Additives Amendment established the following test for safety: "Safety requires proof of a reasonable certainty that no harm will result from the proposed use of an additive." H.R. REP. NO. 85-2284, 85th Cong., 2d Sess. 4 (1958); S. REP. NO. 85-2422, 85th Cong., 2d Sess. 2 (1958). This passage refers only to health considerations; no passage in the statute or the legislative history authorizes FDA to balance any economic considerations against harmfulness. FDA, however, has acted as though it had this authority to balance. *See* Freedman, *"Reasonable Certainty of No Harm:" Reviving the Safety Standard for Food Additives, Color Additives, and Animal Drugs*, 7 ECOLOGY L. Q. 245 (1978). For an argument that the prohibition of balancing is a sound policy for food additives, see text accompanying notes 877-892 *infra*.

    493.   FDCA § 409(c)(3)(A), 21 U.S.C. § 348(c)(3)(A) (1970). Note that cancer must be caused by *ingestion* of the chemical. The term "appropriate tests" usually is interpreted to require ingestion studies. *See, e.g.* Food & Drug Admin. Advisory Comm. on Protocols for Safety Evaluation, *Panel on Carcinogenesis Report on Cancer Testing in the Safety Evaluation of Food Additives and Pesticides*, 20 TOXICOLOGY & APPLIED PHARMACOLOGY 419, 436 (1971).

    494.   See note 492 *supra*. The more serious the health risk, the more likely it is to be true that the benefits of additives fail to outweigh their risks. Thus the *per se* approach excluding the consideration of benefits from decisions regarding food additives is most sensible when the effect involved is cancer or some other usually fatal illness.

    For a critical view of the Delaney Clause, see Blank, *The Delaney Clause: Technical Naïveté and Scientific Advocacy in The Formulation of Public Health Policies*, 62 CALIF. L. REV. 1084 (1974). For views in support of the Clause, on grounds other than those presented above, see *Comments on the Scientific Basis for the "Delaney Clause"*, *supra* note 52; Turner, *The Delaney Anticancer Clause: A Model Environmental Protection Law*, 24 VAND. L. REV. 889 (1971).

any substance the intended use of which results or may reasonably be expected to result, directly or indirectly, in its becoming a component or otherwise affecting the characteristics of any food[,] includ- ing any substance intended for use in producing, manufacturing, packing, processing, preparing, treating, packaging, transporting, or holding food . . . .[495]

Food packaging and other food-contact materials (*e.g.*, the surfaces of processing equipment) are considered food additives if a substance migrates from the materials into foods, or if there is a reasonable expectation that such migration will occur.[496] FDA, rather that the proponent of use, bears the burden of proof on this issue. If migration is established to occur or can be reasonably expected to occur, the materials may not be used without a food additive regulation. If the migrating substance is a carcinogen, the Delaney Clause prohibits use of the materials, and FDA may not issue a regulation.

Under the 1958 Amendment, some substances that meet all the characteristics of food additives are nonetheless exempted from the requirement of obtaining a food additive regulation. These are substances that are "generally recognized as safe" (GRAS) by qualified experts.[497] The GRAS status of a substance is subject to revocation at any time upon the appearance of evidence that its use is not safe.[498] A substance that loses its GRAS status becomes a food additive, and a proponent must obtain a food additive regulation in the normal manner to continue using it.[499]

Certain other substances that otherwise would be treated as food additives are excluded from section 409 regulation by a "grandfather" clause in the 1958 Amendment.[500] The clause exempts from the requirements of section 409 those substances and uses that FDA had approved before the passage of the 1958 Amendment.[501] These so-called "prior-sanctioned" substances may be regulated, if at all, only under section 402(a)(1), an older provision of the FDCA. Under this section FDA may prohibit the sale of a food "[if] it bears or contains any poisonous or deleterious substance which may render it injurious to health."[502] Hence, the section permits FDA

495. FDCA § 201(s), 21 U.S.C. § 321(s) (1970).

496. 21 C.F.R. § 170.3(e) (1977).

497. FDCA § 201(s), 21 U.S.C. § 321(s) (1970). For the definition of GRAS and the procedures for obtaining and maintaining GRAS status, see 21 C.F.R. §§ 170.20-.38 (1977).

498. *Id.* §§ 170.38, .35. FDA has set up "interim" food additive regulations for substances formerly listed as GRAS, *id.* § 170.30(e), in the case where

new information raises a substantial question about the safety . . . of the substance but there is a reasonable certainty that the substance is not harmful and that no harm to the public health will result from the continued use of the substance for a limited period of time [while further studies are conducted].

Id. § 180.1(a).

499. *Id.* §§ 170.30(l), 170.3(e).

500. FDCA § 201(s)(4), 21 U.S.C. § 321(s)(4) (1970).

501. *Id.*

502. *Id.* § 402(a)(1), 21 U.S.C. § 342(a)(1) (1970). If a substance loses its prior-sanctioned

to regulate prior-sanctioned packaging and other food-contact materials through the foods with which they come in contact.

Although there are significant differences between section 402(a)(1) and section 409 that make the latter a generally more effective tool in the regulation of PVC materials, the policy and theoretical issues facing the agency are identical under the two sections. As to whether under section 402(a)(1) a food "bears or contains" a substance leached from the materials, FDA has determined to use the same test that applies to food additives under section 409, *i.e.*, whether the substance migrates, or may reasonably be expected to migrate. In proceedings under section 402(a)(1) FDA bears the burden of proof on the harmfulness of a substance as well as on its presence. While this is often an important difference between the sections, it makes no difference here because VC is well established to be a carcinogen. The absence of a Delaney Clause in section 402(a)(1) also makes no difference. Since no level of exposure to a carcinogen may be considered safe, its presence in food at any concentration "may render [the food] injurious to health."[503] As a result of the identity of the substantive issues for PVC regulation under section 402(a)(1) and section 409, in the discussion below the regulation of prior-sanctioned uses of PVC is treated together with regulation of the rest of its food-contact uses.[504]

---

status by being condemned under this section, the proponent of its use may apply for a food additive regulation under § 409. If the proponent can show that some lower concentration of the substance is "safe," *i.e.*, is reasonably certain to be harmless, FDA may issue a regulation permitting its use. *See id.* § 409(c)(5), 21 U.S.C. § 348(c)(5) (1970). Of course, if the substance is a carcinogen, the Delaney Clause, § 409(c)(3)(A), 21 U.S.C. § 348(c)(3)(A) (1970), prevents issuance of a food additive regulation.

503.   FDA has taken this position. *See FDA Proposed Rules for Food-Contact PVC, supra* note 164, at 40,533. See text accompanying notes 34-57 *supra*.

504.   There are, however, a number of procedural reasons why § 409 generally is a preferable regulatory mechanism to § 402(a)(1). A decision with regard to a food additive is reviewable in a court of appeals, where the proponent of use must overcome substantial judicial deference to administrative action. See note 490 *supra*. Added to the fact that the proponent has the burden of proof on safety anyway, judicial deference makes it very difficult for the proponent to challenge successfully an FDA decision. In a subsequent FDA action in a district court to enjoin the sale of such a substance, to assess civil or criminal penalties, or to seize the substance under FDCA §§ 301-304, 21 U.S.C. §§ 331-334 (1970), the nonexistence of a food additive regulation promulgated under § 409 is conclusive proof that the substance is "adulterated." *Id.* § 402(a)(2)(C), 21 U.S.C. § 342(a)(2)(C) (1970). Moreover, the substance itself, not only food containing it, is "adulterated." *Id. See* Natick Paperboard Corp. v. Weinberger, 525 F.2d 1103 (1st Cir. 1975).

By contrast, under § 402(a)(1), in order to demonstrate that a substance is "adulterated," FDA has the burden of proving *de novo* to a district court that a substance "may render [food] injurious to health," in any proceeding under §§ 301-304. The agency lacks the benefit of an initial presumption against safety and of judicial deference to its decisions. Moreover, since the agency lacks a simple, conclusive means to show "adulteration"—*e.g.*, the absence of a food additive regulation—the agency has the difficult task of making its case in each district court in whose jurisdiction the offending activity is taking place. Finally, the additive itself may not be condemned; FDA can reach only foods containing it. These shortcomings of § 402(a)(1) were the major reasons for passage of the 1958 Food Additives Amendment, which contains § 409.

To some extent, FDA can mitigate these problems and approximate the effect of a food additive decision for a substance that it may reach only under § 402(a)(1). The agency can

3. FDA's Early Regulation of PVC Food-Contact Materials

PVC food packaging and other food-contact materials first came into use in the late 1940s and early 1950s.[505] FDA approved these uses before passage of the 1958 Food Additives Amendment, and they became prior-sanctioned uses under the new law.[506] In the late 1950s and in the 1960s, FDA also designated many new PVC uses GRAS and issued food additive regulations for many others.[507] The regulations typically dealt with the migration problem only by setting limits on "total extractives" and not on VC or any other individual substances.[508] The agency appears to have known at the time that VC was among the substances that migrate into food, but before the discovery of the chemical's ability to cause cancer and other chronic diseases there was little reason to treat migrated VC separately. Nonetheless, FDA appears not to have required adequate long-term feeding studies on animals to investigate the carcinogenic potential or chronic toxicity of VC or of any other extractives. While FDA debates how to regulate PVC, the prior-sanctioned uses remain unregulated, and the GRAS status and food additive regulations remain in effect for uses that were not prior-sanctioned.

4. FDA's Aborted Regulation of PVC in 1973

By the spring of 1973, FDA had learned that VC was migrating into foods from some materials at higher levels than the agency had previously assumed. The agency had received reports that VC concentrations as high as 20 ppm were leaching into gin and vodka packaged in PVC bottles.[509] FDA had ample reason to be concerned about the safety of such levels even then. Although the connection between the chemical and human cancer had not yet been recognized, the scientific literature contained reports that inhalation of VC produced chronic diseases in workers[510] and that inhalation of very high levels produced cancer in rats.[511] FDA proposed to withdraw its approval of PVC's use in liquor bottles, stating that it had not established a

---

publish its belief that foods containing the substance are adulterated and its intention to prosecute actions against the food and its makers and distributors. FDA then must rely on these parties to withdraw the food voluntarily and to refrain from putting the agency to proving its case in court. This is in fact what FDA proposed to do regarding "prior-sanctioned" PVC uses. See *FDA Proposed Rules for Food-Contract PVC, supra* note 164, at 40,533. But since the food industry knows that the agency's cost of litigating under § 402(a)(1) is substantial, publication of such belief and intention is a less effective deterrent to the sale of the products than is the nonexistence of a food additive regulation under § 409.

505. *See FDA Proposed Rules for Food-Contract PVC, supra* note 164, at 40,533.
506. *Id.*
507. *Id.* Food additive regulations covering PVC materials are now codified at 21 C.F.R. §§ 172.210, 175.105, .300, .320, 176.170, .180, 177.1010, .1200, .1210, .1630, .1850, .1950-.1980, .2250, 179.45 (1977).
508. *See, e.g. id.* § 177.1950(c)(2).
509. FDA, *Prior-Sanctioned Polyvinyl Chloride Resin, Notice of Proposed Rulemaking,* 38 Fed. Reg. 12,931 (1973) [hereinafter cited as *FDA Proposed Rules for PVC Liquor Bottles*].
510. *See* EPA SCIENTIFIC AND TECHNICAL REPORT, *supra* note 90, at 3.
511. *Oncogenic Response of Rats to VC, supra* note 139.

safe level for the ingestion of VC.[512] However, the distillers voluntarily stopped using PVC bottles, and the agency dropped pursuit of the rulemaking.[513]

Despite this instance of relatively high migration, and despite the evidence of VC's potential toxicity, FDA did not then require testing of other PVC packaging and food-contact materials for migration, nor did it require an assessment of VC's ability to cause either cancer or less serious effects when ingested with food. The agency displayed no further interest in PVC until mid-1975, more than a year after VC's human carcinogenicity became known.

5. FDA's 1975 Proposal for PVC

In July 1975, the Health Research Group (HRG) petitioned FDA to withdraw its approval for all food-contact uses of PVC.[514] The petition cited findings of VC migration in a wide variety of food, drug, and cosmetic products packaged in the plastic.[515] HRG requested FDA to presume that VC migrates from any PVC food-contact material, to hold therefore that all such materials are food additives, and to end their use in compliance with the Delaney Clause.[516]

In September of that year, FDA proposed less sweeping regulations that would end the use of some PVC materials but would permit the use of others to continue.[517] The agency held that VC met the criteria of the Delaney Clause, *i.e.*, that it had been shown to cause cancer when ingested by animals.[518] However, FDA declined to hold that all PVC food-contact materials presented a reasonable expectation of VC migration.

In its proposal FDA divided PVC materials into three groups: "rigid," "semi-rigid," and "flexible." Materials in the first two groups—such as

---

512. *FDA Proposed Rules for PVC Liquor Bottles, supra* note 509, at 12,931.

513. The proposed rulemaking was not terminated until the date of the broader proposal in 1975. FDA, *Prior-Sanctioned Polyvinyl Chloride Resin, Termination of Notice of Proposed Rulemaking*, 40 Fed. Reg. 40,529 (1975).

514. Health Research Group, Citizen Petition Regarding Vinyl Chloride Food Packaging (July 1, 1975) [hereinafter cited as Health Research Group Petition].

515. *Id.* at 3-4. Drugs and cosmetics packaged in PVC are considered in text accompanying notes 772-775 *infra*.

516. *Id.* at 1. The petition does not differentiate between those PVC materials subject to food additive regulations and those that are prior-sanctioned. It appears that HRG would have FDA treat them all in the same manner. See text accompanying notes 500-504 *supra*.

517. *FDA Proposed Rules for Food-Contact PVC, supra* note 164.

518. *Id.* at 40,532-33. At that time, tests on the effects of VC when ingested by animals had not yet been completed. FDA cited an April 1975 preliminary report of experiments in progress, in which angiosarcoma of the liver and thymus had been induced in rats fed VC dissolved in olive oil. *Id.* at 40,532 (citing *Oncogenic Effects of VC Administered Orally to Rats: Preliminary Report, supra* note 142). The agency concluded that the completed study would confirm that VC is carcinogenic when ingested by rats, and that this preliminary evidence, taken together with abundant information on VC's human and animal carcinogenicity when inhaled, was sufficient to support a finding that the substance is carcinogenic by ingestion. *FDA Proposed Rules for Food-Contact PVC, supra* note 164, at 40,532-33.

bottles for salad oil and wrappers for cheeses and perserved meats—had been shown to contain relatively high concentrations of VC residual, and to leach detectable concentrations of VC into foods and food-simulating test solvents.[519] The agency proposed to end the use of these substances.[520] Tests to that date, however, had failed to detect the migration of VC from materials in the third group—such as food wrap, coatings for cans, fruits, and vegetables, and components of processing equipment.[521] The agency proposed to conclude that these materials posed no reasonable expectation of migration, and thus that they were neither food additives subject to the Delaney Clause nor substances subject to regulation under section 402(a)(1). Rejecting HRG's request, FDA refused to presume that migration occurs from these materials at levels lower than the minimum amount the testing methods were capable of registering.[522]

To assess the reasonableness of FDA's position regarding "flexible" materials, it is necessary to review certain chemical characteristics of PVC, the basics of its production process, and the limitations of detection techniques. The polymerization of VC does not incorporate all VC molecules into polymer chains; some remain physically trapped in the plastic. Not all of this VC residual can be removed by "stripping"—the application of heat and vacuum to newly-formed resin—or by other post-polymerization processes. The amount of VC remaining in finished PVC products depends on many factors, including: (1) the degree to which the resin was stripped; (2) the resin's age and conditions of storage before processing; (3) the amount of heat applied and the amounts of plasticizing and coloring agents added in processing; (4) the thickness of the final product; and (5) the product's age and conditions of storage before coming into contact with food.[523]

When PVC comes in contact with food, residual VC diffuses from the plastic into the food, an area of lower concentration. The concentrations that migrate are a function of such factors as: (1) the amount of residual in the material; (2) the solubility of VC in the particular food contacted; (3) the length of time the food is stored in contact with the material; and (4) the

---

519. For "rigid" PVC FDA reported VC levels as high as 8.4 ppm in apple cider, 6.5 ppm in vegetable oil, two ppm in mineral oil, 1.5 ppm in malt vinegar, and just less than one ppm in wine. Levels between 10 ppb and one ppm were reported in other samples of these products and in other foods, drugs, and cosmetics. FDA's data indicated that up to 20 ppb VC could leach into foods from "semi-rigid" PVC. Tests showed the presence of as much as 180 ppm in the PVC materials themselves. *Id.* at 40,531. *See also* Health Research Group Petition, *supra* note 514, at 3-4.

On the uncertainties regarding the hazards of human consumption of such levels, see note 167 *supra* and accompanying text.

520. *FDA Proposed Rules for Food-Contact PVC, supra* note 164, at 40,533-37.

521. *Id.* at 40,531.

522. *Id.* at 40,531, 40,533-37.

523. *Id.* at 40,530-31; Health Research Group Petition, *supra* note 514, at 1-2. *See also* Letter to Hearing Clerk, Food and Drug Administration, from Jerome Heckman, General Counsel, The Society of the Plastics Industries, commenting on FDA Proposed Rules for Food-Contact PVC, at app. E (Dec. 19, 1975) [hereinafter cited as SPI Comments on FDA Proposal]

temperature of storage.[524]

The minimum levels of VC that can actually be detected as residual in PVC or in solution in foods depend on the sensitivity of the detection techniques. As would be expected, experimental results showed that levels of residual and migrated VC declined with appropriate changes in the above factors, until the levels dipped below the minimum concentrations that the techniques used in the particular test could detect.[525]

FDA put forward these experimental results to support its conclusion that no reasonable expectation of VC migration existed for "flexible" PVC materials. Tests reportedly capable of detecting one ppm residual in the plastic had failed to find any VC present in food wrap, cap liners, can coatings, and other such materials. FDA's own tests of several "flexible" items, reportedly sensitive to 350 ppb, had not detected any residual. Tests of undisclosed sensitivity had failed to find migrated VC in solutions stored in contact with these materials.[526] The weakness of this evidence is that it is not probative of the absence of VC concentrations lower than the test methods can detect.

In addition to stating its test results, FDA also made a theoretical argument in support of its conclusion. The agency contended that the processing of "flexible" products—which involves raising PVC to high temperatures and "spreading out" the polymers by the addition of plasticizing and coloring agents—releases nearly all residual VC before the materials come in contact with foods. Using a set of assumptions that it characterized as "exaggerated," FDA predicted that food wrapped in PVC film containing one ppm VC would pick up only two ppb of VC. The agency asserted that under more plausible assumptions, there was no "realistic possibility" of VC migration from these materials.[527] This conclusion, however, does not follow. The "exaggerated" prediction tends to prove only that less than two ppb VC will migrate into foods from "flexible" materials; it does not eliminate the reasonable expectation that some small amount of VC diffuses even from the "flexible" materials.[528]

---

524. *See* sources cited in note 523 *supra*.

525. *See FDA Proposed Rules for Food-Contact PVC, supra* note 164, at 40,530-31. See the discussion of reasons why the use of detection sensitivities as the basis of a regulation is unsound policy in the discussion of the OSHA standard, in text accompanying notes 259-262, 291 *supra*.

526. *Id*. at 40,531.

527. *Id*. As an example of the "exaggerated" assumptions, FDA posited that all VC residual in the material would migrate into the food. The agency pointed out, however, that some VC would move out to the air. On the implications of VC migration from packaging into indoor air, see text accompanying notes 793-795 *infra*.

528. The FDA Proposal briefly described a theory that could support the "no migration" conclusion: at residual levels somewhere below one ppm, all residual VC molecules may be tightly bound to "active sites" in PVC materials. Migration could occur only at higher residual concentrations than those found in "flexible" packaging materials. The theory was suggested by experiments in which VC dissolved in test solvents apparently was absorbed by powdered PVC material. The proponent of the theory, however, had not yet suggested a chemical or physical mechanism to account for the "active sites" theory. Ultimately, FDA neither endorsed or rejected the theory in its proposal, and the agency did not rely on the theory to

In its proposal, FDA also designated two official detection techniques for determining the presence of VC. One was capable of detecting a minimum of 20 ppb of migrated VC in food-simulating solvents; the other, a minimum of 350 ppb of VC residual in PVC materials.[529] The agency's reasons for setting official test methods are not clear. The stated reason was to create standard and reliable test methods, because the results of tests reported to the agency by manufacturers were inconsistent.[530] The agency gave no explanation of why the above sensitivity levels were selected, and it did not discuss whether any of the more sensitive test methods available were equally reliable. The agency's purpose may have been to establish an official "undetectable" level for VC in solution and in plastic materials, and to treat materials that leached lower levels as presenting no reasonable expectation of migration. This position would have strained the statutory definition of a food additive beyond the point already reached by the general approach of defining reasonable expection in terms of detectability. Under this rule a material could be held to present no reasonable expectation of migration even though migration had actually been detected by an unofficial method more sensitive than FDA's.

Finally, FDA held open the possibility that the final rulemaking might ban even fewer PVC materials than the proposal. The agency stated that it was considering issuing general specifications for PVC food-contact materials in place of the three categories set out in the proposal. The specifications might cover permissible thickness, degree of plasticization, method of polymerization, permissible residual levels, amount of heat applied, and other characteristics.[531] FDA noted that methods of reducing the VC content of resins and finished products were improving.[532] The agency invited the industry to demonstrate that the improved methods permitted the manufacture of some or all of the "rigid" and "semi-rigid" materials such that they too would present, by FDA's criteria, no reasonable expectation of VC migration.[533]

6. Subsequent History of the Proposal

Commenting on the proposal at the end of 1975, PVC manufacturers seconded FDA's position that migration could not reasonably be expected unless it had actually been detected.[534] They also took FDA's suggestion

---

support its conclusions regarding "flexible" materials. *FDA Proposed Rules for Food-Contact PVC, supra* note 164, at 40,531. *See* Gilbert, *Migration of Minor Constituents from Food Packaging Materials*, 41 J. FOOD SCIENCE 955 (1976), for an explanation of the theory.

529. *FDA Proposed Rules for Food-Contact PVC, supra* note 164, at 40,531.

530. *Id.*

531. *Id.* at 40,534.

532. *Id.* The agency stated that although PVC resins formerly contained up to 2000 ppm VC residual, new manufacturing methods by that time enabled production of resins with as little as one or two ppm residual by the time the resins were ready for fabrication into food-contact materials. *Id.* at 40,530.

533. *Id.* at 40,534.

534. SPI Comments on FDA Proposal, *supra* note 523, at 13-15, 25-27; Comments of Tenneco Chemicals, Inc., on FDA Proposal 2 (Dec. 18, 1975).

and presented evidence that residual levels in all PVC materials then manufactured were far lower than those in the materials upon which the earlier
tests had been performed. Manufacturers of "rigid" bottles and "semi-
rigid" plastic sheet reported that their materials then contained residue
levels lower than those in the "flexible" materials that FDA proposed to
allow to continue in use. They also reported their failure to find migrated
VC from these products, using detection techniques more sensitive than the
two offical FDA test methods.[535]

The Health Research Group maintained its position that all PVC food-
contact materials should be presumed to leach VC into foods. HRG
criticized FDA's interpretation of the reasonable expectation requirement as
a deliberate evasion of the policy against adding any amount of a carcinogen
to foods. HRG contended that PVC materials should be banned from all
food-contact uses until manufacturers could prove that the materials were
completely free of VC residual.[536]

More than two years have elapsed since the comments were filed,
without the promulgation of final regulations by FDA. From time to time,
representatives of the agency have stated that a decision would be forthcom-
ing several months in the future, but the agency has let each such deadline
pass.[537] However, there have been recent indications that FDA plans to
revive its effort to regulate food-contact PVC.[538] Moreover, in light of the

---

535. A number of manufacturers reported that their bottles contained less than one ppm
VC residual and that with tests sensitive to 20 ppb, no migrated VC was detected in any solvent,
even after storage for prolonged periods at high temperatures. Two manufacturers reported no
migration detected with tests they claimed to be even more sensitive. SPI Comments on FDA
Proposal, *supra* note 523, at 67-70. One manufacturer reported that its "semi-rigid" sheet PVC
contained less than 0.35 ppm VC residual; others reported residual contént less than 0.5 ppm.
Tests sensitive to 20 ppb, and one test claimed to be sensitive to one ppb, failed to detect any
migration from sheet material. *Id.* at 65-78.
    At least one company referred to the "active sites" theory, although the company put
forward no additional support for it. *See* SPI Comments on FDA Proposal, *supra* note 523, at
77. See also note 528 *supra*.
    536. Letter from Anita Johnson and Sidney Wolfe, Health Research Group, to Hearing
Clerk, Food and Drug Administration (Dec. 19, 1975) (commenting on FDA proposal).
    537. For example, in December 1976, an attorney for FDA stated that the agency planned
to complete the PVC proceedings in June 1977. Personal communication with Stuart Pape,
Associate Counsel, Food and Drug Administration, Dec. 29, 1976.
    538. In January 1978, FDA revealed that it intends to promulgate the rules proposed in
1975 sometime in spring of this year. The agency also stated that by the end of 1978 it would
propose new rules to end the use of the remaining food-contact PVC materials, following the
precedent of the acrylonitrile decision discussed in text accompanying notes 540-545 *infra*.
FDA Plans Further Ban of PVC Materials, Interagency Memo Confirms, FOOD CHEMICAL
NEWS, Jan. 16, 1978, at 41 [hereinafter cited as *FDA Plans Further PVC Ban*]. The agency
revealed its intentions in a memorandum to the Interagency Regulatory Liason Group, a body
created in August 1977 by EPA, OSHA, FDA, and the Consumer Product Safety Commission
to help the four agencies learn of each others' activities regarding chemicals of mutual interest,
and to facilitate cooperation between them. *Id. See* EPA, *Regulation of Toxic and Hazardous
Substances, Interagency Agreement*, 42 Fed. Reg. 54,856 (1977) [hereinafter cited as *IRLG
Agreement*]. For further discussion of this coordination effort, see text accompanying notes
851-868 *infra*.

agency's action regarding acrylonitrile, discussed immediately below, it appears that FDA will revise its approach to determining when there is a reasonable expectation of migration.[539]

7. *Correcting the Approach to Migration: The Regulation of Acrylonitrile*

In September 1977, in proceedings to end the use of beverage bottles composed of acrylonitrile copolymer, FDA adopted the interpretation of the reasonable expectation requirement that it had incorrectly rejected in the PVC proposal.[540] The material is a plastic very similar to PVC.[541] Acrylonitrile monomer, which differs only slightly from VC, is polymerized into a solid, and as with PVC, a residual of the monomer remains in the plastic.[542] Experiments on bottles composed of the plastic had shown the migration of the monomer into food-simulating solvents. Subsequently, however, the manufacturers had reduced the residual level to the point that migration became undetectable. The manufacturers contended, as they had contended regarding PVC, that migration could not reasonably be expected if it were not detected.[543]

FDA rejected this argument and held that all acrylonitrile copolymer bottles presented a reasonable expection of migration and therefore were food additives.[544] The agency stated the following rule, which applies with equal force to PVC:

> Once the applicability of the diffusion principle has been reasonably confirmed, projections based on the diffusion process are sufficient to satisfy the burden of proof with respect to migration, even though the amounts projected to migrate are below the level of analytical detectability. The reasonable expectation of migration, arrived at on the basis of the diffusion principle, is not unalterable, however. The expectation can be rebutted, but only if an adequate showing is made that migration is not reasonably to be expected. Such a showing could be made through a demonstration that an unusual or different physical process occurs at some point that prevents migration.[545]

Regarding acrylonitrile bottles, FDA finally has come to a correct view of the reasonable expectation requirement, one consistent with the policy against the intentional addition of any carcinogens to food, and consistent with a fair reading of the food additive definition. As noted above, it appears that by the end of 1978 FDA will propose to apply this interpretation to

539. *See FDA Plans Further PVC Ban, supra* note 538.
540. *FDA Acrylonitrile Decision, supra* note 484.
541. Slesin & Sandler, *supra* note 11, at 377-379.
542. *FDA Acrylonitrile Decision, supra* note 484, at 48,528.
543. *Id.* at 48,528-29.
544. *Id.* at 48,530.
545. *Id.*

PVC.[546] For now, however, FDA continues to move cautiously. The manufacturers have sued the agency over the acrylonitrile decision,[547] and it may be that FDA intends to await a judicial decision before acting with regard to any other material.[548]

The agency's most serious failure in the regulation of PVC is its unjustifiable delay in decision making. There were indications that VC is carcinogenic as early as 1971. Yet in 1973, when FDA learned that high VC concentrations were leaching from liquor bottles, the agency took no new steps to assess the chemical's toxicity or the amounts leached from other PVC materials. More than two years elapsed between the discovery that VC causes human cancers and FDA's proposed regulations. A proposal probably would not have been made even then without the pressure of the Health Research Group's petition.[549] FDA's interest in regulating PVC at all has itself motivated the manufacturers to reduce the VC residual content of the materials and the levels of VC migration. Interest alone, however, is not action enough to satisfy FDA's duty to ensure the safety of food. The agency has missed at least one self-imposed deadline for completing the proceeding.[550] Meanwhile, all PVC food-contact materials—even ones with detectable migration—remain in unrestricted use.

E.   The Aerosol Bans—The Food, Drug, and Cosmetic Act, The Federal Environmental Pesticide Control Act, and the Federal Hazardous Substances Act

1.   The Key Issues in the Regulation of Aerosols

Two areas where regulatory jurisdiction is especially fragmented are the regulation of VC-propelled aerosols and the regulation of the chemical's transportation. Preceding sections have shown that agencies find the problems of decision making under uncertainty and balancing health and economic interests quite difficult. The next two sections show the complicating effect that jurisdictional fragmentation can have on the decision making process.

Fragmented jurisdiction has two particularly deleterious features. First, it creates opportunities for one agency facing a difficult problem or contro-

---

546.   See text accompanying notes 538-539 *supra*.

547.   Monsanto Corp. v. Kennedy, No. 77-2023 (D.C. Cir., filed Nov. 17, 1977). Challenges also have been filed by other companies and by the Society of the Plastics Industries; the cases are likely to be consolidated.

548.   This is the opinion of the General Counsel for the Society of the Plastics Industries. Personal communication with Jerome Heckman, General Counsel, The Society of the Plastics Industries, Dec. 19, 1977. In fact, FDA has not yet extended the acrylonitrile decision even to the chemical's uses in food-contact materials other than bottles. *FDA Acrylonitrile Decision, supra* note 484, at 45,841. FDA's position is correct, even though it has fairly drastic results. The agency should not be reluctant to apply the rule to other materials.

549.   Personal communication with Stuart Pape, Associate Counsel, Food and Drug Administration, Dec. 29, 1976.

550.   See note 537 *supra*.

versial issue to argue that another agency should handle it, or simply to delay action with the hope that another agency will step forward. Second, the statutes may differ from one another—even if only marginally—on such issues as burdens of proof, the amount of evidence of harm needed to support regulation, and whether economic factors may be considered.

Hence, outcomes may differ depending upon which statute is applied. Differences among the statutes create an incentive for industries, consumer and environmental groups, and the agencies themselves to struggle over which statute and agency should regulate a substance. The importance of these two features—the tendency of agencies to avoid difficult or controversial regulatory issues and the possibility of reaching different results under different statutes—is magnified where problems of uncertainty and balancing are great, because the parties have greater reason to believe that the minor differences among the statutes will yield different regulatory results. Conversely, in decisions where these problems are relatively minimal, jurisdictional fragmentation also is less important.

Prior to 1973, VC was widely used as a propellant in a broad range of aerosol products, including cosmetics, drugs, and pesticides. Because of increases in the price of VC, sometime in late 1973 or early 1974 all of the manufacturers of aerosol products stopped using the chemical as a propellant.[551] Nevertheless, when the human cancer hazard was identified in January 1974, there were still at least three and a half million cans containing VC in the possession of manufacturers, distributors, and consumers.[552] All three of the agencies with jurisdiction over these cans—FDA, EPA, and

---

551. The exact date on which manufacturers stopped using VC as an aerosol propellant is uncertain. Probably they did not all stop at the same time. At one point FDA noted that some manufacturers had stopped using the chemical before 1973. FDA, *Vinyl Chloride as an Ingredient of Drug and Cosmetic Aerosol Products, Notice of Proposed Rule Making*, 39 Fed. Reg. 14,215, 14,216 (1974) [hereinafter cited as *FDA Proposed VC Aerosol Ban*]. CPSC stated that the use of VC had ended in early 1974. CPSC, *Self-Pressurized Household Substances Containing Vinyl Chloride, Notice of Environmental Assessment and Reconsideration*, 40 Fed. Reg. 11,170, 41,171 (1975) [hereinafter cited as *CPSC VC Environmental Assessment*]. All indications are that the use of VC was ended for financial reasons. Personal communication with Judy Pitcher, Acting Director, Division of Special Economic Studies, CPSC, Jan. 30, 1978. There is no evidence that any company's cessation of VC use before the Goodrich disclosure in January 1974 was motivated by insider's information about the cancer hazard.

552. This estimate is probably on the low side. CPSC estimated that there were about 3.3 million cans containing VC on the market that were subject to its jurisdiction. *CPSC Environmental Assessment, supra* note 551, at 41,171. Most uses of VC as a propellant apparently were under CPSC's control. Personal communication with Judy Pitcher, *supra* note 551. FDA noted that the 1973 production of hair sprays containing VC by just two companies was more than 1.6 million units. *FDA Proposed VC Aerosol Ban, supra* note 551, at 14,215. According to EPA figures there were at least 19,000 pesticide aerosol cans containing VC on the market. EPA, *Vinyl Chloride, Emergency Suspension Order Concerning Registrations for Certain Products and Intent to Cancel Registrations*, 39 Fed. Reg. 14,753 (1974) [hereinafter cited as *EPA VC Aerosol Suspension*]. Thus, it is likely that the number of cans on the market in early 1974 exceeded 3.5 million cans. The difficulty of establishing the exact number illustrates the problems of information gathering that result from jurisdictional fragmentation.

the Consumer Product Safety Commission (CPSC)—acted quickly in response to the VC aerosol hazard. In the first nine months of 1974, even before OSHA completed its promulgation of the workplace standard, the three agencies banned the future use of VC as a propellant and ordered or requested manufacturers to recall stocks currently on the market.[553]

Since the manufacturers had already stopped using the substance in aerosols, the recall orders and requests were the only disputed aspect of the regulations. Manufacturers sought judicial review only of the CPSC regulations, which were the only ones with a mandatory recall. In 1977, after a long delay, the Ninth Circuit Court of Appeals vacated these regulations on procedural grounds.[554] In March 1978, CPSC repromulgated the prospective portion of the ban, dropping the now largely moot attempt to obtain the recall of existing stocks.[555]

The major reason for the prompt regulatory action by these agencies was the fact that regulating aerosols presented the agencies with no serious balancing issue. The discussion below examines the actions of these three agencies more closely; its major purpose, however, is to expose the differences among the applicable statutes and to demonstrate the potential for jurisdictional conflict in regulating a substance that requires more difficult choices to be made.[556]

2. The Statutes Governing Aerosol Products

The following discussion presents the relevant portions of the statutes under which the three agencies addressed VC aerosols. There are substantial differences among the statutes in terms of burdens of proof and criteria for determining if a substance may remain in use. Even though the agencies' decisions were more or less a foregone conclusion in this relatively easy case, these statutory differences would likely become important in a more difficult case.

---

553. FDA, *Vinyl Chloride as an Ingredient of Drug and Cosmetic Aerosol Products*, 39 Fed. Reg. 30,830 (1974) [hereinafter cited as *FDA VC Aerosol Ban*]; *EPA VC Aerosol Suspension*, *supra* note 552; CPSC, *Self-Pressurized Household Substances Containing Vinyl Chloride Monomer, Classification as Banned Hazardous Substance*, 39 Fed. Reg.' 30,112 (1974) [hereinafter cited as *CPSC VC Aerosol Ban*].

554. Pactra Indus., Inc. v. CPSC, 555 F.2d 677 (9th Cir. 1977). The court held that CPSC had improperly denied the aerosol manufacturers a hearing where they could dispute the need for recalling the products on the market. *Id*. at 684 (construing the hearing provisions of FDCA § 701(e), 21 U.S.C § 371(e) (1970), made applicable to CPSC's actions under the Federal Hazardous Substances Act, § 3(a)(2), 15 U.S.C. § 1261(a)(2) (1970)). The case is discussed further in notes 580, 605 *infra*.

555. CPSC, *Self-Pressurized Household Substances Containing Vinyl Chloride Monomer, Classification as Banned Hazardous Substance*, 43 Fed. Reg. 12,308 (1978) [hereinafter cited as *CPSC Reinstatement of VC Aerosol Ban*].

556. For example, the next section of the Article considers the regulation of VC in transportation, where the problems of fragmentation are more evident.

Although a lay person probably would consider VC aerosol products to be one undifferentiated group, regulatory authority over the products was divided three ways along complex lines. FDA had jurisdiction over VC-propelled "drugs" under the 1962 New Drug Amendments to FDCA[557] and over "cosmetics" under provisions of FDCA dating from 1938.[558] EPA was responsible for VC-propelled "pesticides" under the 1972 Federal Environmental Pesticide Control Act (FEPCA).[559] The remainder of VC-propelled products suitable for consumer use were "household substances" subject to CPSC regulation under the 1966 amendments to the Federal Hazardous Substances Act (FHSA).[560] Whether a substance is a drug, a cosmetic, a pesticide, or a household product is not always clear.[561]

Generally speaking, controls on drugs and pesticides are more stringent than those on cosmetics or household products. For the former pair, the burden is on the proponent of use to show that a substance is safe, rather than on the agency to show that it is unsafe. Under the New Drug Amendments, the proponent must show that a new drug, including its components, is "safe" and effective for its intended use before FDA may permit it to

---

557. A drug is defined as any article "intended for use in the diagnosis, cure, mitigation, treatment, or prevention of disease in man or other animals." FDCA § 201(g)(1)(B), 21 U.S.C. § 321(g)(1)(B) (1970). Each component of such articles is considered a drug. *Id.* § 201(g)(1)(D).

558. Cosmetics are defined as "articles intended to be rubbed, poured, sprinkled, or sprayed on, introduced into, or otherwise applied to the human body or any part thereof for cleansing, beautifying, promoting attractiveness, or altering the appearance," and their components. *Id.* § 201(i), 21 U.S.C. § 321(i) (1970).

559. Pub. L. No. 92-516, 86 Stat. 983, 7 U.S.C. §§ 136-136y (Supp. V 1975), amending the Federal Insecticide, Fungicide, and Rodenticide Act, 7 U.S.C. §§ 135-135k (1970). FEPCA defines a pesticide as:

(1) any substance or mixture of substances intended for preventing, destroying, repelling, or mitigating any pest, and (2) any substance or mixture of substances intended for use as a plant regulator, defoliant, or dessicant.

FEPCA § 2(u), 7 U.S.C. § 136(u) (Supp. V 1975). A mixture of substances includes both active and so-called "inert" ingredients, such as propellants. *Id.* § 2(a), (m).

For a general description of the statute, its basic principles, and the legislative history, see Comment, *The Federal Environmental Pesticide Control Amendments of 1972: A Compromise Approach*, 3 ECOLOGY L. Q. 277 (1973) [hereinafter cited as *FEPCA: A Compromise Approach*].

560. Pub. L. No. 89-756, § 3(a), 80 Stat. 1303 (1966), adding 15 U.S.C. § 1261(q) (1970). FHSA applies to hazardous substances found or used in households. 15 U.S.C. § 1261(p), (q)(1) (1970). Hazardous substances are defined in pertinent part as:

Any substance or mixture of substances which is (i) toxic . . . , if such substance's [*sic*] or mixture of substances may cause substantial personal injury or substantial illness during or as a proximate result of any customary or foreseeable handling or use
. . . .

Id. § 1261(f)(l)(A) (1970). Pesticides subject to FEPCA and foods, drugs, and cosmetics subject to FDCA are now excluded from this definition. *Id.* § 1261(f)(2) (Supp. V 1975). A toxic substance is defined as having "the capacity to produce personal injury or illness to man through ingestion, inhalation, or absorption through any body surface." *Id.* § 1261(g) (1970).

The administration of FHSA was transferred in 1972 from FDA to CPSC by the Consumer Product Safety Act. *Id.* § 2079(a) (Supp. V 1975).

561. See text accompanying note 608 *infra*.

enter commerce.[562] When doubts arise as to the safety or effectiveness of a drug already in use, the proponent of continued use must refute these doubts or approval for use must be withdrawn.[563] To register a pesticide under FEPCA, *i.e.*, to obtain a permit for its use, the proponent must show that the product and its components are effective for their intended use and that under customary use they will not cause "unreasonable adverse effects on the environment."[564] As with drugs, when evidence arises that a registered pesticide is causing unreasonable adverse effects, the proponent of continued use must refute the evidence.[565] If the proponent fails, EPA must cancel the product's registration.[566]

For both drugs and pesticides, the agencies can suspend a substance's approval or registration—*i.e.*, order an immediate halt to its use after opportunity for a very limited and brief hearing—if the substance presents an imminent hazard of harm.[567] In addition, EPA may order an emergency suspension of a pesticide, effective without any prior hearing, when the harm is so imminent that the time required for the hearing would allow the harm to occur.[568]

---

562. FDCA § 505(d), 21 U.S.C. § 355(d) (1970).

563. *Id.* § 505(e), 21 U.S.C. § 355(e) (1970). If a drug was generally recognized as safe and effective by qualified experts in 1962, it was grandfathered past the requirement applicable to new drugs that the applicant show safety and effectiveness. *Id.* § 201(p)(1), 21 U.S.C. § 321(p)(1) (1970). These, however, become subject to regulation as new drugs whenever new information contradicts their general recognition as safe or effective. This was the case with VC-propelled drugs.

564. FEPCA § 3(c)(5)(C)-(D), 7 U.S.C. § 136a(c)(5)(C)-(D) (Supp. V 1975). "Unreasonable adverse effects on the environment" is defined as

any unreasonable risk to man or the environment, taking into account the economic, social, and environmental costs and benefits of the use of any pesticide.

Id. § 2(bb), 7 U.S.C. § 136(bb) (Supp. V 1975). EPA may classify a pesticide (*i.e.*, restrict its uses) as necessary to prevent unreasonable adverse effects. *Id.* § 3(d)(1)(B), 7 U.S.C. § 136a(d)(1)(B) (Supp. V 1975).

565. *Id.* § 3(b), (d), 7 U.S.C. § 136a(b),(d) (Supp. V 1975).

566. *Id.*

567. FDCA § 505(e), 21 U.S.C. § 355(e) (1970); FEPCA § 6(c)(1), (d), 7 U.S.C. § 136d(c)(1), (d) (Supp. V 1975). FDCA does not define the circumstances that create an imminent hazard. Under FEPCA, an imminent hazard

exists when the continued use of a pesticide during the time required for cancellation proceeding [*sic*] would be likely to result in unreasonable adverse effects on the environment . . . .

Id. § 2(*l*), 7 U.S.C. § 136(*l*) (Supp. V 1975).

Some cancellation proceedings may last as long as two years, and the suspension decision is to take account of the likely length of cancellation proceedings. Therefore, as the length of those proceedings increases, more harms meet the definition of imminence, and it becomes more likely that suspension should be ordered. *See* Environmental Defense Fund v. EPA, 465 F.2d 528, 540, 4 ERC 1523, 1531 (D.C. Cir. 1972); Environmental Defense Fund v. EPA, 510 F.2d 1292, 1300, 7 ERC 1689, 1692-93 (D.C. Cir. 1975). *See generally* Spector, *Regulation of Pesticides by the Environmental Protection Agency*, 5 ECOLOGY L.Q. 233 (1975).

568. See note 567 *supra*. Under FEPCA, EPA may also make regulations for the safe disposal of pesticides whose registrations have been cancelled. FEPCA § 19, 7 U.S.C. § 136q (Supp. V 1975). In 1974, under the 1970 Solid Waste Management Act, Pub. L. No. 91-512, §

In all of these determinations, with the exception of emergencies noted above, proponents of the use of drugs and pesticides have the right to adjudicatory hearings.[569] In fact, the drug and pesticide laws provide for the most formal, trial-type proceedings of all the toxic substances control statutes.[570] Both EPA and FDA must support their determinations concerning approvals and registrations with substantial evidence in the record.[571]

Both agencies may seize products from the market if they lack or have lost the required approval or registration.[572] Neither agency, however, has the authority to order manufacturers to recall supplies of such products from distributors and consumers, potentially a more powerful remedy than bringing many separate seizure actions. However, both agencies may request that the manufacturers recall the products voluntarily, holding in reserve the threat of seizure actions. Manufacturers generally attempt to avoid seizure actions because they often result in widespread unfavorable publicity.

Controls on cosmetics and household products are not so stringent. For these products, the agencies have the burden of showing that a substance is unsafe. A cosmetic is "adulterated" under FDCA if it contains a "poisonous or deleterious substance which may render it injurious to users" when used according to labeled instructions or as is customary.[573] To control a dangerous cosmetic FDA must sue the manufacturer or distributor in federal district court, seeking a finding that the product is adulterated and an injunction against its sale.[574] The agency may also seize products that

---

104, 84 Stat. 1227 (1970), EPA could issue non-enforceable guidelines for the disposal of any hazardous waste. The 1970 Act was superseded by the 1976 Resource Conservation and Recovery Act, 42 U.S.C.A. §§ 6901-6931 (West Supp. 1978), under which the agency may set binding rules for the disposal of such substances. RCRA is discussed in text accompanying notes 722-731 *infra*.

569. FDCA § 505(d)-(e), 21 U.S.C. § 355(d)-(e) (1970); FEPCA § 6(d), 7 U.S.C. § 136(d) (Supp. V 1975).

570. With respect to FEPCA, Congress is now considering an amendment that would reduce the administrative burden of conducting adjudications for each pesticide registration. Under this amendment, the major focus of EPA's regulation would be on the ingredients, or groups of ingredients common to numerous individually registered products, rather than on the products themselves. EPA would set generic standards for these ingredients through rulemaking proceedings, evaluating whether they can be used without "unreasonable adverse effects on the environment." The agency then would apply the relevant generic standards to individually registered products in adjudications. But since the major issues concerning the acceptability of the central ingredients already would have been resolved, the adjudication could be a short, perhaps summary, proceeding. *See* S. 1698, 95th Cong., 1st Sess. § 3 (1977); H.R. 8681, 95th Cong., 1st Sess. § 4 (1977). For discussion of these amendments, see Schulberg, *The Proposed FIFRA Amendments of 1977: Untangling the Knot of Pesticide Registration*, 2 HARV. ENVT'L L. REV. — (1978) (in press).

571. FDCA § 505(f), 21 U.S.C. § 355(f) (1970); FEPCA § 16(b), 7 U.S.C. § 136n(b) (Supp. V 1975).

572. FDCA § 304, 21 U.S.C. § 334 (1970); FEPCA § 13, 7 U.S.C. § 136k (Supp. V 1975).

573. FDCA § 601(a), 21 U.S.C. § 361(a) (1970).

574. FDCA §§ 301-302, 21 U.S.C. §§ 331-332 (1970). For further discussion, see note 971 *infra*.

probably will be found to be adulterated.[575] While to support an action regarding drugs the agency needs only substantial evidence, FDA must prove its case against a cosmetic by a preponderance of evidence, the normal standard in civil actions. The difficulty of carrying this burden, however, is mitigated by the fact that FDA need show only that the substance "may" be injurious.[576] In practice, FDA can approximate the effect of a banning rule for cosmetics by publishing a notice of products it intends to seize and complain against, giving the grounds on which the agency believes the action would be upheld.[577]

For hazardous household products, the primary purpose of FHSA is to reduce dangers by requiring cautionary labeling and protective packaging.[578] CPSC may ban a substance when the agency finds that labeling and packaging requirements would not provide sufficient protection and that "the objective of the protection of the public health can be adequately served" only by a ban.[579] A person affected by such a rule has the opportunity for a hearing.[580] Rules made under FHSA, unlike the drug and pesticide rules, must be made on "a fair evaluation" of the evidence in the record of these proceedings.[581]

CPSC's powers to remove a dangerous household product from the distribution network are broader than FDA's or EPA's. Like the other agencies, CPSC may seize products in commerce.[582] In addition, the agency

---

575.   FDCA § 304, 21 U.S.C. § 334 (1970). *See* Ewing v. Mytinger & Casselberry, Inc., 339 U.S. 594 (1950) (upholding pre-suit seizure when probable cause exists that the substances are adulterated).

576.   FDCA § 601(a), 21 U.S.C. § 361(a) (1970).

577.   This is how FDA proceeded against VC-propelled cosmetics. It promulgated 21 C.F.R. § 700.14 (1977), which essentially is a statement of position on the agency's readiness to sue to remove any such products from the market. *See FDA VC Aerosol Ban, supra* note 553, at 30,830.

578.   FHSA §§ 2(p), 3(b), 15 U.S.C. §§ 1261(p), 1262(b) (1970).

579.   *Id.* § 2(q)(1), 15 U.S.C. § 1261(q)(1) (1970).

580.   *Id.* § 3(a)(2), 15 U.S.C. § 1262(a)(2) (1970), requires that rules declaring a substance to be banned must be set according to the procedures of FDCA § 701(e), 21 U.S.C. § 371(e) (1970). Section 701(e)(1) calls for issuance of a proposal, a period for written or oral comments, and then promulgation of a rule. Section 701(e)(2) permits one adversely affected by such a rule to file objections to the rule and request a public hearing up to 30 days after the promulgation date. Such a filing stays the rule until CPSC holds the hearing and responds to the objections. The provision for a hearing *after* the promulgation date, rather than within the comment period, is unusual. CPSC's refusal to grant such a hearing was the Ninth Circuit's ground for vacating the agency's VC regulations. Pactra Indus., Inc. v. CPSC, 555 F.2d 677 (9th Cir. 1977), discussed further in note 605 *infra* and accompanying text.

581.   FHSA directs CPSC to follow the provisions of FDCA § 701(e) except with regard to the standard of proof that CPSC and a reviewing court must use. In this regard FHSA instructs the agency to apply the "fair evaluation" standard of FDCA § 409(f)(2), (g)(3), 21 U.S.C. § 348(f)(2), (g)(3) (1970). FHSA § 3(a)(2), 15 U.S.C. § 1262(a)(2) (1970). The "fair evaluation" standard, which has never been explicated by a court, is discussed in note 490, *supra*, and in text accompanying notes 975-986 *infra*.

582.   FHSA § 6, 15 U.S.C. § 1265 (1970).

may order manufacturers to recall and repurchase banned substances from distributors and consumers.[583]

The statutes applicable to aerosols take different positions on whether the harmfulness of a substance must be balanced against its utility. FEPCA's requirement that adverse effects be "unreasonable" explicitly requires EPA to balance a pesticide's health and environmental effects against its agricultural and economic benefits.[584] FHSA's standard that a ban be the only means of "adequately" protecting public health requires that CPSC seek less burdensome means of controlling a hazard. It is possible that the term also implies an obligation to balance health costs and economic benefits.[585] In contrast, FDCA's controls over drugs and cosmetics are modified by no adjective or adverb that requires FDA to undertake such balancing; nothing but health considerations are to enter into its decisions.[586]

3. Agency Actions Against VC as an Aerosol Propellant

In February 1974, within a month of the discovery of VC's human carcinogenicity, the Health Research Group petitioned the three agencies to ban the use of the chemical as a propellant and to recall the products then on the market.[587] FDA commenced action first. The agency proposed a ban on drug and cosmetic uses in April, citing generally the evidence at that time of cancer in humans and animals.[588] FDA noted that peak exposures from aerosols could exceed routine occupational exposures. The agency did not cite any precise figures on VC's toxicity, nor did it consider benefits or substitutes. FDA announced that it had asked drug and cosmetic manufac-

---

583. *Id.* § 15, 15 U.S.C. § 1274 (1970).

584. *See generally* Spector, *supra* note 567, at 235-36.

585. In its VC proceedings, CPSC put forward a somewhat equivocal statement of its views on this question:

Although the Commission is not required by the Federal Hazardous Substances Act to consider the economic consequences of its actions, as a matter of policy the Commission has weighed economic factors in deciding upon courses of action.

CPSC, *Self-Pressurized Household Substances Containing Vinyl Chloride Monomer, Ruling on Objection*, 39 Fed. Reg. 36,576, 36,577. (1974) [hereinafter cited as *CPSC Ruling on Objection to VC Recall*].

586. The bare term "safe" in FDCA § 505(e), 21 U.S.C. § 355(e) (1970), might be interpreted to mean that a new drug must be *absolutely* safe. However, the statute is generally taken to allow FDA to weigh risks of a drug's side-effects against the *health* benefits that it offers. *See generally* Merrill, *Compensation for Prescription Drug Injuries*, 59 VA. L. REV. 1, 9-12 (1973). Thus, to postulate the extreme case, drugs are permitted for the treatment of otherwise terminally ill patients if they promise a chance of cure or mitigation, even if they also carry a risk of highly dangerous side-effects. This balancing, however, does not extend to any *economic* benefits the drug may have, which may not be balanced against side-effects. *Id.*

587. The Health Research Group's Petition to CPSC is printed as an appendix to CPSC's proposal. CPSC, *Self-Pressurized Household Substances Containing Vinyl Chloride, Proposed Classification as a Banned Hazardous Substance*, 39 Fed. Reg. 18,115, 18,116-17 (1974) [hereinafter cited as *CPSC Proposed VC Aerosol Ban*]. Health Research Group filed substantially identical petitions with FDA and EPA the same day. Health Research Group, Public Citizen's Health Research Group Asks for Ban on Vinyl Chloride as a Propellant in Aerosols (Feb. 21, 1974) (press release).

588. *FDA Proposed VC Aerosol Ban, supra* note 551, at 14,215-16.

turers to recall voluntarily the products remaining on the market and that several already had done so.[589] The agency proposed two regulations, one removing the drugs' certification of safety, and the other deeming the cosmetics adulterated.[590] Apparently not persuaded that the situation presented an imminent hazard, FDA did not immediately suspend the drugs' certification.[591] The rules were promulgated in August.[592]

EPA acted next and was the first agency to take final action. Several days after FDA's proposal, apparently differing with that agency on the imminence of the hazard, EPA issued an emergency suspension of VC-propelled pesticides.[593] EPA requested the manufacturers to recall existing stocks.[594] To support the emergency suspension EPA cited the fact that at least 14 workers already had died of liver angiosarcoma, and that VC had been shown to cause cancer in animals at levels as low as 50 ppm. The agency termed this evidence "strongly suggestive" of causation. EPA had recently completed tests showing that aerosol users might be exposed to short-term concentrations of up to 400 ppm. The agency concluded that although the health implications of short-term exposures were uncertain, the only "prudent" step was to assume that any exposure to VC increased one's cancer risk.[595] Regarding the economic consequences of its action, EPA noted that there were few economic benefits associated with the use of VC as a propellant, that substitute propellants were readily available, and that no pesticide product would be made unavailable by the ban.[596]

In May, CPSC proposed an order to ban VC-propelled aerosols and to require their repurchase.[597] The agency cited the evidence upon which FDA and EPA had relied. Applying the analysis required under FHSA, CPSC concluded that lesser measures such as a warning label would not provide sufficient protection, particularly since no new VC-propelled products were

---

589. *Id.*

590. *Id.* At the same time FDA also called for information on VC levels in food, drugs, and cosmetics packaged in PVC, and on the risks therefrom. See note 607 *infra*.

591. Neither the proposal nor the statement accompanying the promulgation, *FDA VC Aerosol Ban, supra* note 553, shows that FDA ever formally considered using its suspension powers.

592. *Id.*

593. *EPA VC Aerosol Suspension, supra* note 552, at 14,753.

594. *Id.*

595. *Id.* at 14,753-54.

596. *Id.* at 14,754. EPA gave notice of its intent to cancel these registrations unless a hearing were requested, or unless the manufacturers amended their registrations to demonstrate that VC was no longer used. *Id.* No one requested a hearing, and the registrations that were not properly amended were formally cancelled in January, 1975. EPA, *Vinyl Chloride, Pesticide Products Containing Vinyl Chloride*, 40 Fed. Reg. 3,494 (1975).

Although under FEPCA the agency had the authority to promulgate binding regulations for the disposal of recalled aerosols, EPA confined itself to preparing non-binding guidelines in early 1975 for safely incinerating or burying them. EPA, *Vinyl Chloride, Recommended Procedures for Disposal of Aerosol Cans*, 41 Fed. Reg. 23,226 (1976). See note 568 *supra*.

597. *CPSC Proposed VC Aerosol Ban, supra* note 587.

being made and the hazard came from those already on the market. The agency concluded that a ban and repurchase was required in order to protect consumers' health adequately.[598]

The CPSC proposal appears to have been the only one to raise significant objections from manufacturers. During the comment period, some manufacturers objected that the health risks were too small to justify imposing on manufacturers the expense of recalling existing products.[599] In August, CPSC rejected this contention and promulgated the rule, scheduled to become effective in October.[600] To controvert the manufacturers' objections the agency relied on the evidence of harm cited in the proposal, on reports of additional liver angiosarcoma cases in the interval since the proposal, and on the manufacturers' failure to suggest a safe level of exposure. CPSC concluded that the risks were sufficiently large and immediate to justify the expense of the recall.[601] The manufacturers then requested a hearing on the evidence.[602] In October, CPSC rejected the request, concluding that the manufacturers had not raised any "factual information which the Commission believes would lead to a conclusion contrary to that reached by it."[603] The agency stated that the manufacturers' disagreement with the agency as to the measures that the facts justified under FHSA was a legal and policy matter not capable of resolution in an evidentiary hearing.[604] The Ninth Circuit held that, on the contrary, a hearing was statutorily mandated, and vacated CPSC's regulations in the spring of 1977.[605] As noted above, the ban was reinstated prospectively in March 1978.[606]

---

598. *Id*. at 18,115-16.

599. *CPSC VC Aerosol Ban, supra* note 553, at 30,112-14.

600. *Id*. at 30,114.

601. *Id*.

602. *CPSC Ruling on Objection to VC Recall, supra* note 585, at 36,576-77. In addition to the above objections, the manufacturers alleged that CPSC was required to file an environmental impact statement under the National Environmental Policy Act. *Id*. at 36,577.

603. *Id*.

604. *Id*. at 36,578.

605. Pactra Indus., Inc. v. CPSC, 555 F.2d 677, 684 (9th Cir. 1977). Decision on the main issue of the case, the propriety of CPSC's denial of a hearing, was delayed by the drawn-out disposition of a NEPA claim. In December 1974, the court stayed the recall order until CPSC prepared an EIS or, as required by NEPA, submitted a declaration that the recall was not a "major federal action" subject to the EIS requirement. Pactra Indus., Inc. v. CPSC, No. 74-2902 (9th Cir., Dec.15, 1974) (order staying recall until compliance with NEPA). In September, 1975, nine months later, CPSC stated that no EIS was needed and reaffirmed the recall order. *CPSC VC Environmental Assessment, supra* note 551. In November, the court lifted the stay and reinstated the recall order. Pactra Indus., Inc. v. CPSC, No. 74-2902 (9th Cir., Nov. 6, 1975) (order lifting stay). Somewhat redundantly, in February, 1976 the agency reaffirmed that the recall was in effect. CPSC, *Self-Pressurized Household Substances Containing Vinyl Chloride, Notice of Court Order Affecting Repurchase Requirements*, 41 Fed. Reg. 5425 (1976). At this point it was highly unlikely that there were cans still about.

606. *CPSC Reinstatement of VC Aerosol Ban, supra* note 555.

4. Evaluating the Aerosol Regulations

The three agencies' decisions to act promptly were justified by the hazard posed by the use of VC as a propellant. Although that use had ended in early 1974 for economic reasons, prospective bans were needed to assure that VC-propelled products were not reintroduced. The recalls were justified in light of the possibility that even short-term exposures were a cancer hazard and in light of the relatively low expense involved in an effort to retrieve existing stocks.[607]

As noted above, regulation of VC's use as a propellant did not bring out the potential for jurisdictional conflict between the three agencies. Because of the one-sided nature of the balance of risks and benefits in this case, each of the statutes called for the same result, regardless of the differences in their burdens of proof and other substantive criteria. Consequently, no manufacturer had reason to hope that its product would fall under a more lenient provision, and so had no incentive to argue that a particular product, such as a disinfectant spray, was a household product subject to FHSA rather than a pesticide subject to FEPCA, or that another product, such as a breath spray, was a cosmetic subject to the 1938 provisions of FDCA rather than a drug subject to the New Drug Amendments. No consumer group, hoping to call into play the more stringent statute, had an incentive to argue the reverse. In addition, because the decisions were not difficult or controversial, no agency had an incentive to avoid taking responsibility. The potential for jurisdictional conflict exists, however, and there are products over which such conflicts have occurred.[608]

---

607. The three agencies' success in this context should not obscure other failures. Although they acted quickly with regard to aerosols, they did not take steps at the same time to control the other uses of VC under their jurisdictions. When FDA proposed its aerosol ban, it requested information on migration of VC from PVC packaging into foods, drugs, and cosmetics. *FDA Proposed VC Aerosol Ban, supra* note 551, at 14,125; FDA, *Human Drugs Containing Vinyl Chloride or Packaged in Polyvinyl Chloride Containers, Notice to Drug Manufacturers, Packers, and Distributors*, 39 Fed. Reg. 14,238 (1974). FDA's only subsequent action on these uses was the October, 1975 proposal regarding food packaging; the agency has neither finalized this proposal nor followed up its call for information on drug and cosmetic packaging. EPA delayed promulgation of a hazardous air pollutant standard until October, 1976. CPSC has not even investigated the extent to which household items made from PVC may be a source of VC exposure. The agencies' rapid action on VC's aerosol uses makes more apparent their delay in acting on the other sources of exposure. See text accompanying notes 425-437, 514-533 *supra*, and 772-795 *infra*.

608. An example of a product over which there have been such conflicts, although not under these laws, is the sunlamp. There has been a dispute over when a sunlamp is subject to the 1976 Medical Device Amendments to FDCA, codified in scattered sections of 21 U.S.C. §§ 301-360k (West Supp. 1978), and when it is subject to the 1972 Consumer Product Safety Act, 15 U.S.C. §§ 2051-2081 (Supp. V 1975). Personal communication with Judy Pitcher, *supra* note 551.

Even when divided control over such products does not lead to jurisdictional conflict and inconsistent regulations, it does result in a duplication of effort. There is some value in having three independent inquiries into essentially identical facts; it is less likely that analytical mistakes will go undetected. Nonetheless, considering the backlog of other toxic substances meriting these agencies' attention, it is probable that there are better uses for administrative resources than to double- and triple-check decision making for one substance.

The agencies' experience with VC appears to have led them to this conclusion. In their subsequent actions to control fluorocarbons, another aerosol propellant, the agencies have acted together.[609] Along with OSHA, the three agencies have also established an official liaison among themselves through which to share information and coordinate action on chemicals coming under the jurisdiction of more than one of them.[610] That effort is discussed below.[611]

F. Emissions from Transportation of VC—Four Transportation Statutes and the Occupational Safety and Health Act

1. The Key Issues Regarding VC Transportation

The release of VC and other toxic substances while in transit may be a major source of risk for transportation workers and the general public.[612] The history of VC spills and other accidents has been discussed above.[613] Despite the need for at least an investigation of the extent of the hazard and the desirability of controls on this source of exposure, there has been little study and little regulation of the cancer hazard from VC transportation.[614]

---

609. For a discussion of the agencies' coordinated action on fluorocarbons, see text accompanying notes 842-849 *infra*.

610. *See* IRLG Agreement, *supra* note 538.

611. See text accompanying notes 851-868 *infra*.

612. Rail, trucking, and vessel shippers and carriers are required to report release of hazardous materials to the Department of Transportation. 49 C.F.R. §§ 171.15-.16 (1976) (rail and trucking reporting); *id.* § 176.48 (vessel reporting). In 1974, 8,500 hazardous materials accidents were reported to DOT, which has stated that "only a small portion of reportable incidents are actually reported." U.S. Dep't of Transp., Hazardous Materials Incidents Reports Received During 1974, at 1 (May 7, 1975). One EPA official expects the number of actual spills to double from a current 1,700 per year "to [at least] 3,000 spills per year by 1980 before leveling off." *Toxic Materials News in Brief*, 5 Toxic Materials News 104, 105 (1978). Without accurate statistics on release, possible epidemiological connections between accidents and illnesses will remain almost impossible to draw.

613. See text accompanying notes 158-160 *supra*.

614. No epidemiological studies of the effects of VC on transportation workers have been reported. No estimates have been made of the number of people who may be exposed to VC by accidents, nor of the doses they may receive. While some attempts have been made to relate VC emissions from factories to cancer and birth defect rates in nearby communities, there has been no attempt to determine what portion of the so-called "background" level of angiosarcoma of the liver may be connected to the release of VC in transportation. Personal communica-

The major reason that transportation regulation lags so far behind the regulation of factory emissions is the fragmentation and lack of clarity of the present statutory and administrative regime. The ambiguity of this regime can hardly be overemphasized. Practically speaking, existing rules under OSH Act and the Clean Air Act apply to VC transportation only while rail tank cars, tank trucks, or tank vessels are on the premises of VC and PVC factories for loading and unloading.[615] Five statutes apply to the control of risks from VC transportation between the factories: the 1975 Hazardous Materials Transportation Act,[616] the 1972 Ports and Waterways Safety Act,[617] the Dangerous Cargo Act,[618] the Federal Railroad Safety Act,[619] and OSH Act.[620] The first four statutes are administered by agencies within the Department of Transportation (DOT), and the last by OSHA, in the Department of Labor. Some modes of transport are potentially subject to more than one statute. Although the scope of some of these statutes is well-defined, for several of them it is unclear whether they authorize regulations meant to protect transportation workers alone, only the general public, or both. The basic features of this complex tangle are displayed somewhat tentatively in Table II. To date, regulations aimed at the cancer hazard have been set only for water transportation of VC.

The regulation of VC transportation poses more difficult balancing issues than the regulation of VC aerosols. As a result, the jurisdictional uncertainty and controversy that were largely dormant in the aerosol area are highly visible here.

Although conceptual division of the authorities in this area is not clear, some sense may be made of the statutory arrangements by considering, first, the protection of the general public near transportation facilities, and second, the protection of transportation workers.

---

tion with Mary Williams, Chemical Engineer, Office of Hazardous Materials Operations, Materials Transportation Bureau, DOT, Oct. 28, 1976.

615.   OSHA's regulations state that the standard "applies to the transportation of vinyl chloride or polyvinyl chloride except to the extent that the Department of Transportation may regulate the hazards covered by this section." 29 C.F.R. § 1910.1017(a)(3) (1977). However, the standard's provisions are aimed primarily at the handling of the chemical only at the VC and PVC plants. *See, e.g., id.* § 1910.1017(e) (regulated areas). Nothing in the OSHA standard applies specifically to transportation except with regard to loading and unloading at these plants.

The EPA standard is directed at the owners and operators of VC and PVC plants. Some requirements pertain to the loading and unloading of rail tank cars, tank trucks, and vessels, but not to other phases of transportation. *See* 40 C.F.R. § 61.65 (1977).

616.   Pub. L. No. 93-633, 88 Stat. 2156, 49 U.S.C. §§ 1801-1812 (Supp. V 1975).

617.   Pub. L. No. 92-340 § 201, 86 Stat. 424, 46 U.S.C. § 391a (Supp. V 1975).

618.   Pub. L. No. 76-809, 54 Stat. 1023, 46 U.S.C. § 170(7) (1970).

619.   Pub. L. No. 91-458, 84 Stat. 971 (1970), 45 U.S.C. §§ 421-441 (1970).

620.   29 U.S.C. §§ 651-678 (1970). In addition, EPA has responsibilities for hazardous pollutant spills from vessels and onshore facilities under the Federal Water Pollution Control Act. See text accompanying notes 711-721 *infra*.

TABLE II

STATUTES APPLICABLE TO VC TRANSPORTATION

	Mode of Transport			Persons Protected			
	Rail	Truck	Water	General Public	Rail Workers	Truck Workers	Port and Waterway Workers
Hazardous Materials Transportation Act Materials Transportation Bureau	*	*		*	?	?	
Ports and Waterways Safety Act and Dangerous Cargo Act Coast Guard			*	*			*
Federal Railroad Safety Act Federal Railroad Administration	*			*	?		
Occupational Safety and Health Act Occupational Safety and Health Administration	*	*			*	*	

2. The Safety of the General Public Near Transportation Facilities

a. The Hazardous Materials Transportation Act—railroad and trucking

The Hazardous Materials Transportation Act (HMTA) authorizes the Secretary of Transportation to make regulations to protect "health and safety" from the movement of dangerous materials around the country.[621] The Act defines a "hazardous material" as "a substance or material in a quantity and form which may pose an unreasonable risk to health and safety or property when transported in commerce."[622] When, "in his discretion," the Secretary finds that a chemical meets this definition, he must designate it a hazardous material.[623] He may then set regulations for its "safe transportation" by railroad, truck, airplane, or vessel.[624] The regulations may cover the handling and routing of hazardous materials, the manufacture and labeling of shipping containers[625] and the number and training of transport

---

621. HMTA §§ 103-106, 49 U.S.C. §§ 1802-1805 (Supp. V 1975).
622. *Id.* § 103(2), 49 U.S.C. § 1802(2) (Supp. V 1975).
623. *Id.* § 104, 49 U.S.C. § 1803 (Supp. V 1975).
624. *Id.* § 105(a)-(b), 49 U.S.C. § 1804(a)-(b) (Supp. V 1975).
625. *Id.* § 105(a), 49 U.S.C. § 1804(a) (Supp. V 1975), states:
   Such regulation may govern any safety aspect of the transportation of hazardous materials which the Secretary deems necessary or appropriate, including, but not limited to, the packing, repacking, handling, labeling, marking, placarding, and routing . . . of hazardous materials and the manufacture, fabrication, marking, maintenance, reconditioning, repairing, or testing of a [hazardous materials package or container].

personnel.[626] The Secretary has delegated his responsibilities under the Act to the Materials Transportation Bureau (MTB),[627] which has established standards for hundreds of substances.[628] Since VC apparently is not transported by air carriers, and since MTB apparently leaves the regulation of water transport to the Coast Guard under statutes to be discussed below, the following discussion concerns only rail and truck transportation.

MTB's current regulations for VC, as for other substances, are aimed at reducing the risks of fire, explosion, and acute toxicity, rather than the risks of cancer or other subtle and latent effects. The agency classifies VC in the "flammable gas" category.[629] Containers of VC in transport must thus carry warnings of the fire hazard, but not of carcinogenicity.[630] Containers must be designed to resist leakage, and tank trucks and rail tank cars must be handled carefully.[631] Of course, measures to decrease the risk of fire incidentally lower the risk of exposure to the carcinogen. Nevertheless, measures that are meant to keep VC releases below combustible concentrations may not be sufficient to keep releases below concentrations that pose a cancer risk.

In late 1976, MTB publicly began to consider taking action to reduce releases of VC and similar chemicals further than its existing regulations accomplish. The agency requested views on whether HMTA gives it authority to set regulations aimed at protecting the public from "low-level" exposures to chemicals—*i.e.*, exposures that pose risks of chronic and latent health and environmental effects—and if so, how much of that authority should be exercised.[632] The agency also asked for opinions on the

---

626.   *Id*. § 106(a), 49 U.S.C. § 1805(a) (Supp. V 1975), authorizes the promulgation of regulations regarding personnel, monitoring equipment, inspection requirements, and other specifications.

627.   49 C.F.R. § 1.53(a)(5) (1977). Under the Interstate Commerce Act, 49 U.S.C. § 304(a)(3) (1970), another agency within DOT, the Bureau of Motor Carrier Safety, has promulgated a rule requiring truckers of hazardous materials to avoid heavily populated areas "[u]nless there is no practicable alternative." 49 C.F.R. § 397.9 (1976). This somewhat vague control over routing adds nothing of substance that cannot be accomplished under HMTA, but it raises the possibility that yet another agency in DOT has hazardous materials responsibilities.

628.   *See generally* 49 C.F.R. pts. 171-179 (1976). The enforcement of MTB rules is divided among the agencies with direct responsibilities for the several transportation modes, such as the Federal Highway Administration, the Federal Railroad Administration, and the Coast Guard. 49 C.F.R. § 107.301 (1976).

629.   49 C.F.R. § 172.101 (1976).

630.   49 C.F.R. §§ 172.417, .532 (1976).

631.   For instance, certain leak-prone types of gauges may not be used. 49 C.F.R. § 173.315(h) (1976). To reduce the chances of punctures during derailments, railroad tank cars must have shields at each end designed to deflect the coupling gear of adjacent cars. 49 C.F.R. § 179.100-23 (1976). There have been complaints, however, that the installation of these shields is not proceeding quickly enough. Only a few dozen of the 20,000 jumbo tank cars on the rails have been fitted with these shields. Kramer, *Rail Tank Car Safety Speedup Urged*, Washington [D.C.] Post, Apr. 5, 1978, § E, at 1, col. 3.

632.   Department of Transportation, *Materials Transportation Bureau, Environmental and Health Effects Materials, Advance Notice of Proposed Rulemaking*, 41 Fed. Reg. 53,824 (1976) [hereinafter cited as *DOT Advance Notice*].

type of data and evaluation that should be used to determine the extent of such hazards, the means and costs of control and the levels of risk and benefit to be considered "reasonable" under the statute.[633] MTB has received a number of comments, but has not yet decided upon a course of action.[634]

The statute would support an MTB decision to protect workers and others against long-term health effects of VC and of other chemicals. The main concern of Congress and DOT obviously has been risks of acute toxicity, fire, and explosion.[635] Nevertheless, the statute's definition of a hazardous material uses the language of risk and possibility typical of other statutes directed at long-term health effects,[636] and it refers not only to human safety, but to human health as well.[637] Some of the legislative history supports this view; the House Committee implied that it desired latent and uncertain effects to be minimized by stating: "In making the designation [that a material is hazardous] it is expected that *potential* damage to human health and the safety of people and property be considered."[638]

If MTB were to decide to protect the public from the carcinogenic threat in VC transport, the agency would have to address the following issues. First, it would have to develop better data on the number of people,

633. *Id*. at 53,825-26.

634. *See MTB Receives Comments on Transportation Controls for Certain Classes of Materials*, 1 BNA CHEM. REG. REP.—CURR. REP. 542 (1977).

Recently, an offshoot of this proposal has brought MTB closer to regulating such materials. Under the 1976 Resource Conservation and Recovery Act, EPA has certain responsibilities to regulate the transportation of hazardous wastes, as a part of an overall hazardous waste disposal system. See text accompanying notes 722-731 *infra*. Concerned that the EPA regulations and the existing MTB rules will subject transporters to duplicative or inconsistent requirements, the two agencies are working toward an agreement whereby MTB would assume substantial responsibilities, in cooperation with EPA, for the safe movement of substances that pose carcinogenic risks and other long-term health and environmental risks. *See Existing Transportation Safety Laws Should Apply to TSCA, RCRA, Santman Says*, 1 BNA CHEM. REG. REP.—CURR. REP. 1756 (1978); Personal communication with Walt Kovalick, Chief, Guidelines Branch, EPA Hazardous Waste Management Division, Feb. 22, 1978.

635. In fact, one might argue that Congress did not intend this statute to cover risks of cancer and other chronic diseases. As examples of the need for the bill, the House Report recounts incidents involving bombs and munitions and such acutely toxic or explosive chemicals as chlorine, liquefied petroleum gas, hydrochloric acid, ammonia, sulfuric acid, and cyanide. H.R. REP. NO. 1083, 93rd Cong., 2d Sess. 15 (1974), *reprinted in* [1974] U.S. CODE CONG. & AD. NEWS 7669, 7675. Several reported incidents involved VC leakages and fires, *id.*, and although the carcinogenic potential of this chemical was well known at the time of the Report, the Committee made no direct reference to it. The discussion in the text immediately below, however, presents the contrary argument.

636. *Compare* HMTA § 103(2), 49 U.S.C. § 1802(2) (Supp. V 1975) ("unreasonable risk to health and safety") *with* FEPCA § 2(bb), 7 U.S.C. § 136(bb) (Supp. V 1975) ("unreasonable adverse effects on the environment") *and* Consumer Product Safety Act § 7(a), 15 U.S.C. § 2056(a) (Supp. V 1975) ("unreasonable risk of injury"). *See also* OSH Act § 6(b)(5), 29 U.S.C. § 655(b)(5) (1970) (protection "to the extent feasible" against "material impairment of health or functional capacity").

637. HMTA § 103(2), 49 U.S.C. § 1802(2) (Supp. V 1975).

638. H.R. REP. NO. 1083, 93rd Cong., 2d Sess. 20 (1974), *reprinted in* [1974] U.S. CODE CONG. & AD. NEWS 7669, 7680 (emphasis added).

especially workers, exposed once or repeatedly to short-term, high-level exposures to VC. The agency would also need information on the contribution of transportation releases to low-level, sustained exposure of the general public. Second, MTB would need to learn more about the relative cancer risk from short-term, high-level exposures; most of the toxicological and epidemiological work to date has focused on the effects of sustained exposures.[639] Third, the agency would have to develop more information on the impact of additional requirements for packing and handling VC on transportation costs.[640]

b.   The Ports and Waterways Safety Act and the Dangerous Cargo Act— water transport

Under the Ports and Waterways Safety Act (PWSA), the Commandant of the Coast Guard, a branch of DOT, is authorized to establish minimum standards for the design, construction, maintenance, and operation of vessels carrying bulk cargoes that create "substantial hazards to life, property, and the marine environment."[641] The Commandant also may set rules for the handling and stowage of such cargoes.[642] In addition, "[i]n order to secure effective provisions against the hazards of health life, limb, or property created by explosives or other dangerous articles or substances," the Dangerous Cargo Act authorizes the Commandant to set rules for "marking, handling, storage, stowage, and use of explosives or other dangerous articles or substances on board such vessels."[643] Both statutes apply to vessels in any navigable waters of the United States.[644] The statutes are aimed at protection of both ship crews and the general public surrounding ports and waterways.[645]

---

639. See text accompanying note 167 *supra*.

640. The possibility that transportation would become much more expensive would not necessarily be a justification for refusing to impose the requirements. The health hazard to the public near transportation routes is a cost associated with VC production and use that should be internalized. In the long run, industries would find ways to reduce transportation costs; for example, they could group VC and PVC facilities closer together, thereby reducing both costs and hazards of transportation.

641. 46 U.S.C. § 391a(1),(3) (Supp. V 1975); 49 C.F.R. § 1.46(n)(4) (1977).

642. 46 U.S.C. § 391a(3) (Supp. V 1975); 49 C.F.R. § 1.46(n)(4) (1977).

643. 46 U.S.C. § 170(7)(a) (1970).

644. 46 U.S.C. § 391a(2) (Supp. V 1975); 46 U.S.C. § 170(1) (1970).

645. The House Report on the 1952 amendments to the Dangerous Cargo Act states:
     Under the Dangerous Cargo Act the Coast Guard is concerned with the safety of the vessel and its crew and passengers.

H.R. REP. NO. 2346, 82d Cong., 2d Sess. (1952), *reprinted in* [1952] U.S. CODE CONG. & AD. NEWS 2285, 2285-86. The legislative history of PWSA is concerned primarily with ecological damage and human casualties caused by bulk carrier collisions, groundings, and the like. *See*, *e.g.*, S. REP. NO. 724, 92d Cong., 2d Sess. 1-5 (1972), *reprinted in* [1972] U.S. CODE CONG. & AD. NEWS 2766, 2766-69. However, the statement of policy, list of cargos covered by the PWSA, and the nature of regulations which the Coast Guard is authorized to promulgate all demonstrate a broader concern with human health risks than the legislative history would indicate. *See* 46 U.S.C. § 391a(1)-(3) (Supp. V 1975). The Coast Guard apparently views both acts as conferring authority to regulate handling of hazardous substances for the protection of

To reduce the risks of fire, explosion, and acute toxicity, the Coast Guard has established rules similar to MTB's for hundreds of chemicals.[646] Prior to the recognition of VC's carcinogenicity, the agency designated VC a dangerous cargo and promulgated specific design, construction, and handling standards for the chemical.[647] In addition, since 1974 the Coast Guard has imposed tighter regulations to protect crew members, and incidentally the general public, from the VC cancer hazard.[648] The Coast Guard is the only transportation agency which has protected either group. These regulations are discussed below.

3. The Safety of Transportation Workers.

Workers involved in the transportation of VC are protected by the OSHA standard only when they participate in loading and unloading operations on the premises of VC and PVC plants. Transportation workers, however, are present regularly at loading and unloading operations elsewhere and, of course, during leaks and other accidents. In those circumstances, the general measures against fire, explosion, and acute toxicity may not be sufficient to protect them from the cancer hazard. Regard for their safety may require equipment standards and work practices permitting fewer leaks, or it may even require the use of respiratory protective equipment as in VC and PVC factories. Only the Coast Guard has required any of these steps; MTB and the Federal Railroad Administration have only recently begun to analyze the need for them.

The four statutes administered by agencies within DOT authorize more or less clearly the promulgation of standards to protect transportation workers. In addition, until those agencies act, OSHA also has the authority to set such standards. Since only the Coast Guard has acted, there are many areas of untested ambiguity, both as to what each agency within DOT may do, and as to the conditions under which OSHA may step in. The probable resolution of these ambiguities is set out below.

a. OSHA's dependent jurisdiction

OSHA has authority to issue rules to protect transportation workers, but may not set standards regarding "working conditions of employees with respect to which other Federal agencies . . . exercise statutory authority to prescribe or enforce standards or regulations affecting occupational safety or health."[649] OSHA's power to protect railroad, trucking, and waterway workers depends, therefore, on three factors: (1) whether other agencies

---

bulk cargo workers. In promulgating the VC regulations discussed in the text accompanying notes 650-661 *infra*, the Coast Guard cited no substantive authorizing statute other than the Dangerous Cargo Act and PWSA. Coast Guard, *Vinyl Chloride Carriage Requirements*, 40 Fed. Reg. 17,024, 17,026 (1974) [hereinafter cited as *Coast Guard VC Requirements*].

646. 46 C.F.R. pts. 40 (1977), 151 (1976).
647. 46 C.F.R. §§ 151.01-10(b), 151.05-1 (1976).
648. 46 C.F.R. §§ 40.15-1 (1977), 151.50-34 (1976).
649. OSH Act § 4(b)(1), 29 U.S.C. § 653(b)(1) (1970).

have authority over these employees' "working conditions"; (2) the definition of an "exercise" of such authority; and (3) the definition of "affecting" occupational health. These factors can be clarified through an exploration of the DOT agencies' actions regarding the VC transportation workers.

b.   Worker protection under the Ports and Waterways Safety Act and the Dangerous Cargo Act

As noted above, two statutes, PWSA and the Dangerous Cargo Act, confer on the Coast Guard the authority to establish standards to protect crew members as well as the general public.[650] Under this authority the agency has set rules protecting crews of VC tankers from the chemical's cancer hazard. In the period immediately after the recognition of the cancer hazard, the Coast Guard sought to provide a measure of emergency protection for tanker crews. In May 1974, shortly after OSHA set the emergency temporary standard limiting exposure to 50 ppm, the Coast Guard established interim measures to reduce the exposure of crews during loading and unloading, exposures which then exceeded 50 ppm.[651] The agency adopted OSHA's conclusion that VC is carcinogenic and poses a "grave danger" to employees exposed to concentrations exceeding 50 ppm.[652] These regulations were essentially "housekeeping" measures, *i.e.*, steps that could be taken with existing equipment to eliminate unnecessary exposure to VC.

For a time, OSHA's and the Coast Guard's responses diverged. In July, after OSHA had proposed the one ppm standard, the Coast Guard proposed rules to lower VC concentrations only below 50 ppm.[653] These rules would have eliminated gauges of a leaky design, prohibited venting VC to the atmosphere, required the purging of pipes into onshore containers prior to disconnecting them, required continuous monitoring for leaks, and required a halt to transfer operations whenever airborne concentrations greater than 50 ppm were detected.[654] Aware of the divergence between its proposal and OSHA's, the Coast Guard held open the possibility that the 50 ppm level would be lowered, depending on the results of the OSHA hearings then taking place.[655]

The Coast Guard apparently delayed promulgating a rule to replace its interim measures until the resolution of the plastics industries' challenge to OSHA's final one ppm standard. In April 1975, about three months after the Second Circuit Court of Appeals upheld OSHA's standard, the Coast Guard adopted similar regulations.[656] The final rules lowered the permissible VC

650.   See text accompanying notes 641-645 *supra.*
651.   Coast Guard, *Vinyl Chloride, Proposed Carriage Requirements*, 39 Fed. Reg. 26,752 (1974) *citing* Coast Guard Message 131513Z (May 13, 1974) [hereinafter cited as *Proposed Coast Guard Requirements*].
652.   *Id.*
653.   *Id. See also* Coast Guard, *Vinyl Chloride, Supplemental Notice*, 39 Fed. Reg. 33,711 (1974).
654.   *Proposed Coast Guard Requirements*, *supra* note 651, at 26,752-53.
655.   *Id.*
656.   *Coast Guard VC Requirements*, *supra* note 645.

concentration from the 50 ppm level that had been proposed to the one ppm level selected by OSHA.[657] These rules were not challenged, and they became effective in July 1975.[658]

The Coast Guard and OSHA rules are substantially identical responses to substantially the same hazards. The Coast Guard rules clearly are the "exercise" of authority over "working conditions" that the jurisdictional section of OSH Act contemplates.[659] Thus, so long as these regulations are in effect, OSHA is precluded from regulating the VC exposure of water transportation workers.

Like the OSHA standard, the Coast Guard regulations do not completely eliminate the worker's risk of cancer. Unlike OSH Act, however, the two water transportation statutes lack any term such as "feasible" that explicitly authorizes the weighing of health risks and economic benefits. Implicitly, the Coast Guard has interpreted these statutes to allow such balancing. This is probably an acceptable interpretation; there is nothing in the statutes' legislative history to suggest that Congress meant the absence of such a term to carry the restrictive meaning that it does elsewhere,[660] and there are no policy reasons to treat water transportation safety differently in this regard than safety in land transportation or in factories.[661]

c. *The Federal Railroad Safety Act—railroad workers*

Another agency in DOT may have the authority to set standards for railroad workers exposed to VC. Under the Federal Railroad Safety Act (FRSA),[662] the Federal Railroad Administration (FRA) "shall . . . . prescribe, as necessary, appropriate rules, regulations, orders, and standards for all areas of railroad safety."[663] That "all areas of railroad safety" includes the safety of railroad workers is made clear by the legislative history; the House Report repeatedly refers to injuries to employees, as well as injuries to bystanders, as evidence of the need for the statute.[664] It is less

657. 46 C.F.R. §§ 40.15-1(a) (1977), 151.01-25, .50-34 (1976).

658. *Coast Guard VC Requirements*, *supra* note 645, at 17,025.

659. OSH Act § 4(b)(1), 29 U.S.C. § 653(b)(1) (1970), quoted in text accompanying note 651 *supra*.

660. *See, e.g.*, the discussions of the Food Additives Amendment, in text accompanying notes 489-494 *supra*, and of the hazardous air pollutant section of the Clean Air Act, in text accompanying notes 375-377 *supra*.

661. It should be noted, however, that although the water transportation statutes appear to permit balancing risks and benefits, it was not necessary that the Coast Guard settle on the same exposure limit as OSHA, one ppm. Differences in the number of workers involved, the cost of exposure control measures, and other factors might have led the Coast Guard and OSHA reasonably to choose different levels. There is no evidence, however, that the Coast Guard did more than use OSHA's estimation of the appropriate level.

662. Pub. L. No. 91-458, 91st Cong., 2d Sess., 84 Stat. 971 (1970), 45 U.S.C. §§ 421-441 (1970). The administration of this statute was assigned to the Federal Railroad Administration in 49 U.S.C. § 1655(f)(3)(A) (Supp. V 1975).

663. FRSA § 202, 45 U.S.C. § 431(a) (1970).

664. H.R. Rep. No. 1194, 91st Cong., 2d Sess. 8-10 (1970), *reprinted in* [1970] U.S. Code Cong. & Ad. News 4104, 4106-07.

clear that the phrase encompasses the authority to protect workers from toxic substances. It may be argued that the use of the word "safety" alone implies that in FRSA Congress was concerned solely with the traditional railroad hazards of physical harm from engines, rolling stock, and other equipment and machinery connected with railroad operations. On the other hand, there is no bright line between "safety" hazards and "health" hazards to suggest that the use of one term rather than the other is meaningful in this context.[665]

Despite the ambiguity of the term "safety," FRA has tentatively asserted its authority to set health as well as safety standards. In the course of a March 1975 "Advance Notice of Proposed Rulemaking" announcing its intention to set standards regarding certain obviously physical rail yard workplace hazards, FRA asserted that it possesses "broad authority to regulate railroad occupational safety and health."[666] The agency declared its intention to issue standards "as necessary," for "all railroad working conditions or work places," regarding both safety and health.[667] FRA stated that it planned to adopt certain existing OSHA standards, modified as necessary to suit railroad occupational situations.[668] None of the contemplated standards applied to toxic substances. In July 1976, the agency reaffirmed its intention to issue a "comprehensive code" of standards "to protect the safety and health of railroad employees."[669] At that time FRA proposed rules covering only certain physical safety hazards, but it announced that this would be the first in a series of installments to construct this safety and health code.[670] Despite this promise, no FRA standards exist as yet to protect workers from VC or any other toxic substance, and FRA's interpretation of the statute has not been tested.

The March 1975 Advance Notice and the July 1976 proposal, however, have been the occasion for testing the definition of an "exercise" of a federal agency's authority sufficient to exclude OSHA[671] in circumstances more ambiguous than the actions of the Coast Guard. Three 1976 appellate cases affirmed OSHA's authority to enforce its generally applicable occupational safety and health regulations against railroads.[672] The cases rejected the view that either the Advance Notice or the proposal pre-empts OSHA's authority. Although the cases were not consistent in all particulars, they

---

665. Consider, for example, the hazards of fire. The flames ordinarily are considered a safety hazard. The smoke, however, ordinarily is considered a health hazard.

666. Federal Railroad Administration, *Advance Notice of Proposed Rulemaking*, 40 Fed. Reg. 10,693 (1975) [hereinafter cited as *FRA Advance Notice*].

667. *Id*. at 10,693.

668. *Id*.

669. Federal Railroad Administration, *Railroad Occupational Safety and Health Standards, Proposed Rules*, 41 Fed. Reg. 29,153 (1976).

670. *Id*. at 29,153-54.

671. *See* OSH Act § 4(b)(1), 29 U.S.C. § 653(b)(1) (1970).

672. Southern Ry. Co. v. OSHRC, 539 F.2d 335 (4th Cir. 1976), *cert. denied* 429 U.S. 999 (1977); Southern Pac. Transp. Co. v. Usery, 539 F.2d 386 (5th Cir. 1976); Baltimore & O. R.R. Co. v. OSHRC, 548 F.2d 1052 (D.C. Cir. 1976).

implied that in order to block OSHA from extending the protection of toxic substances standards to railroad workers, FRA must set such rules itself, or at least must formally consider and reach a conclusion upon the need for them.[673]

Recently FRA terminated its proposed rulemaking and issued a statement of policy attempting to clarify its relationship with OSHA.[674] Discus-

---

673. The three courts all rejected the theory that FRA regulation of some aspect of railroad worker safety is sufficient to exclude OSHA from the entire area. Sensitive to the railroads' burden of complying with overlapping, independent regulatory regimes, yet desiring to leave OSHA the broad jurisdiction that Congress intended, the Fourth and Fifth Circuits each developed tests for the "exercise" of statutory authority and the scope of the "working conditions" to which it applies, under OSH Act § 4(b)(1).

The Fourth Circuit's solution, while adequate to the case at hand, may lead to undesirable results in the future. The court rejected OSHA's claim that it may regulate any "particular, discrete hazard" that FRA rules leave uncovered. The court defined "working conditions" as "the environmental area in which an employee customarily goes about his daily tasks," and it held that whenever FRA establishes rules applicable to such an environmental area, OSHA is foreclosed. Southern Ry. Co. v. OSHRC, 539 F.2d 335, 339 (4th Cir. 1976). This geographic definition would preclude OSHA from protecting workers from exposure to VC or another toxic substance in any location —loading area, repair facility, even on the tracks themselves— for which FRA has prescribed safety rules, even if the FRA rules do not reach the hazard OSHA desired to control.

The Fifth Circuit developed a solution that will avoid this difficulty. The court adopted an approach oriented to the type of hazard rather than the geographic area. In its view, "comprehensive FRA treatment" of a hazard would displace otherwise applicable OSHA regulations. Moreover, it held that FRA could defeat OSHA jurisdiction by stating a "formal position" that certain hazards should be unregulated, or regulated no more than FRA prescribed. Failing these FRA actions, OSHA retains jurisdiction. Southern Pac. Transp. Co. v. Usery, 539 F.2d 386, 391-92 (5th Cir. 1976).

These tests would have no import for the regulation of VC if FRA were eventually held to lack authority to set toxic substance standards. Then OSHA's way would be unobstructed. But assuming FRSA confers this power, the Fifth Circuit's test is preferable to the Fourth Circuit's. The Fourth Circuit's focus on geography would permit FRA to preclude OSHA from regulating VC without ever considering action against this kind of hazard. The Fifth Circuit's focus on hazards, however, permits OSHA to regulate the sources of exposure to VC or other substances, so long as FRA declines to do so, or to consider the need to do so.

The Fourth and Fifth Circuits, which had only the Advance Notice before them, agreed that the mere announcement of an intention to propose regulations was not an "exercise" capable of barring action by OSHA. 539 F.2d at 339-40; 539 F.2d at 392. The District of Columbia Circuit, which had before it the proposed rules as well, held that a proposal is not an "exercise" either. Baltimore & O. R.R. Co. v. OSHRC, 548 F.2d 1052, 1054-55 (D.C. Cir. 1976). The cases imply that only a final agency action—such as a promulgation of rules or a determination that a hazard should not be regulated—would be an "exercise" within the meaning of OSH Act § 4(b)(1). *Compare* the foregoing cases *with* Dunlop v. Burlington N. Ry., 395 F.Supp. 203, 205 n.1 (D. Mont. 1975) (holding that the Advance Notice was an "exercise" with respect to the specified OSHA rules, but declining to decide if the whole railroad industry was exempted from OSHA regulation thereby) *and* Organized Migrants in Community Action v. Brennan, 520 F.2d 1161, 8 ERC 1442 (D.C. Cir. 1975) (holding that EPA pesticide regulations were an "exercise" pre-empting OSHA from setting standards to protect farmworkers from pesticide exposure in the fields).

674. Federal Railroad Administration, *Railroad Occupational Safety and Health, Termination, Policy Statement*, 43 Fed. Reg. 10,583 (1978). The agency maintained its view that it has "broad authority" to regulate "all areas of railroad safety." *Id.* at 10,584. However, the agency has determined to *exercise* that authority at this time only with respect to "conditions and procedures necessary to achieve safe movement of equipment over the rails," *i.e.*, with respect

sing toxic substances control specifically for the first time, FRA implied that
the existence of MTB rules with respect to a given substance pre-empts
OSHA's jurisdiction to regulate that substance.[675] FRA is thus suggesting
that OSHA is pre-empted even though the MTB rules do not address the
long-term effects of low exposures, which would be the focus of OSHA
standards. Under the doctrine of the three cases discussed above, the
effectiveness of so broad a pre-emption is doubtful.[676]

Thus the agencies' responsibilities in the toxic substances control area
are still unclear. For its part, OSHA has taken no steps to extend the
coverage of the VC standard to railroad workers either. OSHA has little
incentive to do so, since any moves in this direction still could be blocked
and rendered a waste of effort by FRA action.

Therefore, railroad workers currently are not protected by either
agency from the possible VC cancer hazard. Nominally, they have two
agencies to look to for this protection, but practically, neither agency is
likely to act as long as the present uncertain relationship continues. If the
agencies can resolve the relationship more clearly, the railroad employees
may be able to obtain more attention to their needs from whichever agency
emerges with the responsibility for protecting their health.

d.   The Hazardous Materials Transportation Act—railroad and trucking workers

Regulations explicitly directed at the protection of railroad and trucking
workers probably also could be set under HMTA. The Act does not define
the class of persons whose health and safety is to be protected from
unreasonable risks; it is likely, though, that the statute authorizes MTB to
set very strict controls in order to protect workers, who are more heavily
exposed to hazardous materials than is the general public. Such rules may
emerge from the agency's effort now underway to determine its responsibilities regarding substances that have long-term health and environmental
effects.[677] However, until such rules are set, with explicit reference to the
greater hazard of the workers, OSHA retains the authority to protect them. It
would be useful then for OSHA and DOT to execute a jurisdictional
agreement regarding HMTA as well as FRSA.

4.   Evaluating the Control of VC in Transportation

As in the case with aerosols, the costs of jurisdictional complexity in
the regulation of hazardous materials transportation are high. Investigations

---

to the safety of track, roadbed, associated devices and structures (such as signals, bridges, and
tunnels), equipment, and employee behavior. *Id.* at 10,585-86.

675.   *See id.* at 10,587, 10,589. FRA also specifically asserts that it is exercising jurisdiction
over employee exposures in locomotive cabs and in cabooses, thereby pre-empting OSHA from
regulating in these areas. *Id.* at 10,589.

676.   See note 673 *supra* and accompanying text.

677.   See text accompanying notes 632-633 *supra*.

of hazards and rulemaking proceedings are duplicative. Agencies that are reluctant to enter a field as difficult as the regulation of carcinogens are encouraged to leave the responsibility to others, even when their own statutes would support regulation. Industries run the risk of inconsistent responsibilities. Proponents of regulation for these substances must bear the cost of multiple proceedings.

Indeed, the case for consolidating these hazardous materials transportation responsibilities is even greater than the case for consolidating control over aerosols and other consumer products. Whereas there are a few problems that affect aerosols across the board, and a substantial number of such problems regarding other consumer products, there are hundreds of chemicals in transportation that run afoul of this complex regulatory tangle.[678] The scenario of slow regulation will be repeated often. It may be possible to achieve a substantial degree of coordination through administrative means; three of the four relevant agencies are already within one department, DOT. Short of consolidating these three agencies' responsibilities, DOT could still make improvements by defining their jurisdictions clearly. This is particularly the case with regard to the conflicting jurisdictions of MTB and FRA concerning the protection of railroad workers. It is also important that agreements be concluded between OSHA and the transportation agencies. If these four agencies cannot work this problem out alone, Congress, which is responsible for the jurisdictional fragmentation in the first place, should take action. Regarding VC, at the very least MTB, FRA, and OSHA should follow the lead of the Coast Guard in providing the general public and transportation workers with adequate protection from the cancer hazards of releases of VC in transport.

G. Miscellaneous Sources of Vinyl Chloride Exposure and the Statutes for Their Control

Two basic categories of sources of VC exposure remain to be discussed. First, VC enters both the air and drinking water through the effluent and sludge waste of VC and PVC plants, and through spills in water transportation accidents. Second, residual VC leaches from a wide variety of PVC products, such as water pipe, drug and cosmetic packaging, medical devices, latex paints, and other consumer and industrial products. The discharges to water are probably the most important of these sources, because they can contaminate drinking water. The other sources probably amount to less exposure than any of those already discussed, and probably pose a correspondingly smaller health hazard.

A bewildering number of statutes and agencies would be involved in an

---

678. For a sense of the potential magnitude of the hazardous materials transportation problem, note the size of the list of substances that MTB now regulates. 49 C.F.R. § 172.101 (1976). Although not all of these substances present a risk of cancer or other health and environmental effects at low exposures, VC is by no means the only one.

effort to regulate all of these sources of exposure.[679] This section completes the case study by surveying the statutes and the regulatory efforts applicable to these sources. It also explores how the 1976 Toxic Substances Control Act[680] could be used in future instances of extreme jurisdictional fragmentation to reduce the number of separate actions that must be taken.

There are no regulations in effect yet for any of these sources of VC exposure, although regulations are in preparation for most of the sources affecting water.[681] The reasons for the lack of action differ from source to source. Several of the newer laws are only just being implemented, and it would be premature to expect regulations directed at a particular substance.[682] In some of these areas VC does not deserve the highest priority; there are other chemicals that are more toxic or to which people are more heavily exposed.[683] In some of these areas, especially water, it is appropriate to regulate VC in a group with other chemicals posing similar hazards and susceptible to the same means of control; preparing such group regulations takes longer than preparing regulations for any one substance.

1. VC Entering Air and Drinking Water From Factory Effluent, Water Transport, Sludge Waste, and PVC Pipe

VC enters water in several ways, and once in water, there are various ways people can be exposed to it. VC is deposited in rivers and groundwater by the effluent and sludge from VC and PVC factories and by spills from vessels and on-shore loading facilities.[684] VC does not dissolve readily in water, and most VC deposited in the rivers apparently is volatilized into the air.[685] This airborne VC may be a source of low-level exposure for people living near the discharge points.

A portion of the discharged VC remains in the water and, along with hundreds of other synthetic organic chemicals from similar sources,

---

679. The applicable statutes are: Federal Water Pollution Control Act, Pub. L. No. 92-500, 86 Stat. 816 (1972), as amended by Clean Water Act of 1977, Pub. L. No. 95-217.91 Stat. 1566, codified at 33 U.S.C. §§ 1251-1376 (Supp. V 1975 & West Supp. 1978); Safe Drinking Water Act, Pub. L. No. 93-523, 88 Stat. 1660 (1974), as amended by the Safe Drinking Water Amendments of 1977, Pub. L. No. 95-190, 91 Stat. 1393, codified at 42 U.S.C. §§ 300f-300j-9 (Supp. V 1975 & West Supp. 1978) (The 1977 amendments do not affect this discussion.); Resource Conservation and Recovery Act of 1976, Pub. L. No. 94-580, 90 Stat. 2795, 42 U.S.C.A. §§ 6901-6987 (1977); Medical Device Amendments to the Food, Drug, and Cosmetic Act, Pub. L. No. 94-295, 90 Stat. 539, codified in scattered sections of the Food, Drug and Cosmetic Act, 21 U.S.C.A. §§ 301-392 (West Supp. 1978); the food additive and cosmetic provisions of the Food, Drug, and Cosmetic Act, 21 U.S.C. §§ 301-392 (1970 & Supp. V 1975); and Federal Hazardous Substances Act, 15 U.S.C. §§ 1261-1274 (1970).
680. Pub. L. No. 94-469, 90 Stat. 2003 (1976), 15 U.S.C. §§ 2601-2629 (West Supp. 1978).
681. See text accompanying notes 710, 717-721, 749-752 *infra*.
682. With regard to the Medical Device Amendments and the Resource Conservation and Recovery Act, see text at notes 730-731, 776-787 *infra*.
683. With regard to toxic effluents and drinking water, see text accompanying notes 710, 749-752 *infra*.
684. EPA Task Force Report, *supra* note 85, at 5-7, 19. *See* EPA PRELIMINARY REPORT ON DRINKING WATER CARCINOGENS, *supra* note 89, at 35-39.
685. EPA Task Force Report, *supra* note 85, apps. at 31-32.

contaminates the drinking water of communities that depend on polluted rivers or groundwater.[686] These chemicals, alone or in combination, are suspected of causing cancer in persons drinking contaminated water.[687] In 1975, EPA reported the detection of VC in samples from a number of water systems, including the water supplies of Miami and Philadelphia, two of ten major cities surveyed.[688]

In addition to the VC entering raw drinking water supplies, VC leaches from PVC pipe and other PVC components of water distribution systems, especially when the plastic is relatively new.[689] Miles of PVC pipe are used in the distribution systems of many new communities,[690] and PVC pipe is used extensively in new homes.[691] The migrated VC can be ingested with the water or, if it escapes from the water in use in an enclosed space such as a bathroom or a kitchen, it can be inhaled.[692]

The regulation of these water-related sources of exposure is mainly the responsibility of EPA, although FDA has asserted the authority to regulate PVC pipe. The actions these agencies are contemplating are summarized below.

---

686. VC is one of 253 different specific organic chemicals that have been found in American drinking water. Many others may also be present although as yet unidentified. Some are known carcinogens; most have not been tested. EPA PRELIMINARY REPORT ON DRINKING WATER CARCINOGENS, *supra* note 89, at 3, 7, 26-30, 35-39.

687. One study found a correlation between high cancer incidence in certain areas of Louisiana and high concentrations of organics in drinking water. Page, Harris, & Epstein, *Drinking Water and Cancer Mortality in Louisiana*, 193 SCIENCE 55 (1976). A National Academy of Sciences study, conducted pursuant to § 1412(e) of the Safe Drinking Water Act, 42 U.S.C. § 300g-1(e) (Supp. V, 1975), also found a strong association between these drinking water contaminants and cancer rates. EPA, *Interim Primary Drinking Water Regulations; Control of Organic Chemical Contaminants in Drinking Water*, 43 Fed. Reg. 5756, 5758 (1978), *citing* NATIONAL ACADEMY OF SCIENCES, DRINKING WATER AND HEALTH (June 1977).

688. EPA PRELIMINARY REPORT ON DRINKING WATER CARCINOGENS, *supra* note 89, app. I at 14, app. II at 7. The precise origins of this VC have not been traced. The only possible sources, however, seem to be effluent from VC and PVC factories, and leaching from VC-bearing sludge. *Id*. at 35-39; EPA Task Force Report, *supra* note 85, at 5, 19. Chloroform and other compounds belonging to a chemical group called trihalomethanes form spontaneously from the interaction of organic compounds in raw water supplies with chlorine added for disinfection. EPA, *Control of Organic Chemical Contaminants in Drinking Water, Proposed Rules*, 43 Fed. Reg. 5756, 5759 (1978) [hereinafter cited as *EPA Proposed Drinking Water Regulations*]. VC, however, is not thought to be formed in such reactions. Personal communication with Ervin Bellack, Chemist, Criteria and Standards Division, EPA Office of Drinking Water, Feb. 22, 1978.

689. *See* EPA PRELIMINARY REPORT ON DRINKING WATER CARCINOGENS, *supra* note 89, at 17; *FDA Proposed Rules for Food Contact PVC*, *supra* note 164, at 40,534-35.

690. As an example, in Williamson County, Texas, EPA reported that more than one milligram of VC per liter of water was added by two eight-month-old stretches of PVC pipe, one three miles long and the other 9.5 miles long. Dressman & McFarren, *Determination of Vinyl Chloride Migration From Polyvinyl Chloride Pipe Into Water Using Improved Gas Chromatography Method*, 70 J. AM. WATER WORKS ASS'N 29, 30 table 1 (1978).

691. EPA Task Force Report, *supra* note 85, at app. 1, table 2.

692. *See FDA Proposed Rules for Food-Contact PVC*, *supra* note 164, at 40,532.

a. The control of toxic effluents

The Federal Water Pollution Control Act (FWPCA) places a high priority on the regulation of "toxic water pollutants,"[693] substances that pose threats of serious long-term harm to human health or the environment.[694] EPA's implementation of this program got off to a slow start. This led to extensive litigation in the mid-1970s and to an amendment of the statute in 1977. EPA is now preparing to regulate a significant number of these substances.

The control strategy Congress adopted in 1972 for toxic water pollutants was similar to that for hazardous air pollutants under the Clean Air Act.[695] Section 307(a) of FWPCA established a very tight rulemaking schedule and required industries to comply with a standard within a year of the standard's promulgation.[696] Moreover, the section precluded EPA from considering economic factors, requiring each standard to be set at the level that provides "an ample margin of safety."[697] Thus, EPA again faced the problem discussed previously in the hazardous air pollutant setting.[698] Only a complete prohibition of effluent discharge could assure an ample margin of safety from a carcinogen, but a complete prohibition would have caused many industries to close, especially if compliance had to be achieved within a year.

---

693.   FWPCA § 307(a), 33 U.S.C.A. § 1317(a) (West Supp. 1978). A "toxic pollutant" is one

> which after discharge and upon exposure, ingestion, inhalation or assimilation into any organism, either directly from the environment or indirectly by ingestion through food chains, will, on the basis of information available to the Administrator, cause death, disease, behavioral abnormalities, cancer, genetic mutations, physiological malfunctions (including malfunctions in reproduction) or physical deformations, in such organisms or their offspring.

FWPCA § 502(13), 33 U.S.C. § 1362(13) (Supp. V 1975).

The term "any organism" obviously includes humans. The specification of inhalation and the explicit reference to direct environmental exposure indicate that the definition is intended to encompass the inhalation of chemicals which volatilize from water as well as the ingestion of them in water. EPA must set standards that limit or prohibit each pollutant so designated,

> tak[ing] into account the toxicity of the pollutant, its persistence, degradability, the usual or potential presence of the affected organisms in any waters, the importance of the affected organisms and the nature and extent of the effect of the toxic pollutant on such organisms . . . .

Id. § 307(a)(2), 33 U.S.C. § 1317(a)(2) (Supp. V 1975).

694.   FWPCA § 502(13), 33 U.S.C. § 1361 (Supp. V 1975).

695.   See text accompanying notes 364-375 *supra*.

696.   FWPCA § 307(a)(6), 86 Stat. 857 (1972) (prior to 1977 amendment). The original list of toxic pollutants was to be compiled and regulations made within 15 months of FWPCA's enactment. *Id.* § 307(a)(1)-(2), 86 STAT. 856 (1972) (prior to 1977 amendment).

697.   FWPCA § 307(a)(4), 33 U.S.C. § 1317(a)(4) (Supp. V 1975). Concerning this section the House Report states that the cost of complying with such regulations should not be considered in the rulemaking: "The Committee considers that the discharge of toxic pollutants are [*sic*] much too dangerous to be permitted on merely economic grounds." H.R. REP. No. 911, 92d Cong., 2d Sess. 113 (1972).

698.   See text accompanying notes 350-386 *supra*.

In the subsequent years, EPA fell far behind in implementing section 307(a).[699] The agency hesitated to impose the large economic consequences of the strict regulations that the section apparently required. By mid-1976, the agency had designated only nine substances as toxic pollutants and had not promulgated any regulations. In the proposals and in opinions of EPA's General Counsel, the agency had narrowly interpreted the definition of toxic pollutants and had asserted that the criteria for standards did permit consideration of economic factors.

Between 1972 and 1976, three environmental groups brought four suits to compel more aggressive implementation of section 307(a) and related sections of FWPCA.[700] In 1976, EPA and these environmental groups settled the suits and established a new framework for controlling toxic water pollutants. Under the terms of the settlement, EPA agreed to set standards for 65 pollutants or groups of pollutants and for 21 categories of sources that discharge them.[701] VC and the plants in which it is made and polymerized were included in the lists.[702] The parties agreed that EPA would rely primarily on "effluent limitations" set under section 301(b) for categories of sources, rather than on standards set under section 307(a) for individual pollutants.[703]

EPA further agreed to set section 301(b) effluent limitations for all 21 source categories by the end of 1979.[704] The agency also assented to take

699. The following discussion of events up to the 1977 amendments relies heavily on two informative articles on the problems encountered in implementing § 307(a). *See* R. Hall, *The Evolution and Implementation of EPA's Regulatory Program to Control the Discharge of Toxic Pollutants to the Nation's Waters*, 10 NAT. RES. LAW. 507 (1977); K. Hall, *The Control of Toxic Water Pollutants Under the Federal Water Pollution Control Act Amendments of 1972*, 63 IOWA L. REV. 609 (1978).

700. Natural Resources Defense Council v. Train, 8 ERC 2120 (D.D.C. 1976). The other groups were the Environmental Defense Fund and Citizens for a Better Environment.

701. Settlement Agreement (NRDC v. Train), 8 ERC 2120, 2122 (D.D.C. 1976) [hereinafter cited as Settlement Agreement].

702. Settlement Agreement, *supra* note 701, apps. A-B.

703. Settlement Agreement, *supra* note 701, para. 1. There are two major differences between § 307(a) and § 301(b), Pub. L. No. 92-500, 86 Stat. 816, amended by Clean Water Act of 1977 § 42(a), codified at 33 U.S.C.A. § 1311(b) (West Supp. 1978). First, § 307(a) required rapid rulemaking and did not permit consideration of economic factors; § 301(b)(2)(A) expressly provides for the use of "best available technology *economically achievable*," commonly known as "BAT" (emphasis added), and § 301(b)(2)(B) sets the compliance deadline at no later than mid-1983.

Second, § 307(a) standards were to be aimed at individual pollutants; in contrast, § 301(b) effluent limitations are to be set on an industry-by-industry basis. *See* E.I. DuPont de Nemours & Co. v. Train, — U.S. —, 97 S. Ct. 965, 9 ERC 1753 (1977). The pollutant-by-pollutant approach had raised planning difficulties for industries which discharge more than one pollutant, and could result in an economically wasteful system under which an industry could be subjected to a series of standards set without regard to overall efficiency. The effluent limitation system avoids these problems, albeit at the risk that a particular toxic pollutant may be inadequately regulated. For a more complete discussion of these issues, see R. Hall, *supra* note 699, at 516-19; K. Hall, *supra* note 699, at 611-24.

704. Settlement Agreement, *supra* note 701, paras. 1, 7. EPA also agreed to set corre-

more stringent action under section 307(a) and the other provisions of FWPCA when, because of the economic considerations that went into the selection of the control methods, or because of the distant compliance date, the effluent limitations would fail to protect health and the environment adequately from one or more toxic pollutants.[705]

In 1977, Congress amended FWPCA[706] to make "mid-course corrections" on the basis of the experience gained in the first years of the statute's implementation.[707] The amendments relating to toxic water pollutants essentially codify the terms of the settlement agreement, with minor changes. Section 307(a) itself now designates the 65 substances from the settlement as toxic water pollutants (although EPA may amend the list), and it requires EPA to set effluent limitations for their sources in accordance with sections 301 and 304.[708] The amendments extend the timetable somewhat to give EPA and the industries additional time for compliance; the section 301 standards for dischargers of these pollutants must be set by mid-1980 and achieved by mid-1984.[709]

According to EPA's current schedule for regulating toxic water pollutants, "best available technology" effluent limitations for plastics factories, including VC and PVC plants, are to be proposed in early 1979 and promulgated later that year. Currently, EPA and contractors for the agency are studying the health, technological, and economic issues involved in setting the limitations for these factories and in determining whether standards beyond the effluent limitations will be needed.[710]

---

sponding "new point source performance standards" and "pretreatment standards" for publicly owned treatment works under §§ 306, 307(b)-(c). *Id.*, paras. 2-3, 8.

705.   The other steps include establishing water quality criteria under § 304(a), setting ambient water quality standards under §§ 301 and 303, and setting toxic water pollutant standards under § 307(a) itself (33 U.S.C. §§ 1311, 1313, 1314(a), 1317(a) (Supp. V 1975 & West Supp. 1978)). Settlement Agreement, *supra* note 701, paras. 11-12. *See* R. Hall, *supra* note 699, at 519-25; K. Hall, *supra* note 699, at 616-24.

706.   Clean Water Act of 1977, Pub. L. No. 95-217, 91 Stat. 1567, amending 33 U.S.C. §§ 1251-1376 (Supp. V 1975).

707.   *See generally* R. Hall, *The Clean Water Act of 1977*, 11 NAT. RESOURCES LAW. — (to appear), manuscript at 4 [hereinafter cited as R. Hall, *The 1977 Clean Water Act*]. This article is a thorough summary of the changes made in FWPCA.

708.   FWPCA § 307(a)(2), 33 U.S.C.A. § 1317(a)(2) (West Supp. 1978). *See* STAFF OF HOUSE COMM. ON PUB. WORKS & TRANSP., 95TH CONG., 1ST SESS., DATA RELATING to H.R. 3199 (CLEAN WATER ACT OF 1977), at 3-4, table 1 (Comm. Print No. 95-30, 1977) (listing pollutants to be regulated under § 307(a)(2)). The list in *id.* is identical to Appendix A of the Settlement Agreement, *supra* note 701. The amendments required EPA to publish this list of toxic pollutants within 30 days of the law's enactment. FWPCA § 307(a)(i), 33 U.S.C.A. § 1317(a)(1) (West Supp. 1978). This was done in January, 1978. *See* EPA, *Publication of Toxic Water Pollutant List*, 43 Fed. Reg. 4108 (1978).

709.   FWPCA § 301(b)(2)(C)-(D), 33 U.S.C.A. § 1311(b)(2)(C)-(D) (West Supp. 1978). The amendments did not adopt the list of 21 source categories. This raises the question of whether the settlement is superseded entirely, or only as directly affected by the amendments. See R. Hall, *The 1977 Clean Water Act*, *supra* note 707, manuscript at 26-31.

710.   *See* Environmental Protection Agency, Quarterly Briefing—Settlement Agreement, Schedule, BAT Review Industries (Apr. 27, 1977) (mimeograph).

b. The control of hazardous substances spills

FWPCA also empowers EPA to take certain steps to control spills of "hazardous substances" carried in water transport.[711] Under section 311 EPA must designate a list of substances that "present an imminent and substantial danger to the public health or welfare" when spilled from vessels or onshore facilities.[712] The agency must establish stiff civil penalties for the discharge of such substances.[713] The 1977 amendments make clear that EPA may take action to clean up the spill, and may add the cost of doing so to the penalties assessed against the discharger.[714]

EPA has been slow to implement these provisions. In late 1975, EPA proposed to designate more than 300 acutely toxic substances as hazardous and proposed a set of penalties for spilling them.[715] After a long delay, these regulations were promulgated in March 1978.[716]

No regulations, however, have been proposed for regulating spills of carcinogens. There has been some confusion concerning whether EPA may list carcinogens in general, or VC in particular, as hazardous pollutants. The agency's 1975 proposal implied that only acutely toxic substances may present an "imminent hazard."[717] However, in a related context at least one circuit court has stated that the concept of imminent hazard is not limited to acute toxicity, but also embraces future effects such as cancer that are the result of present exposures.[718] With respect to VC itself, EPA's 1974 VC Task Force concluded that since most spilled VC would leave the water for the air, regulation under section 311 was inappropriate.[719] However, there is no basis in the statute or in the legislative history for excluding from consideration the health hazards posed by the evaporation of a spilled substance. EPA acknowledged this point in the March promulgation.[720]

---

711. FWPCA § 311, 33 U.S.C.A. § 1321 (West Supp. 1978).

712. *Id.* § 311(b)(2)(A), 33 U.S.C.A. § 1321(b)(2)(A) (West Supp. 1978).

713. *Id.* § 311(b)(2)(B), 33 U.S.C.A. § 1321(b)(2)(B) (West Supp. 1978). The Senate Report explained that these penalties should be set high enough to discourage the water transportation of substances that pose an "unacceptable environmental risk" if spilled. S. REP. No. 414, 92d Cong., 1st Sess. 67 (1971), *reprinted in* [1972] U.S. CODE CONG. & ADM. NEWS 3668, 3733.

714. *See* R. Hall, *The 1977 Clean Water Act, supra* note 707, manuscript at 40-41.

715. EPA, *Designation of Hazardous Substances, Notice of Proposed Rulemaking*, 40 Fed. Reg. 59,960 (1975) [hereinafter cited as *EPA Proposed Designation of Hazardous Substances*].

716. EPA, *Designation of Hazardous Substances*, 43 Fed. Reg. 10,474 (1978) [hereinafter cited as *EPA Designation of Hazardous Substances*] (to be codified in 40 C.F.R. §§ 116.1-.4).

717. The proposal set out a number of acute toxicity criteria and then stated that these criteria were applied "in order to limit the designation to those substances which could reasonably be anticipated to present an imminent and substantial danger to public health or welfare . . . ." *EPA Proposed Designation of Hazardous Substances, supra* note 715, at 59,961.

718. Environmental Defense Fund v. Ruckelshaus, 439 F.2d 584, 595-97, 2 ERC 1114, 1121-22 (D.C. Cir. 1971). This case concerned the definition of "imminent hazard" in the context of pesticide regulation.

719. EPA Task Force Report, *supra* note 85, at 17.

720. *EPA Designation of Hazardous Substances, supra* note 716, at 10,476.

Now that VC's ability to cause cancer in animals when inhaled at very low doses has been established,[721] it seems that EPA should consider whether VC spilled in this manner merits regulation under section 311.

c. The control of sludge wastes

Subchapter III of the 1976 Resource Conservation and Recovery Act (RCRA)[722] establishes a federal program of hazardous waste management under which EPA can regulate the disposal of PVC industrial wastes, in order to reduce the escape of trapped VC into the air and water. The statute set an April 1978 deadline for the promulgation of criteria for identifying hazardous wastes, taking into account numerous kinds of health and environmental damage, including potential human toxicity.[723] EPA was also required to establish a list of substances that it determines meet the definition of a hazardous waste.[724]

By the same date, the agency was to set regulations applicable to persons who generate, transport, or dispose of substances that meet the promulgated criteria for a hazardous waste, or that have been specifically listed as such.[725] There are two main features of these regulations. First, the agency must set performance standards for disposal sites and practices.[726] Each owner or operator of a disposal facility must obtain a permit to handle hazardous wastes; EPA may grant the permit only after the applicant has demonstrated compliance with the applicable performance standards.[727] Second, EPA must establish reporting and monitoring requirements, including a manifest system designed to provide accurate information on the characteristics and amounts of wastes and the locations of their disposal.[728]

---

721. See text accompanying note 143 *supra*.

722. RCRA §§ 3001-3011, 42 U.S.C.A. §§ 6921-6931 (1977).

723. A hazardous waste is defined as
a solid waste, or combination of solid wastes, which because of its quantity, concentration, or physical, chemical, or infectious characteristics may—
(A) cause, or significantly contribute to an increase in mortality or an increase in serious irreversible, or incapacitating reversible, illness; or
(B) pose a substantial present or potential hazard to human health or the environment when improperly treated, stored, transported, or disposed of, or otherwise managed.
RCRA § 1004(5), 42 U.S.C.A. § 6903(5) (1977).
The term "solid waste" means any garbage, refuse, . . . and other discarded material, including solid, liquid, semi-solid, or contained gaseous material resulting from industrial, commercial, mining, and agricultural operations, and from community activities . . . .
Id. § 1004(27), 42 U.S.C.A. § 6903(27) (1977). Criteria for identifying hazardous wastes must be promulgated within eighteen months of the statute's enactment. *Id*. § 3001(a), 42 U.S.C.A. § 6921(a) (1977).

724. *Id*. § 3001(b), 42 U.S.C.A. § 6921(b) (1977). The same April 1978 deadline applied.

725. *Id*. §§ 3002-3004, 42 U.S.C.A. §§ 6922-6924 (1977).

726. *Id*. § 3004, 42 U.S.C.A. § 6924 (1977).

727. *Id*. § 3005, 42 U.S.C.A. § 6925 (1977).

728. *Id*. §§ 3002-3004, 42 U.S.C.A. §§ 6922-6924 (1977); H.R. REP. NO. 1491—PART I, 94th Cong., 2d Sess. 26-28 (1975), *reprinted in* [1976] U.S. CODE CONG. & AD. NEWS 6238, 6264-66. The implementation of the reporting requirements and the permit program may be delegated to

A weakness of the statute is that it does not authorize EPA to require the generators of hazardous wastes to pretreat the wastes or otherwise to alter their production processes and practices.[729] Thus under RCRA the PVC manufacturers cannot be required to strip VC from the wastes. There is, however, an indirect incentive for the manufacturers to do so. Hazardous wastes cannot be disposed of except at a permitted facility in an approved manner. If disposal standards were to limit strictly the leaching of VC to air and water, the manufacturers might find it cheaper to strip sludge than to pay the high cost of containing the VC in a disposal site. That incentive probably would operate most strongly on manufacturers who handle the disposal of their own wastes.

EPA did not meet the April 1978 deadlines for promulgating these regulations.[730] Although the criteria defining a hazardous waste are certain to cover VC-bearing sludge, it presently is uncertain whether the initial list of specific wastes will include this sludge.[731]

d.   *The control of contaminants of drinking water sources*

Under the 1974 Safe Drinking Water Act (SDWA),[732] EPA has the responsibility to protect the public health from the hazards of chemical and other contaminants of drinking water supplied through "public water systems."[733] One major congressional goal in passing the statute was the rapid control of synthetic organic chemicals of industrial and urban origin that are present in many "raw" drinking water sources.[734] Despite the urgency attached to this and other objectives of the Act, this program, like the toxic water pollutant control effort, was not immediately implemented. Recently, however, EPA has proposed regulations that would significantly reduce the

---

states which demonstrate to EPA that they have an adequate hazardous waste management program. RCRA § 3006, 42 U.S.C.A. § 6926 (1977).

729.   Hazardous waste generators are subject only to labeling, record keeping, reporting, and disclosure requirements, and the manifest system. RCRA § 3002, 42 U.S.C.A. § 6922 (1977); H.R. REP. NO. 1491-PART I, 94th Cong., 2d Sess. 26-27 (1976), *reprinted in* [1976] U.S. CODE CONG. & AD. NEWS 6238, 6264-65.

730.   *See EPA Regulatory Agenda*, 43 Fed. Reg. 14,602, 14,607-08 (1977)(current schedule for proposal of RCRA regulations).

731.   Personal communication with Walt Kovalick, Chief, Guidelines Branch, EPA Hazardous Waste Management Division (Feb. 22, 1978).

The Senate bill would have expressly required the list of hazardous wastes to include any mixture of wastes containing any substance which had been designated a hazardous air pollutant under Clean Air Act § 112 or a toxic or hazardous pollutant under FWPCA §§ 307(a), 311(b), unless the EPA Administrator affirmatively determined otherwise. *See* S. 3622, § 212(a), in S. REP. NO. 988, 94th Cong., 2d Sess. 49 (1976). This provision was dropped from the final bill, in favor of giving EPA more discretion. Clearly, however, Congress expected hazardous air pollutants and toxic water pollutants to be candidates for inclusion as hazardous wastes.

732.   SDWA §§ 1401-1450, 42 U.S.C. §§ 300f-300j-9 (Supp. V 1975 & West Supp. 1978).

733.   *Id.* § 1411, 42 U.S.C. § 300g (Supp. V. 1975).

734.   *See, e.g.*, H.R. REP. NO. 1185, 93d Cong., 2d Sess. 8-10 (1974), *reprinted in* [1974] U.S. CODE CONG. & AD. NEWS 6454, 6459-60.

levels of many chemicals, including VC, in the tap water of major metropolitan areas.

SDWA established a two-stage process for setting standards to protect health from drinking water contaminants.[735] First, EPA was to set "national interim primary drinking water regulations."[736] These must protect health "to the extent feasible," defined as the protection offered by the use of "technology, treatment techniques, and other means, which the Administrator determines [were] generally available (taking costs into consideration)" when the statute was enacted.[737] The standards were to be set by June 16, 1975, and can be amended or supplemented at any time.[738]

The interim standards were to be effective for only an interim period. In 1975 and 1976, EPA and the National Academy of Sciences were to conduct intensive research to develop more information on the effects of the covered substances and on control methods, and to identify any additional contaminants, their effects, and the means and costs of controlling them.[739] The purpose of the research was to identify levels of the contaminants at which health would be protected from known or anticipated adverse effects with an adequate margin of safety.[740] On the basis of this research, EPA is to issue "revised national primary drinking water regulations"[741] which must specify maximum contaminant levels or treatment techniques that EPA judges are as close to the recommended levels as "feasible."[742] EPA may amend the regulations to take account of improved control methods.[743]

The legislative history of SDWA gives EPA some additional guidance in setting the interim and revised standards. In view of the vast number of discrete chemicals in drinking water, Congress expected EPA to make

---

735. *See generally* Douglas, *Safe Drinking Water Act of 1974—History and Critique*, 5 ENVT'L AFF. 501, 518-24 (1976).

736. SDWA § 1412(a), 42 U.S.C. § 300g-1(a) (Supp. V 1975).

737. *Id.* § 1412(a)(2), 42 U.S.C. § 300g-1(a)(2) (Supp. V 1975).

738. *Id.* § 1412, 42 U.S.C. § 300g-1 (Supp. V 1975).

739. *Id.* § 1412(e), 42 U.S.C. § 300g-1(e) (Supp. V 1975). The report was delivered some months after its statutory due date. *See* EPA, *Interim Primary Drinking Water Regulations, Control of Organic Chemical Contaminents in Drinking Water*, 43 Fed. Reg. 5756 (1978), *citing* NATIONAL ACADEMY OF SCIENCES, DRINKING WATER AND HEALTH (June 1977).

740. SDWA §§ 1412(b),(e), 42 U.S.C. §§ 300g-1(b),(e) (Supp. V 1975).

741. *Id.* §§ 1412(b)(2)-(3), 42 U.S.C. §§ 300g-1(b)(2)-(3) (Supp. V 1975).

742. *Id.* § 1412(b)(3). The term "feasible" level is defined in the same manner as for the interim regulations, except that control methods which EPA requires need not be limited to those available when the statute was passed. They are to be the "best available" controls. *Id.*

The section does not provide a time frame in which the judgment of what methods are the "best available" is to be made. In an analogous context where EPA had to make a determination concerning whether particular technology had been "adequately demonstrated" to be available, it was held that EPA was authorized to base its requirements not on what was available when the decision was made, but on what the agency judged would be available at the future time when the regulations became effective. *See* Portland Cement Ass'n v. Ruckelshaus, 486 F.2d 375, 391-92, 5 ERC 1593, 1603-04 (D.C. Cir. 1973), *cert. denied*, 417 U.S. 921 (1973) (construing § 111(a)(1) of the Clean Air Act).

743. Amendments of regulations for particular contaminants are authorized by SDWA §

regulations for groups of similar substances whenever possible.[744] For substances without identifiable threshold doses, such as carcinogens, Congress intended that the revised regulations be set as close to zero as feasible.[745]

As it has elsewhere, EPA has fallen behind the statutory schedule. The interim regulations currently in effect were set at the end of 1975, and they cover only six organic pesticides and a few other substances.[746] EPA has set no revised regulations to date. In February 1978, however, the agency proposed additional interim regulations for synthetic organic chemicals entering raw water supplies from industrial and urban pollution (such as VC), and for organic chemicals that result from the reaction of chlorine, added for disinfection, with chemicals naturally present in the water.[747] Many chemicals in both categories are known or suspected carcinogens, and contaminated drinking water has been related to increased rates of cancer in certain areas, notably New Orleans.[748]

The proposed regulations would require drinking water systems serving more than 75,000 people to install granular activated carbon filtration systems, which are capable of removing a large percentage of the amounts of most of the synthetic organic chemicals present, including VC.[749] These regulations generally would be effective three and a half years after promulgation, although some systems might have to take some short-term control

---

1412(b)(4), 42 U.S.C. § 300g-1(b)(4) (Supp. V 1975). Although an explicit statement of the power to add new revised primary drinking water standards for contaminants unregulated in the first standard setting is curiously absent, the power may fairly be implied from the totality of § 1412(b). It would make little sense to give EPA only one chance to identify and regulate all harmful pollutants. In the legislative history there is no indication of Congress' desire to so limit EPA, and such a limitation would be contrary to the structure of all the other health and environmental statutes discussed in this Article, each of which gives the administering agency the power to add standards for unregulated substances as developing information warrants. *See generally* Environmental Defense Fund v. Costle, — F.2d —, 11 ERC 1209, 1212-13 (D.C. Cir. 1978) (reviewing the interim regulations and discussing legislative intent).

The Act also calls for the settling of "national secondary drinking water regulations" to reduce contamination by substances that give an odor or color to drinking water, or otherwise affect "public welfare." SDWA § 1401(2), 42 U.S.C. § 300f(2) (Supp. V 1975). No such standards have yet been established.

744. H.R. REP. No. 1185, 93rd Cong., 2d Sess. 10-11 (1974), *reprinted in* [1974] U.S. CODE CONG. & AD NEWS 6454, 6463-64.

745. *Id.* at 20, *reprinted in* [1974] U.S. CODE CONG. & AD. NEWS at 6472-73.

746. EPA, *National Interim Primary Drinking Water Regulations*, 40 Fed. Reg. 59,566 (1975), codified at 40 C.F.R. §§ 141.1-.40 (1977). The Environmental Defense Fund brought suit to challenge, among other aspects of these regulations, EPA's decision not to regulate the full spectrum of organic chemicals. The District of Columbia Circuit Court of Appeals decided the case in February 1978, one day after EPA proposed more complete interim regulations for organics (discussed in the text immediately below). In view of the fact that the proposal was substantially the relief EDF wished the court to order, the court avoided a decision on the merits and remanded the matter to EPA with instructions to report its progress and intentions to the court within 60 days. In other respects the court affirmed EPA's regulations. Environmental Defense Fund v. Costle, — F.2d —, 11 ERC 1209 (D.C. Cir. 1978).

747. *EPA Proposed Drinking Water Regulations, supra* note 688.

748. See note 686 *supra*.

749. *EPA Proposed Drinking Water Regulation, supra* note 688, at 5756, 5770.

measures as well.[750] The systems subject to the proposal together serve about 52 percent of the population of the United States.[751] These are generally the most contaminated water sources, as they are in heavily industrialized and urbanized areas. If promulgated and enforced, these regulations would significantly reduce exposure to VC, as well as to other substances.[752]

e.   Drinking water contamination from plastic water pipe

PVC pipe is widely used in municipal drinking water distribution systems and in residential construction, and VC leaches into water from this pipe. Although improved "stripping" techniques have reduced the amount of VC residual in the plastic material,[753] some residual is still present in new pipe,[754] and VC presumably continues to migrate from old pipe currently in use.[755]

The control of hazards from water pipe provides another illustration of the problem of jurisdictional fragmentation. Both FDA and EPA assert authority over PVC pipe, although neither has actually taken any action to control VC leaching. The pipe problem presents the obverse of the problem discussed in the aerosols section.[756] With respect to aerosols, the regulatory decision was unambiguous under all three statutes, and no single agency had an interest in raising the latent jurisdictional issues. In the case of PVC pipe, however, the potential exists for significantly different results, depending upon which agency has regulatory authority, and consequently the jurisdictional issue is more important.

Under the Food Additives Amendment to FDCA, drinking water is considered a food,[757] and pipe materials that may reasonably be expected to leach substances into water therefore are subject to regulation as food additives.[758] Where a carcinogenic substance may be expected to migrate from piping into the water, the use of that substance must be prohibited.[759]

As part of its 1975 proposal regarding PVC food packaging and other food-contact materials, FDA proposed to ban the future use of PVC water pipe, unless the manufacturers showed that VC migration from new pipe could not reasonably be expected, *i.e.*, that it could not be detected.[760] Like the food packaging rules, this rule has never been promulgated, although

750.   *Id.* at 5756-57.

751.   *Id.* at 5764.

752.   The agency is also considering expanding the control requirements to systems serving between 10,000 and 75,000 people sometime in the future. *Id.* at 5757, 5765.

753.   Dressman & McFarren, *supra* note 690, at 30.

754.   *Id.*

755.   *See* note 689 and text accompanying notes 689-692 *supra*. *But see* note 689 *supra*.

756.   See text accompanying notes 551-611 *supra*.

757.   Food is defined as "articles used for food *or drink* for man or other animals . . . ." FDCA § 201(f)(1), 21 U.S.C. § 321(f)(1) (1970) (emphasis added).

758.   *Id.* § 201(s), 21 U.S.C. § 321(s) (1970).

759.   *Id.* § 409(c)(3)(A), 21 U.S.C. § 348(c)(3)(A) (1970) (the Delaney Clause).

760.   *FDA Proposed Rules for Food Contact PVC, supra* note 164, at 40,534-35.

FDA has indicated recently that it plans to revive and complete the proposal.[761]

However, FDA is uncertain whether jurisdiction over pipe belongs to it, to EPA, or is shared.[762] Under SDWA, EPA also appears to have jurisdiction over the material, and the regulation called for by SDWA is not as stringent as that required under the Food Additives Amendment.

Under SDWA, EPA can establish interim or revised drinking water regulations pertaining to the use of PVC pipe in "public water systems."[763] A restriction on the permissible VC residual content of pipe would be authorized under the phrase "other means" in the definition of "feasible" control methods.[764] Unlike the Food Additives Amendment, however, SDWA requires EPA to balance health concerns with economic considerations.[765] If the hazard were judged to be sufficiently serious, it seems that the term "feasible" would authorize a complete ban on the use of a piping material and even the replacement of pipe now in use. EPA's present position seems to be that the VC hazard posed is not serious enough to justify either prohibiting the manufacture of new pipe or forcing replacement of pipe currently installed.[766] Certainly in comparison with the other hazards from drinking water that have not yet been controlled,[767] PVC pipe does not deserve the highest priority.

Due to the uncertainty of the jurisdictional issue, FDA has suggested that it and EPA make a joint determination of how to regulate PVC pipe.[768] Joint action will be complicated, if not barred, however, by the inconsistent demands of the Food Additives Amendment and SDWA. EPA is required to consider economic factors, but FDA cannot. Moreover, the manufacturers contend that the explicit grant to EPA of authority over drinking water safety contained in SDWA pre-empts the older, more general authority of FDA under the Food Additives Amendment.[769] This is a persuasive argument, but

---

761. *FDA Plans Further PVC Ban, supra* note 538. Since FDA's interpretation of the reasonable expectation requirement has changed, it is conceivable that any pipe containing PVC would be subject to a ban. See text accompanying notes 540-546 *supra*.

762. *FDA Plans Further PVC Ban, supra* note 538.

763. SDWA §§ 1411, 1412(a), (b)(3), 42 U.S.C. §§ 300g-1(a), (b)(3) (Supp. V 1975). The Act gives EPA broad authority to set regulations regarding contaminants that "may have any adverse effect" on health. *Id.* § 1401(1)(B), 42 U.S.C. § 300f(1)(B) (Supp. V 1975). There is no restriction on the sources or the contaminants that may be covered.

764. *Id.* § 1412(a)(2), (b)(3), 42 U.S.C. § 300g-1(a)(2), (b)(3) (Supp. V 1975).

765. *Id.*

766. Referring to the reduction in the VC residual level accomplished since 1974, one EPA official stated that the PVC pipe problem "sort of solved itself." Personal communication with Ervin Bellack, Chemist, Criteria and Standards Division, EPA Office of Drinking Water, Feb. 22, 1978.

767. See text accompanying notes 747-752 *supra*.

768. *FDA Plans Further PVC Ban, supra* note 538.

769. Comments on FDA Proposed Rules for Food-Contact PVC by Jerome Heckman, General Counsel, The Society of the Plastics Industries 36-41 (Dec. 19, 1975).

its validity depends upon whether SDWA gives EPA the authority to deal
with all the hazards that FDA can reach. The answer to this question turns
on the meaning of the term "public water system."

EPA does not have jurisdiction over pipe which is not in a "public
water system."[770] This term is defined in part as "a system for the
provision to the public of pipe water for human consumption, if such system
has at least fifteen service connections or regularly serves at least twenty-
five individuals."[771] This definition creates two problems of jurisdiction.
First, since the purpose of the definition apparently is to exclude from
regulation small, generally private systems, such as back yard wells, it
seems clear that only FDA has authority over the use of PVC pipe in such
systems. Second, the definition raises the issue of whether a "public water
system" ends at the service connection or at the tap, *i.e.*, whether the
limitation in SDWA is intended to keep EPA out of the business of regulating piping materials used in homes. If so, then only FDA has jurisdiction of
domestic piping connected into "public water systems."

It could be held that EPA's authority pre-empts FDA's jurisdiction for
the sources that SDWA covers, but that FDA retains authority over the
sources that SDWA does not cover. This holding would lead to the banning
of PVC in the "non-public" uses over which FDA has control, but to no
action by EPA, which must balance economic factors against health hazards
under SDWA. It may seem anomalous that the treatment of water pipe
should vary so greatly depending on its location, but this may be the result
the statutes demand. In any event, litigation is likely however the agencies
resolve the jurisdictional issue, and this prospect deters FDA from acting.

2. Drug and Cosmetic Packaging, Medical Devices, and Consumer Products

PVC has many uses in the home. VC residual in packaging and plastic
products can leach into drug and cosmetic products that are ingested or
applied to the skin. It can also leach into the air of enclosed interior spaces,
where it may be inhaled. Neither FDA nor CPSC, the agencies responsible
for the control of hazards from these sources, appears to have given any
significant attention to these uses of PVC, even to the extent of investigating
the dimensions of the hazard.

a. Drug and cosmetic packaging

In the course of its 1974 aerosol proceedings[772] FDA called for information on the levels of VC migration from drug and cosmetic packaging and

---

770. SDWA § 2(a), 42 U.S.C. § 300g-5 (Supp. V 1975).
771. *Id.* § 1401(4), 42 U.S.C. § 300f(4) (Supp. V 1975).
772. See note 607 *supra*.

the levels of human exposure to be expected from these sources. The primary source of exposure is leaching from bottles for such products as mouthwashes.[773] Since such products generally are not swallowed, exposure from them will be less than that from food products containing an equivalent amount of VC. Here, as elsewhere, better "stripping" of the PVC material has reduced the VC migration levels since 1974.[774] Nonetheless, some exposure presumably still occurs.

FDA has the authority to regulate drug and cosmetic packaging under the same provisions of FDCA discussed in the aerosols section.[775] To date, the agency has not followed up its call for information. The hazard probably is small compared to the risks from other drugs and cosmetics not yet regulated. There is, however, little social benefit to be derived from much of the packaging, let alone from many of the products it contains; it is to be hoped that in the future FDA will assess whether the need for the packaging justifies even the small risks that may be involved.

b. Medical devices

PVC is also used in a number of medical devices such as blood bags, transfusion tubes, endotracheal tubes, and other articles that may be inserted in the human body for substantial periods of time. From these devices it is possible for VC residue to enter the bloodstream directly, to be inhaled, or to be otherwise absorbed.[776] While the VC residual content of this PVC may be low, the routes of exposure from medical devices are very direct. Thus far, the potential risk has not been seriously investigated.[777]

FDA has authority to regulate these uses of PVC under the 1976 Medical Device Amendments to FDCA.[778] This statute requires all medical devices to be classified into one of three groups, based on recommendations by panels of experts and representatives of manufacturer and consumer interests.[779] Devices placed in Class III are subject to pre-market testing for safety and efficiency.[780] For those placed in Class II, FDA is required to adopt performance standards to ensure that the devices measure up to criteria determined to provide adequately for their safety.[781] Devices placed in Class I are subject to minimal controls.[782]

---

773. *See* Health Research Group Petition, *supra* note 514, at 3-4.

774. See text accompanying note 104 *supra*.

775. See text accompanying notes 562-577 *supra*.

776. Personal communication with Carl W. Bruch, Acting Associate Director for Device Evaluation, FDA Bureau of Medical Devices, Feb. 27, 1978.

777. *Id*.

778. Pub. L. No. 94-295, 90 Stat. 539 (1976), codified in scattered sections of the Food, Drug, and Cosmetic Act, 21 U.S.C.A. §§ 301-392 (West Supp. 1978). For an analysis of these amendments, see Foote, *Loops and Loopholes: The Medical Device Amendments of 1976*, 7 ECOLOGY L.Q. 101 (1978).

779. FDCA § 513, 21 U.S.C.A. § 360c (West Supp. 1978).

780. *Id*. § 515, 21 U.S.C.A. § 360e (West Supp. 1978).

781. *Id*. § 514, 21 U.S.C.A. § 360d (West Supp. 1978).

782. *Id*. §§ 501-502, 510, 516, 518-520, 21 U.S.C.A. §§ 351-352, 360, 360f, 360h-360j (West 1972 & West Supp. 1978).

Medical devices composed of PVC generally have been placed in Class II.[783] They will not be tested before marketing for the extent to which they leach VC into the bloodstream or otherwise into the body, and there are no requirements for the assessment of the extent of the cancer hazard from this source of exposure. Moreover, it will be many years before performance standards for many devices in Class II are actually written.[784] In the meantime, Class II devices will be subject to only minimal controls.[785]

The statute permits FDA to move devices from one class to another, upon its own motion or upon the petition of an interested person.[786] There have been very few petitions or decisions to move Class II devices into Class III, and none has been made for PVC devices.[787]

c. Consumer products

There are numerous PVC consumer products with which people come in contact daily. Commonly used products that contain PVC are floor tiles, curtains, and other home furnishings, phonograph records, toys, and latex paints.[788] VC migration from some of these products into indoor air has been reported.[789] The jurisdiction to regulate these products belongs to CPSC under provisions of FHSA discussed in the aerosols section.[790] Thus far, however, CPSC has shown no interest in investigating the potential hazard from the leaching of VC into indoor air.

EPA has done some investigation in this area. In 1976, EPA sampled the air in interior spaces containing a wide variety of PVC products that the experimenters had selected as potential sources of airborne VC. With a testing method sensitive to a minimum of 10 ppb, EPA detected the presence of VC only from certain brands of latex paint containing PVC. The air in a freshly painted, normally ventilated room contained about 20 ppb of VC; the concentration declined below the detectable level within two days.[791] No VC was detected in several other environments containing new PVC products, including a newly-furnished nursery and the interiors of a new car and a mobile home.[792] The absence of detectable VC concentrations in most common consumer surroundings in these recent tests is reassuring, yet the possibility of very low-level exposure remains and has not been addressed by CPSC.

The consumer product area yields another example of the jurisdictional complexity surrounding regulation of toxic substances. It seems that CPSC,

---

783.   Personal communication with Carl W. Bruch, *supra* note 776.
784.   *Id.*
785.   *See* Foote, *supra* note 778, at 113.
786.   FDCA § 513(e), 21 U.S.C.A. § 360c(e) (West Supp. 1978).
787.   Personal communication with Carl W. Bruch, *supra* note 776.
788.   *See* EPA Task Force Report, *supra* note 85, at app. 1, table 2.
789.   *VC: How Many Unknown Problems?, supra* note 110, at 55.
790.   See text accompanying notes 578-583 *supra*.
791.   EPA Sampling of PVC Consumer Products, *supra* note 163, at 20-22.
792.   *Id.*

as well as FDA, has responsibility for controlling the hazards of food packaging. In its 1975 proposal to regulate the food-contact uses of PVC, FDA noted that VC may migrate from packaging not only from the inside of the package into foods, but from the outside of the package into indoor air.[793] FDA has no authority under the Food Additives Amendment to consider the latter risk of harm in deciding whether to regulate packaging. The responsibility for this source of hazard is CPSC's, under FHSA. The Commission and FDA have formed an agreement recognizing the former's jurisdiction over the toxic effects of food-contact materials that are not mediated through food.[794] As yet, however, CPSC has taken no action regarding this source of VC exposure.[795]

3. The Application of the Toxic Substances Control Act

The 1976 Toxic Substances Control Act (TSCA)[796] gives EPA the authority to regulate existing uses of any "chemical substance or mixture" that "presents or will present an unreasonable risk of injury to health or the environment."[797] The regulatory measures available to the agency range from requiring labels and warnings, to selective restrictions on certain uses, to a complete prohibition on manufacture.[798]

The agency's authority to use TSCA, however, is limited by several provisions of the statute. First, the definition of "chemical substance" specifically excludes pesticides, tobacco, alcoholic beverages, food, food additives, drugs, cosmetics, and medical devices.[799] Measures to control the hazards of these substances may be taken, if at all, only under other laws.

Second, section 9 of the statute directs EPA to use other statutes at its disposal and to defer to other agencies in certain circumstances, in order to

---

793. *FDA Proposed Rules for Food-Contact PVC, supra* note 164, at 40,531. See note 527 *supra*. In fact, FDA treated the migration into the air as a partial reason for leaving the materials in use, arguing that whatever migrated to the air would not make its way into foods. *Id.*

794. FDA, *Food, Food Containers, and Food-Related Articles and Equipment, Memorandum of Understanding With Consumer Product Safety Commission*, 41 Fed. Reg. 34,342, 34,343 (1976).

795. Ironically, prior to the creation of CPSC in 1972, FDA administered FHSA. The administration was transferred to CPSC by § 30(a) of the Consumer Product Safety Act, 15 U.S.C. § 2079(a) (Supp. V 1975). The principal reason for the transfer of authority under FHSA to CPSC was that FDA had been exceedingly lax in carrying out the mandates of the statute. *See* S. REP. NO. 835, 92d Cong., 2d Sess. 3-4, *reprinted in* [1972] U.S. CODE CONG. & AD. NEWS 4573, 4575-76. Between 1966, when FDA was given the authority to ban products under FHSA, and 1972, when CPSC took responsibility under the Act, FDA banned only two products and left many toxic household hazards unexamined and unregulated. *See* H. HEFFRON, R. MEDALIE, S. KURZMAN, & M. PEARLMAN, FEDERAL CONSUMER SAFETY LEGISLATION: REPORT TO THE NATIONAL COMMISSION ON PRODUCT SAFETY 180-87 (1970).

796. 15 U.S.C.A. §§ 2601-2629 (West Supp. 1977).

797. TSCA § 6(a), 15 U.S.C.A. § 2605(a) (West Supp. 1977).

798. *Id.* The means selected must be "the least burdensome" that "adequately" protects against the risk. *Id.*.

799. TSCA § 3(a)(2)(B), 15 U.S.C.A. § 2062(a)(2)(B) (West Supp. 1977).

avoid overlapping or duplicative action.[800] Under section 9(a), if another agency clearly could take action to control a particular hazard "to a sufficient extent," EPA must refer the matter to the other agency and may not regulate the hazard unless the other agency fails to do so.[801] Under section 9(b), if the Administrator determines that a hazard may be controlled "to a sufficient extent" by the use of another statute administered by EPA, the agency must act under that law rather than under TSCA.[802]

In enacting section 9, Congress seems to have intended to preclude action under TSCA when action under another statute could adequately resolve the problem. But if a chemical falls under the jurisdiction of several other agencies, EPA may still not be pre-empted if separate actions by the several agencies would not reduce the risk "to a sufficient extent." It has been argued above that separate action by several agencies can lead to standards that are less protective than they should be, because the separate evaluation of risks and benefits results in an under-weighting of risks.[803] Each agency tends to compare *all* of the chemical's economic benefits to only *part* of the risks—the risks to the segment of the population that the agency is charged to protect. This was the case with OSHA's and EPA's separate treatments of VC.[804] If the benefits are overvalued in this manner, then the standard set by each agency will not be as stringent as it should be. Individually and cumulatively, the separate actions will not reduce the risks "to a sufficient extent," and action under TSCA would not be barred. Thus, in dealing with future instances of jurisdictional fragmentation, consolidated action under TSCA may be preferable to multiple separate actions.[805]

---

800.   *Id.* § 9, 15 U.S.C.A. § 2068 (West Supp. 1977). *See* H.R. REP. NO. 1679, 94th Cong., 2d Sess. 84 (1976), *reprinted in* [1976] U.S. CODE CONG. & AD. NEWS 4539, 4569 (1976) (Conference Report).

801.   TSCA § 9(a), 15 U.S.C. § 2068(a) (West Supp. 1977). This provision requires the Administrator to refer a hazard to another agency for control (through a complicated procedure established by subsections (1) and (2)) if "in the Administrator's discretion" he determines that the risk "may be prevented or reduced to a sufficient extent" by the action of another agency under another statute. *Id.*

The section gives the Administrator broad discretion over whether to act under TSCA or to refer a problem to another agency. In fact, the Conference Report states that this "discretionary determination . . . is not subject to judicial review . . . ." H.R. REP. NO. 1679, 94th Cong., 2d Sess. 84 (1976).

802.   *Id.* § 9(b), 15 U.S.C.A. § 2608(b) (West Supp. 1977). An exception to this rule is in the case where "the Administrator determines, in the Administrator's discretion, that it is in the public interest" to act under TSCA rather than the other statute. The size of this exception is curtailed by the next sentence, which states: "This subsection shall not be construed to relieve the Administrator of any requirement imposed on the Administrator by such other Federal laws." *Id.*

803.   See text accompanying notes 19, 347-348, 470-472 *supra.*

804.   See text accompanying notes 347-348, 470-472 *supra.*

805.   Section 9(b) permits EPA to use TSCA instead of other laws that the agency administers when "the public interest" would be served; this may permit consolidated action in the interest of husbanding EPA's scarce resources. In contrast, section 9(a) does not permit the Administrator to use TSCA rather than referring the matter to another agency simply on the grounds that consolidated action under TSCA would be a more economical use of government resources than separate actions by the several agencies.

It should be noted that EPA has many obligations under TSCA other than to deal with future jurisdictional problems similar to those presented by VC.[806] The agency may not wish to devote its limited resources to reducing hazards that could be dealt with, to some degree at least, under other programs. Thus it may be some time before EPA invokes the aggressive interpretation of section 9 postulated here.

III
GENERAL OBSERVATIONS AND FUTURE DIRECTIONS

The preceding case study has illustrated the three problems identified in the Introduction as central to federal toxic substances regulation: jurisdictional fragmentation, decision making under uncertainty, and balancing incommensurable interests.[807] In Part I it was emphasized that VC is only an example and a forerunner, one among hundreds of substances that will pose the same problems in greater or lesser degree.[808] Part III returns to these central problems. Drawing on the VC case study and, less comprehensively, other events, regulatory actions, and judicial decisions, it offers some general observations about the development of the policies and legal tools for toxic substances control, and it surveys the efforts to cope with these problems.

Prominent among these efforts are recent initiatives by the federal agencies to coordinate their activities related to toxic substances control; these are in part responses to the frustration created by the fragmented control of VC. Some attention is also paid to the possibility of presidential reorganization of the toxic substances programs.

Part III also explores the major elements of the legal framework within which toxic substances control decisions are made. There are four legal devices for directing agency decision making under uncertainty and for guiding the agencies in the balancing of incommensurable interests. First, a statute can either grant or withhold from an agency the authority to balance risks and benefits. Most statutes grant this authority, but with very little guidance for determining the appropriate balance. Some statutes bar agencies from considering economic issues. These statutes are often criticized as unduly harsh or irrational, but there are special conditions under which health-only rules can be justified.

Second, through a variety of terms and phrases, nearly all of the health and environmental statutes grant the agencies the authority to base decisions on uncertain evidence, and to make policy judgments to resolve uncertainties in favor of taking protective action. Here too, however, the statutes give the agencies little guidance on what quantity and kind of evidence is needed to support regulatory action. The argument presented here is that the mean-

---

806. *See* Slesin & Sandler, *supra* note 541.
807. See text accompanying notes 22-80 *supra*.
808. See text accompanying notes 22-80b *supra*.

ings of the various terms and phrases coincide. Recognition of the agreement of these statutes on this point would reduce the incentives of the parties to dispute which agency has jurisdiction in areas of abutting or overlapping authority. It would also remove a barrier to more frequent joint action by the agencies.

Third, the statutes differ in their allocation of the ultimate burden of persuasion. Traditionally the allocation of this burden is thought to have a significant effect on ultimate outcomes when critical issues are shrouded in uncertainty. While the allocation of the burden of persuasion does have some power to affect decisions, it appears that in the toxic substances control decisions of this decade, the burden of persuasion has had less impact than might be expected.

Finally, the statutes differ in their standards for judicial review. It is argued here that, despite these differences, the courts are developing a uniform approach to review. This approach emphasizes the importance of substantive review in keeping administrative decisions within broad limits of rational action, but it also emphasizes the limited capacity of judicial oversight to control closely the agencies' doubt-resolving and interest-balancing judgments.

A.   Mitigating the Problem of Jurisdictional Fragmentation

1.   Overview of the Fragmentation Problem

The present patchwork of toxic substances control statutes is the result of incremental legislation enacted principally over the last 20 years. Congress passed new laws one by one as it perceived relatively narrowly defined needs for additional controls. At no point did Congress take a comprehensive look at the entire problem and attempt to design a single control system that covers the full life-cycle of a chemical, from invention to disposal, through all the media in which it may be found. Even the far-reaching 1976 Toxic Substances Control Act[809] is not such a system. It fills the gaps in the network of controls created by the other laws. It establishes a pre-market screening requirement for many chemicals for which none existed before,[810] and it gives EPA the authority to regulate a chemical hazard when no other agency can adequately control it.[811] But the enormously complex patchwork remains in effect.

As a result, many widely used substances fall under the jurisdiction of more than one agency or law. Perhaps few chemicals will require action by so many agencies under so many statutes as VC. However, there appear to be hundreds that will require two or three separate control actions.[812] EPA,

---

809.   15 U.S.C. §§ 2601-2629 (West Supp. 1978).

810.   TSCA §§ 4-5, 15 U.S.C. §§ 2603-2604 (West Supp. 1978).

811.   *Id.* § 9, 15 U.S.C. § 2608 (West Supp. 1978).

812.   OSHA estimates that there are between 1,500 and 2,000 potential carcinogens in the workplace. *OSHA Proposed Cancer Policy, supra* note 252, at 54,148. Many of the same

OSHA, FDA, and CPSC report that currently, regulations are being developed by two or more of the four agencies for at least 23 substances or groups of substances.[813]

In addition, many business installations and activities, such as factories and transportation, are subject to the independent and perhaps conflicting requirements of multiple laws and agencies. For example, a factory working with a toxic substance can be subject to four separate standards covering its releases into the workplace air, into the general atmosphere, into wastewater, and into solid waste.

As the VC case study shows, there are many instances in which the lines between agencies' jurisdictions are not clear. Often a particular use of a substance or a source of exposure to it can be fairly characterized as falling into more than one jurisdictional category. This creates possibilities for jurisdictional disputes, or for one agency to delay action in the hope that another will act. The case study also shows that the fragmented assessment of risks and benefits increases the likelihood that some benefits will be double-counted and that some risks will not be tallied at all.

The coordination problem exists within agencies as well as between them. Six separate laws affecting toxic substances control are administered by EPA.[814] There are at least four separate program areas affecting toxic substances control within FDA,[815] and there are at least four within DOT.[816]

In several instances Congress has anticipated that zones of regulatory authority will overlap, and it has attempted to enact provisions defining the relationships between separate laws and agencies. Two such provisions,

---

chemicals are released into the general atmosphere, discharged into water, and found in drinking water. *See* EDF Petition for a General Policy on Carcinogenic Air Pollutants, *supra* note 356; EPA, *Publication of Toxic Water Pollutant List*, 43 Fed. Reg. 4108 (1978); *EPA Proposed Drinking Water Regulations, supra* note 688.

813. Interagency Regulatory Liaison Group, Joint Regulatory Developments, March 1, 1978, *reprinted in* 1 BNA CHEM. REG. REP.—CURR. REP. 1916-21 (1978) [hereinafter cited as IRLG List of Substances of Common Concern]. For some of the substances, such as VC, some regulations already are in effect and more are under consideration.

814. These are: Clean Air Act § 112, 42 U.S.C.A. § 7412 (West Supp. 1978); Federal Environmental Pesticide Control Act, 7 U.S.C. §§ 136-136y (Supp. V 1975); Federal Water Pollution Control Act, 33 U.S.C.A. §§ 1251-1376 (West Supp. 1978); Resource Conservation and Recovery Act, §§ 3001-3011, 42 U.S.C.A. §§ 6921-6931 (1977); Safe Drinking Water Act, 42 U.S.C. §§ 201(f), 300f-300j-q (Supp. V 1975); Toxic Substances Control Act, 15 U.S.C.A. §§ 2601-2629 (West Supp. 1978).

815. The statutes governing these programs are: Food, Drug, and Cosmetics Act of 1938, ch. 675, 52 Stat. 1040 (1938) (governing cosmetics); Food Additives Amendments of 1958, Pub. L. No. 85-929, 72 Stat. 1784 (1958) (governing food additives); New Drug Amendments of 1962, Pub. L. No. 87-781, 76 Stat. 779 (1962) (governing drugs); Medical Device Amendments of 1976, Pub. L. No. 94-295, 90 Stat. 539 (1976) (all codified at 21 U.S.C. §§ 301-392 (1970 & West Supp. 1978)).

816. These are: Federal Railroad Safety Act, 45 U.S.C. §§ 421-441 (1970); Hazardous Materials Transportation Act, 49 U.S.C. § 391a (Supp. V 1975); Dangerous Cargo Act, 46 U.S.C. § 170(7) (1970); Ports and Waterways Safety Act, 46 U.S.C. § 391a (Supp. V 1975).

section 4(b)(1) of OSH Act and section 9 of TSCA, have been discussed above.[817] The Consumer Product Safety Act contains two similar provisions.[818] All of these provisions are intended to establish clear lines of responsibility and to promote efficient governmental action. Experience with section 4(b)(1) of OSH Act, however, suggests that these provisions may create more controversy than they avoid.[819]

The major responses to jurisdictional fragmentation have come, and are likely to continue to come, from the executive agencies themselves and from the Office of the President. At the most basic level, agencies that are responsible for more than one toxic substances control program can take internal measures to coordinate their administration and to develop common policies. At the other extreme, it is possible that jurisdictional problems could be attacked through presidential reorganization of existing agencies.

Three types of interagency responses have been employed. The oldest is the conventional interagency agreement or memorandum of understanding to clarify jurisdictions. These are developed on an ad hoc basis as problems arise. Second, recently the agencies have begun to cooperate in various ways to regulate single chemicals that fall under the jurisdiction of more than one agency. A third response is just developing; the agencies are beginning to cooperate on a regular basis in a general manner, prior to the emergence of specific hazards requiring joint action.

Two interagency working groups were established in 1977 for this kind of long-term effort. EPA, OSHA, FDA, and CPSC formed the Interagency Regulatory Liaison Group (IRLG) to coordinate their regulatory programs.[820] At the request of President Carter in his 1977 Environmental Message,[821] some 16 agencies (including these four) have formed another group, the Toxic Substances Strategy Committee (TSSC), under the direction of the Council on Environmental Quality.[822] The agendas of these two groups may include an effort to anticipate jurisdictional complexities and to explore means of resolving conflicts in advance of need.

---

817. 29 U.S.C. § 653(b)(1) (1970); 15 U.S.C. § 2608 (West Supp. 1978). See text accompanying notes 649, 671-674, 800-801 *supra*.

818. The Consumer Product Safety Act assigns the administration of certain statutes, including FHSA, to CPSC. 15 U.S.C. § 2079(a) (West Supp. 1978). The Act then prohibits CPSC from regulating any risk that can be "eliminated or reduced to a sufficient extent" by other agencies' action under OSH Act, the Clean Air Act, or the Atomic Energy Act. *Id*. § 2080.

The Consumer Product Safety Act also governs CPSC's choice of laws. If a risk could be "eliminated or reduced to a sufficient extent" by action under FHSA, CPSC may not use the regulatory provisions of the Consumer Product Safety Act, unless "by rule" CPSC "finds that it is in the public interest" to do so. *Id*. § 2079(d).

819. See note 673 *supra*.

820. EPA, *Regulation of Toxic and Hazardous Substances, Interagency Agreement*, 42 Fed. Reg. 54,856 (1977) [hereinafter cited as *IRLG Agreement*].

821. The President's Message to Congress on Environmental Protection, 123 Cong. Rec. H4796, H4797-98 (Daily ed. 1977).

822. Council on Environmental Quality, *Toxic Substances Strategy Committee, Work Plan*, 42 Fed. Reg. 57,886 (1977) [hereinafter cited as *TSSC Work Plan*].

2. Intra-agency Coordination—The Example of EPA

Three agencies—EPA, FDA, and DOT—each administer more than one toxic substances control program and each faces significant problems of intra-agency fragmentation. EPA is discussed here as an example because it administers the largest number of such programs, and because it has demonstrated the most interest in coordinating them.

Since it was formed by presidential reorganization in 1970,[823] EPA has faced the problem of coordinating closely related programs that have widely different legislative and historical origins. In the toxic substances field, six separate programs are involved. Before 1970, the pesticide program was administered by the Department of Agriculture and by FDA, the air pollution program by another branch of the Department of Health, Education, and Welfare, and the water pollution program by the Department of the Interior.[824] Responsibility for these programs was transferred to EPA upon its creation, and since that time the agency has been given expanded and more difficult responsibilities for toxic substances control in each of these areas. In addition, Congress has given EPA major new programs to administer in the areas of drinking water safety, hazardous waste control, and toxic substances regulation generally.

EPA has always been organized along the lines of these programs. Until 1977, there were two major program divisions, each directed by an Assistant Administrator—the Office of Air and Waste Management and the Office of Water and Hazardous Materials.[825] The former contained lower-level offices concerned with air pollution, solid waste management,[826] noise, and radiation. The latter housed lower-level offices for water pollution, drinking water, pesticides, and toxic substances.[827] In 1977, the agency was reorganized, largely due to the upgrading of concern for toxic substances problems. In that year, TSCA created an Assistant Administrator for Toxic Substances and carved out a separate, top-level office for the new program.[828] In February 1978, EPA shifted the pesticide program from the Office of Water and Hazardous Materials to the Office of Toxic Substances.[829] This step was intended to help integrate these two closely related programs. Shortly before this step, the agency shifted the

823. *Reorganization Plan No. 3 of 1970*, 35 Fed. Reg. 15,263 (1970).

824. *Id.*

825. *See* 40 C.F.R. pt. 1 (1976).

826. Until the passage of the Resource Conservation and Recovery Act in 1976, the solid waste management program was largely informational. *See* Solid Waste Disposal Act of 1970, Pub. L. No. 91-512, 84 Stat. 1227 (1970).

827. As with the solid waste program, before 1976 the Office of Toxic Substances had largely research and informational duties.

828. TSCA § 26(g), 15 U.S.C. § 2625(g) (West Supp. 1978).

829. EPA, Organization and Functions of the Office of Toxic Substances and Pesticide Programs, *reprinted in* 1 BNA CHEM. REG. REP.—CURR. REP. 1766 (1978) [hereinafter cited as Toxic Substances and Pesticide Merger plan].

solid and hazardous waste program, which had been upgraded in 1976 by the passage of RCRA, to the Office of Water and Hazardous Materials.[830] This reflects the realization that solid and hazardous waste problems are more closely related to water pollution control than to the air quality program.[831]

Placing jurisdiction for separate programs in a common agency is no guarantee that they will be implemented in a coordinated fashion. Even though the six toxic substances programs are grouped together under several Assistant Administrators, at a lower level they are administered through distinct units. Some of the programs are even subdivided into additional distinct administrative units.[832] As the case study shows, EPA has dealt with VC pesticide propellants, air emissions, water effluent, and drinking water contamination through four separate, uncoordinated proceedings. Despite the reorganization discussed above, this lack of close cooperation among the program units apparently still exists.[833]

For several years EPA has stated the goal of having a uniform policy for toxic substances control, or at least for controlling carcinogens, and applying it consistently in all of the agencies' regulatory programs.[834] No such policy has yet been articulated; in part, this is due to the inconsistent demands of the major statutes on the issue of risk-benefit balancing, an issue to be considered further below.[835]

3. Interagency Agreements and Memoranda of Understanding

For many years the agencies have concluded bilateral or multilateral interagency agreements and memoranda of understanding[836] to foster cooperative solutions to common problems. Typically, they are concluded on an ad hoc basis to meet a particular narrow problem. Some terminate for all practical purposes, if not formally, after the performance of a specific

---

830. *See* Transfer of the Office of Solid Waste, Environmental Protection Agency Order 112.14 (July 29, 1977), *amending* EPA Organization and Functions Manual (Sept. 29, 1976).

831. Personal communication with Bruce Diamond, Deputy Associate General Counsel for Litigation, EPA, March 10, 1978.

832. *See, e.g.*, the divisions of the air pollution program. 40 C.F.R. § 1.27 (1977).

833. As part of the merger of the toxic substances and pesticides programs, EPA has established a Toxic Substances Priorities Committee with members from all the relevant portions of the agency. This committee is charged with pursuing the goals of uniform toxic substances policy and action. Toxic Substances and Pesticides Merger Plan, *supra* note 829, at 1767. It is too early to appraise the committee's performance.

EPA is also considering the institution of procedures under which new sources could obtain permits for water and air pollutants and solid waste disposal in a single proceeding. *EPA Weighs Advantages of Consolidated Permitting for Water, Air, Solid Waste,* 5 TOXIC MATERIALS NEWS 102 (1978).

834. *See, e.g.*, EPA, *Health Risk and Economic Impact Assessments of Suspected Carcinogens, Interim Procedures and Guidelines*, 41 Fed. Reg. 21,402 (1976).

835. See text accompanying notes 877-901 *infra*.

836. There does not seem to be any significant difference between interagency agreements and memoranda of understanding. The terms are used interchangeably below.

task. Others, such as jurisdictional agreements or agreements to share information, remain in effect indefinitely.

The number and contents of such agreements and memoranda is uncertain. Apparently, no comprehensive compilation of them has ever been made. Some idea of their number and contents may be gained from a compilation of those existing between EPA, OSHA, FDA, and CPSC, the four agencies that make up the IRLG. In July 1977, these agencies reported that a rapid and possibly incomplete search of their files identified 41 agreements or memoranda concerning toxic substances control.[837] Only two of these agreements address areas of abutting or overlapping jurisdiction. One of these, between FDA and CPSC, concerning their joint jurisdiction over food packaging, has been discussed previously.[838] The other, between FDA and EPA, defines the agencies' responsibilities for regulating pesticide residues in food.[839]

The small number of jurisdictional agreements suggests that, through more aggressive use of this technique, some of the jurisdictional disputes noted in the case study could be resolved. Any such effort probably will be under the aegis of the IRLG or the TSSC.

4. *Cooperative Regulation of Particular Substances*

Recently the agencies have begun to act together to regulate particular substances that pose hazards falling into more than one agency's jurisdiction. This concurrent and sometimes joint action is a response to the agencies' experiences with the fragmented regulation of such substances as VC, asbestos, and lead.[840] As noted above, the IRLG lists 23 substances or

---

837. The total breaks down as follows (the number adds up to more than 41 because some fall into more than one category): 38 of these concern the exchange of information or the joint performance of research. One is an agreement for cooperative enforcement of a particular program. Four concern joint regulatory action on particular chemicals. Briefing for Chairman S. John Byington, CPSC, Administrator Douglas M. Costle, EPA, Commissioner Donald Kennedy, FDA, and Assistant Secretary of Labor Eula Bingham, OSHA, Report on Progress of the Interagency Regulatory Liaison Group (July 22, 1977) (unpaginated) [hereinafter cited as IRLG Progress Report]. The Report actually lists 45 agreements. One is the IRLG agreement itself, and is discussed at text accompanying notes 851-866 *infra*. Two concern radiation and one noise, and are unrelated to the subject of this Article.

838. See text accompanying notes 793-795 *supra*.

839. FIFRA Responsibilities Definitions, item no. 36 in the list of agreements in IRLG Progress Report, *supra* note 837.

This compilation does not include any agreements that may exist between these four agencies and DOT. The arrangement between OSHA and DOT concerning the safety and health of transportation workers, and the prospect of an agreement between EPA and DOT over the transportation of hazardous wastes, have both been discussed above. See text accompanying notes 634, 673-674 *supra*.

840. Many separate actions have been taken regarding these substances. Occupational exposure to asbestos has been regulated by OSHA, and asbestos air pollution by EPA. Both CPSC and FDA are considering the need for additional regulations. Lead in paint has been regulated by CPSC, and lead in gasoline by EPA. EPA is developing lead regulations for water discharge, drinking water contamination, and hazardous waste disposal. FDA has set a toler-

groups of substances that are in various stages of regulation by two or more of the four member agencies.[841]

The recent joint regulation of the aerosol propellant uses of fluorocarbons by EPA, FDA, and CPSC is the best example to date of cooperative action. Fluorocarbons are suspected of reducing the amount of ozone in the stratosphere, thereby allowing an increase in the amount of harmful ultraviolet radiation from the sun reaching the earth's surface.[842] In 1977, the three agencies formed an interagency Chlorofluorocarbon Work Group through which to coordinate their research and planning for regulatory action.[843] In March 1978, the three agencies jointly promulgated rules to end nearly all aerosol uses of these substances.

FDA acted under various provisions of FDCA,[844] while EPA acted under TSCA.[845] The FDA rules cover the use of fluorocarbons as an aerosol propellant in foods, drugs, animal food and drugs, cosmetics, and medical devices. The EPA rules cover all other uses, plus the manufacture of the chemical for use as an aerosol propellant.[846] The two agencies established a coordinated set of deadlines that will end the sale of aerosol products propelled by fluorocarbons in April 1979.[847] The EPA rules apply to products that also could be regulated by CPSC.[848] CPSC stated that it would forego separate, unnecessary action.[849]

---

ance for the lead content of milk. OSHA is preparing a permanent lead standard for the workplace. *See* IRLG List of Substances of Common Concern, *supra* note 813.

841. *Id.* Besides VC, asbestos, and lead, the list contains such well-known substances as arsenic, benzene, cadmium, coke oven emissions, DES, mercury, ozone, PCBs, and sulfur dioxide.

842. *See generally* Federal Task Force on Inadvertent Modification of the Stratosphere, Fluorocarbons and the Environment (June 1975).

843. The Group included EPA, FDA, and CPSC, as well as the Department of Commerce, which does not have regulatory authority.

844. FDA, *Certain Fluorocarbons (Chlorofluorocarbons) in Food, Food Additive, Drug, Animal Food, Animal Drug, Cosmetic, and Medical Device Products as Propellants in Self-Pressurized Containers, Prohibition on Use*, 43 Fed. Reg. 11,301 (1978) [hereinafter cited as *FDA Fluorocarbon Rules*].

845. EPA, *Fully Halogenated Chlorofluoroalkanes, Final Rules*, 43 Fed. Reg. 11,318 (1978) [hereinafter cited as *EPA Fluorocarbons Rules*].

846. EPA has chosen to regulate pesticide aerosols not under FEPCA but under TSCA. It will be recalled that under § 3(2)(B)(ii) of TSCA, 15 U.S.C.A. § 2603(2)(B)(ii) (West Supp. 1978), pesticides are not a "chemical substance" subject to regulation under that law. EPA takes the position that it can regulate fluorocarbons under TSCA at the point of their manufacture, on the ground that before they are incorporated into pesticide products they are not pesticides within the meaning of § 3(2)(b)(ii). *See EPA Fluorocarbons Rules, supra* note 845, at 11,320. See also the agency's explanation of the relationship of TSCA to FDCA, *id.*

847. *EPA Fluorocarbon Rules, supra* note 845, at 11,318; *FDA Fluorocarbon Rules, supra* note 844, at 11,302.

848. *See* EPA, *Fully Halogenated Chlorofluorocarbons, Proposed Rules*, 42 Fed. Reg. 24,542, 24,546 (1977).

849. CPSC, *Fully Halogenated Chlorofluoroalkanes as Propellants in Aerosol Consumer Products, Commission Action in Response to the Environmental Protection Agency's Ban*, 43 Fed. Reg. 11,326 (1978).

In sum, the three agencies have proposed to deal with the fluorocarbon hazard through two coordinated, economical regulatory actions. The number of separate proceedings is being held to a minimum. All parties—the regulated industries, the public, and the agencies—are well served by this approach. The major goals of the four agencies that formed the IRLG are to cooperate to a comparable extent on the regulation of 22 other substances currently of joint interest, and to institutionalize such cooperation regarding additional chemicals in the future.[850] It is to be hoped that this sort of joint action will become the rule rather than the exception.

5. Broader Forms of Cooperation

Recently the federal agencies have initiated efforts to cooperate more broadly on a general, programmatic basis. As noted above, two bodies were formed in 1977 for this purpose: the IRLG, composed of EPA, OSHA, FDA, and CPSC,[851] and the TSSC, composed of 16 agencies and chaired by the Council on Environmental Quality.[852] Both bodies have expressed interest in sharing data and data systems, coordinating future research agendas, developing common methods of assessing risks and benefits, and coordinating the setting and enforcing of regulations.[853] Both bodies have formed numerous work groups to pursue these goals. The efforts are just getting underway, and it is too soon to measure their success. However, two objectives deserve further consideration.

First, both the IRLG and the TSSC are acutely conscious of the jurisdictional complexity of federal toxic substances control. Presently, work groups of both bodies are attempting to map the areas of each agency's responsibilities, and to catalogue instances of overlapping, abutting, and conflicting jurisdiction. Both bodies are considering whether to attempt to write comprehensive and anticipatory interagency agreements, on either a bilateral or a multilateral basis, to resolve these complexities before concrete problems arise.[854] The objective would be to avoid both of the extreme results of jurisdictional fragmentation: the setting of duplicative or inconsistent regulations, and the failure of any agency to step forward to deal with a problem.

This is a very important objective, but it will not be easy to achieve. As the VC experience illustrates, some of the jurisdictional problems are subtle. It will be difficult to imagine all of them in advance of concrete situations. Moreover, there are some instances in which the agencies have inconsistent substantive obligations in areas of abutting or overlapping jurisdiction.

---

850. Interagency Regulatory Liaison Group, *Notice of IRLG Work Plans and Public Meetings*, 43 Fed. Reg. 7174, 7192 (1978) [hereinafter cited as *IRLG Work Plans*].

851. *IRLG Agreement, supra* note 820.

852. *TSSC Work Plan, supra* note 822.

853. *Id.* at 57,867-69; *IRLG Work Plans, supra* note 850, at 7174-98.

854. *IRLG Work Plans, supra* note 850, at 7192-93; *TSSC Work Plan, supra* note 822, at 57,867. *See* Environmental Law Institute, An Analysis of Past Federal Efforts to Control Toxic Substances 54 (Apr. 19, 1978) (draft).

FDA's and EPA's overlapping authority over plastic pipe illustrate this problem. As discussed above,[855] EPA is required to balance risks and benefits, but FDA is permitted to consider only health factors. Action that is required under one statute is illegal under the other. Thus, joint action is virtually ruled out. But there is no basis of authority on which either agency could cede control of pipe to the other. Aerosol products provide an example of the same problem in an area of abutting jurisdiction. As discussed above,[856] much may turn on whether a substance is classified a household product or a pesticide. For the former, CPSC is to consider only health factors; for the latter, EPA must balance risks and benefits. Again, the agencies have no statutory guidance as to which rule should govern those products near the jurisdictional line.

Despite these difficulties, the agencies' effort to understand and resolve their jurisdictional conflicts should be well worthwhile. Greater clarity and speedier action would be gained in the more common, less difficult areas of jurisdictional uncertainty.

The second basic objective of the IRLG and the TSSC is the development of a comprehensive policy for the definition and identification of substances that pose a risk of cancer.[857] Both bodies intend this to be a first step in the development of consistent approaches to a wide variety of health and environmental effects.[858] Although many basic aspects of chemical carcinogenesis are uncertain, there is a growing consensus among cancer experts on a number of principles for identifying carcinogenic chemicals.[859] The most important principles are: (1) that it is both impractical and unethical to expose humans deliberately to chemicals to test their carcinogenicity; (2) that epidemiological studies of people already exposed to chemicals are a very useful but insufficient method of assessing carcinogenicity; (3) that animals and humans react basically alike to carcinogens, so that a chemical that causes cancer in animals is likely to do so in humans; (4) that because benign tumors in animals may precede malignant ones or may transform into them, any excess of tumors of either kind in animals is evidence of a cancer risk for humans; (5) that presently it is impossible to identify threshold exposures for carcinogens below which there is no cancer risk; and (6) that although strong carcinogens may be distinguished from

---

855.   See text accompanying notes 754-771 *supra*.

856.   See text accompanying note 608 *supra*.

857.   *IRLG Work Plans, supra* note 850, at 7195-97; *TSSC Work Plan, supra* note 822, at 57,869.

858.   *IRLG Work Plans, supra* note 850, at 7195-98; *TSSC Work Plan, supra* note 822, at 57,869.

859.   These principles are discussed in the text accompanying notes 22-60 *supra*. *See also* Karch, *Explicit Criteria and Principles for Identifying Carcinogens: A Focus of Controversy at the Environmental Protection Agency,* in IIa NATIONAL RESEARCH COUNCIL, DECISION MAKING IN THE ENVIRONMENTAL PROTECTION AGENCY: CASE STUDIES 119 (1977). Karch discusses EPA's attempts to establish such principles for the pesticide program in the early- and mid-1970s.

weak ones, accurate estimates of the size of cancer risks at realistic levels of human exposure presently are not possible.

EPA, OSHA, FDA, and CPSC have all relied on some or all of these principles in developing regulations for VC and other carcinogens. The courts have uniformly accepted agency adoption of these principles as permissible exercises of agency discretion to make policy in an area of uncertainty, under statutes that direct the agencies to protect the public from potential health hazards.[860] Nevertheless, as scientific propositions these principles are still open to reasoned dispute and it has been necessary for each agency to compile extensive records in support of them in each proceeding to regulate a chemical. The scientific accuracy of these principles has been litigated repeatedly. This repetition consumes scarce agency resources and reduces the number of substances that can be regulated. This is one cause of the enormous backlog of potential carcinogens not yet considered by the agencies.[861]

In response to this situation, the agencies currently are considering adopting the cancer principles as general policy. OSHA has already proposed to do so,[862] and EPA, FDA, and CPSC are considering similar action.[863] The IRLG's and the TSSC's attention to this problem should speed and coordinate the adoption of the principles.

It should be noted that the adoption of the principles for identifying carcinogens would have different consequences under different statutes. To decide that a chemical is a carcinogen is not necessarily to decide that it must be banned. OSHA, for example, must set "feasible" exposure standards, a process that involves a balancing of risks and benefits. The cancer principles set out above do not resolve many of the issues raised in the balancing process. For instance, in determining an allowable exposure level, OSHA would have to estimate, at least roughly, the size of the cancer risk a chemical presents. The same is true for all the agencies administering statutes that require risk-benefit balancing.[864] The situation is different

---

860. *See, e.g.*, the following cases upholding regulation of carcinogens on the basis of some or all of these principles: Environmental Defense Fund v. EPA, 510 F.2d 1291, 7 ERC 1689 (D.C. Cir. 1975) (suspension of pesticides aldrin and dieldrin); Society of Plastics Indus., Inc. v. OSHA, 509 F.2d 1301 (2d Cir. 1975) (occupational standard for VC); Synthetic Organic Chem. Mfrs. Ass'n v. Brennan, 503 F.2d 1155 (3rd Cir. 1974) (occupational exposure to ethyleneimine); Bell v. Goddard, 366 F.2d 177 (7th Cir. 1966) (residues of DES in poultry).

861. *See, e.g.*, General Accounting Office, Delays in Setting Workplace Standards for Cancer-Causing And Other Dangerous Substances (May 10, 1977); General Accounting Office, Federal Pesticide Registration Program: Is It Protecting The Public And The Environment Adequately From Pesticide Hazards? (Dec. 4, 1975).

862. *OSHA Proposed Cancer Policy, supra* note 252.

863. EPA held a public meeting in March for comment on EDF's proposal of a policy like OSHA's for regulating carcinogenic air pollutants. EPA, *Regulation of Carcinogenic Air Pollutants, Meeting*, 43 Fed. Reg. 5565 (1978). *See Costle Says EPA Cancer Policy Follows Generally Accepted Scientific Principles*, 1 BNA CHEM. REG. REP.—CURR. REP. 1853 (1978). CPSC is also considering a system similar to that of OSHA. *See Draft Guidelines for CPSC Policy On Carcinogens Have Four Stages*, BNA CHEM. REG. REP.—CURR. REP. 1483 (1977).

864. OSHA recognizes this. *OSHA Cancer Policy Proposal, supra* note 252, at 54,167.

under the minority of statutes that forbid agencies to consider economic factors. Under the Delaney Clause of the Food Additives Amendment, for example, any additive identified as a carcinogen must be banned.[865]

Despite the fact that some of the issues underlying the proposed cancer principles will re-enter most decisions at the stage of selecting the permissible exposure level, the adoption of a government-wide cancer policy is an important goal. If adopted after thorough review by the interagency work groups, the principles would provide the groundwork for individual agency actions and would likely gain increasing recognition in judicial review. Regulation of individual carcinogens could then proceed more rapidly. Most important, the principles for identifying carcinogens would establish a way of sorting chemicals for their priority for regulatory attention. The adoption of the principles would also establish a precedent for the development of general criteria for defining and identifying other health and environmental effects, such as mutagenesis or the capacity to affect the ozone layer.

In addition to advantages of interagency cooperation, certain hazards of the cooperative venture must also be considered. First is a growing risk that the two major coordination efforts will themselves become uncoordinated. The IRLG and the TSSC were created independently, but with very similar purposes. Both bodies have stated repeatedly their intention to cooperate closely.[866] The IRLG has observer status on the TSSC.[867] Yet there is some danger that the two bodies could develop duplicative work programs or conflicting principles and standards.

A second risk is that because the groups must operate by consensus, their efforts may result in actions and recommendations that are less strict than they ought to be. It may be that relatively bold action by one agency is necessary to encourage the other agencies to consider seriously similar action. OSHA's independent proposal of a cancer policy is an example. The possibility that one agency will act aggressively in an area may be lessened by the existence of cooperative work groups acting by consensus.

6.   The Possibility of Executive Reorganization

The tools for reducing jurisdictional fragmentation include presidential reorganization of the agencies with toxic substances responsibilities. Under the Reorganization Act of 1977,[868] the President has broad authority to change the structure of the federal government so as to reduce duplication and overlap and to promote efficiency, coordination, economy, effective

---

Karch notes that the situation is the same for EPA in the pesticide program. Karch, *supra* note 859, at 158.

865.   FDCA § 409(c)(3)(A), 21 U.S.C. § 348(c)(3)(A) (1970). See text accompanying notes 493-504 *supra*.

866.   *TSSC Work Plan, supra* note 822, at 57,869; *IRLG Work Plans, supra* note 850, at 7179.

867.   *TSSC Work Plan, supra* note 822, at 57,870.

868.   Pub. L. No. 95-17, 91 Stat. 29, 5 U.S.C.A. §§ 901-912 (West Supp. 1978).

management, and better delivery of services.[869] Subject to several limitations, the President may shift programs or functions from one agency to another, consolidate programs and functions, or abolish inactive agencies.[870] The reorganization plan must be submitted to Congress, and it becomes effective if it is not disapproved by a resolution of either the House or Senate within 60 days.[871]

The statute empowers the President to create virtually any organizational arrangement that might be desirable for the toxic substances programs. A reorganization plan may merge or realign programs. It may also improve administration through steps short of transferring functions; a plan may require two existing agencies to be coordinated in a given manner.[872]

In 1977, President Carter established the President's Reorganization Project (PRP) within the Office of Management and Budget.[873] This body is required to analyze the need for organizational changes and to draft reorganization plans for presidential consideration.

Reorganization of the toxic substances programs is not currently under active consideration by the PRP, but it is a possible subject for attention in the future.[874] Representatives of the PRP sit as observers in the meetings of the TSSC.[875] Whether the reorganization of these programs will be seriously considered depends largely on how successful the IRLG and the TSSC are at allowing the agencies to solve these problems themselves. Since reorganization is probably not a welcome idea to most of the agencies, the latent possibility of it gives the agencies an incentive to succeed in their coordination efforts. At this point the outcome cannot be foreseen.

B. Legal Tools for Controlling Toxic Substances Control Decisions

Toxic substances regulation is characterized by the difficulties of making decisions on uncertain factual bases and of balancing competing, unlike interests. The uncertainty and balancing problems have been described in general terms in Part I[876] and in the specific context of the VC case study in

---

869. *Id*. § 901(a).

870. *Id*. § 903. The President may not create or abolish an executive department, abolish an independent regulatory agency, or consolidate two such agencies. Nor may the President order an agency to perform a function that is not explicitly authorized by statute. *Id*. § 905.

871. *Id*. § 906.

872. *Id*. § 903(a)(3).

873. Office of the Assistant to the President for Reorganization, *Executive Branch Reorganization, Invitation for Public Comment*, 42 Fed. Reg. 34,958 (1977).

874. The major environmental focus of the PRP has been on the possibility of unifying the natural resources programs of EPA, the Department of the Interior, the Department of Agriculture, and other agencies. The possibility of combining the environmental health functions of EPA with the occupational and public health functions of OSHA, FDA, CPSC, NIOSH, and the National Institute of Health is also under consideration, but the concept has not yet been as fully explored. A recent PRP paper explored this subject. Office of Management and Budget, *President's Reorganization Project, Reorganization Study of Natural Resources and Environmental Functions, Request for Comments*, 42 Fed. Reg. 63,665 (1977).

875. *TSSC Work Plan, supra* note 822, at 57,870.

876. See text accompanying notes 22-80b *supra*.

Part II. This section explores the legal framework within which agencies, Congress, and the courts attempt to resolve these problems of toxic substances regulation.

Because there is a tremendous range of plausible factual conclusions in toxic substances regulatory actions, and because agency decisions necessarily are heavily value-laden, courts can hold only the most extreme decisions to be clearly and unquestionably unreasonable. The first task of the legal framework is to hold toxic substances control decisions within these outer limits. Another, more difficult task is to yield more finely-tuned control over the rules for resolving factual doubts and value conflicts. The possibilities and limitations in this second task are only now becoming clear.

There are four major elements of the legal framework within which toxic substances control decisions are made. One element involves the process for balancing competing factors in administrative decision making. The statutes are divided between those that require agencies to weigh economic interests against health concerns and those that forbid such balancing. Second, all of the statutes permit precautionary regulation on less than certain information that a substance causes harm. Third, burdens of persuasion are allocated to reflect basic policy judgments regarding particular regulatory areas. Fourth, the statutes provide for some degree of judicial review of agencies' factual conclusions and their resolutions of conflicting interests. The following discussion examines each of these elements in its present application.

1. Balancing Rules and Health-Only Rules

Most of the federal health and environmental statutes require the agencies to consider the costs of regulation as well as the health benefits. This requirement is created by terms such as "unreasonable"[877] or "feasible,"[878] or by phrases such as "taking into consideration the cost,"[879] modifying the danger that must exist to justify regulation or limiting the remedial steps that may be taken.

Some statutes, however, contain no such modifiers establishing a duty to balance. From their terms and from their legislative histories, one can see Congress' intent to require that the agency consider health factors alone and take steps to protect health without regard to cost. The major example of this type of statute is the 1958 Food Additives Amendment. The Amendment's general provisions simply require that FDA find an additive to be "safe" before the agency may permit its use.[880] The exclusion of any concern other

---

877.   *E.g.*, TSCA § 6, 15 U.S.C.A. § 2065 (West Supp. 1978); FEPCA § 2(bb), 7 U.S.C.A. § 136(bb) (West Supp. 1978); HMTA § 104, 49 U.S.C. § 1803 (Supp. V 1975).

878.   *E.g.*, OSH Act § 6(b)(5), 29 U.S.C. § 655(b)(5) (1970); SDWA § 1412(a)(2), 42 U.S.C.A. § 300g-1(a)(2) (West Supp. 1978).

879.   *E.g.*, Clean Air Act § 111(a), 42 U.S.C.A. § 7411(a) (West Supp. 1978).

880.   FDCA § 409(c)(3)(A), 21 U.S.C. § 348(c)(3)(A) (1970). *See generally* Freedman, *supra* note 492, at 248-49.

than health is especially clear in the Delaney Clause, which deals specifically with carcinogens.[881] Other examples of this type of statute are the
hazardous air pollutant section of the Clean Air Act[882] and, until it was
amended in late 1977, the toxic water pollutant section of FWPCA.[883] Both
of these sections would have EPA set standards that are sufficient to protect
health "with an ample margin of safety," regardless of the costs of achieving those standards.

At first glance, the two approaches to the consideration of costs seem to
be completely different and mutually exclusive. The contrast has often been
noted by advocates of both positions.[884] Assuming that society is not willing
to accept safety measures regardless of cost, and that people are willing to
trade increases in their risks of death or illness for increases in their
economic well-being,[885] the statutes that forbid balancing of these interests
appear unjustifiable.

Yet, there are conditions under which the "health only" approach is
sound policy. The argument rests on an analogy from the *per se* rules found
in antitrust law against such practices as price fixing.[886] A *per se* rule
prohibiting an agency from considering economic factors is justified in the
following circumstances. First, it must be the case that, in general, the risks
of substances in a given group are judged to outweigh their benefits. But
even if this generalization holds, there may be exceptional members of the
group for which it is not true, and for which benefits do outweigh risks.
Thus, for the *per se* rule to be justifiable on efficiency grounds a second

---

881.   FDCA § 409(c)(3)(A), 21 U.S.C. § 348(c)(3)(A) (1970). See text accompanying notes
490-494 *supra*.

882.   Clean Air Act § 112(b)(1)(B), 42 U.S.C.A. § 7412(b)(1)(B) (West Supp. 1978). See text
accompanying notes 363-381 *supra*.

883.   FWPCA § 307(a), 86 Stat. 857 (1972) (prior to 1977 amendment). See text accompanying notes 693-710 *supra*.

884.   *See* sources cited in note 494 *supra*.

885.   See text accompanying notes 73-78 *supra*.

886.   This *per se* approach originates in antitrust law, and the explanation for it in that
context applies as well to additives:

> There are certain agreements or practices which because of their pernicious effect
> on competition and lack of any redeeming virtue are conclusively presumed to be
> unreasonable and therefore illegal without elaborate inquiry as to the precise harm
> they have caused or the business excuse for their use. This principle of *per se*
> unreasonableness not only makes the type of restraints which are proscribed by the
> Sherman Act more certain to the benefit of everyone concerned, but it also avoids the
> necessity for an incredibly complicated and prolonged economic investigation into the
> entire history of the industry involved, as well as related industries, in an effort to
> determine at large whether a particular restraint has been unreasonable—an inquiry so
> often wholly fruitless when undertaken.

Northern Pac. Ry. Co. v. United States, 356 U.S. 1, 5 (1958). Professor Lawrence Sullivan has
ably articulated the conditions under which the application of a *per se* rule is justified:

> [A] *per se* approach is justified when it applies to conduct which in most instances will
> be harmful to competition, which in few if any will help competition (and then
> probably not greatly) and which is of such a nature that it will be difficult in individual
> cases to identify benefits with certainty or, if they are identified, to measure their
> magnitude relative to harm.

L. SULLIVAN, ANTITRUST 238 (1977).

condition must be met. It must also be the case that the cost of distinguishing the exceptional substances from the ones that follow the general case is greater than the excess of the exceptions' benefits over their risks. That is to say, it must cost more to find the exceptions than they are worth. If these two conditions are met, then society is better served if an agency is not permitted to inquire into and weigh the economic benefits of substances suggested to be harmful.[887]

The group of substances for which these conditions are most likely to be met is food additives;[888] but even as to this category of substances, substantial political controversy exists. Congress will soon have the opportunity to reconsider whether the "health only" approach is appropriate for food additive regulation, or at least for the regulation of potentially carcinogenic additives. The "health only" policy of the Delaney Clause and of the general safety provisions in the Food Additives Amendment came under extreme pressure in 1977 as a result of FDA's attempt to ban the use of saccharin as an additive, and Congress exempted the substance from the requirements of the FDCA, at least temporarily.[889]

It would not be easy to extend the *per se* rule to any other category of toxic substances. Some workplace toxic substances are of little social utility, but many are very valuable. The same is true of air and water pollutants. One could generate little agreement that the two conditions for the *per se* rule are satisfied for these classes of substances. When the conditions are not met, society is better off with honest, complex balancing decisions.

Developments in the implementation of the hazardous air pollutant and toxic water pollutant programs support this analysis. As is discussed

---

887.   Another possible justification for the *per se* rule is that although the best regulatory results might be achieved by honest and neutral balancing of the risks and benefits of each food additive, this cannot be expected of an agency such as FDA. According to this view, FDA is dominated by the industries it is charged with regulating, and the agency is prone to giving economic factors too much weight as a result of industry pressure. Thus the *per se* rule is needed to counterbalance industry pressure; in practice, according to this view, the weighing of risks and benefits will continue to occur behind the scenes and the results will approximate the ideal results to be expected of a neutral agency. However, this approach is likely to *magnify* the error in the agency's decisions rather than cancel it out. In some cases, the agency would apply the *per se* rule to the letter; if one believes that such action gives too little attention to benefits, then these decisions err on the side of over-protection. In other cases, the agency would take no action at all rather than apply the *per se* rule; if one believes that such action gives too little attention to risks, then these decisions err on the side of under-protection. The total divergence from ideal results is large. Thus the justification of the *per se* rule as a counterbalance to industry pressure is flawed. If one believes in case-by-case balancing of risks and benefits, a better strategy would be to increase consumer representatives' pressure on FDA, and thereby cancel the industry bias.

888.   Although sufficient empirical work has not been done, it seems that in general food additives do not confer large economic benefits. Particularly when the hazard involved is a risk of cancer, it is possible that even the most valuable additives are not worth the bargain. Moreover, it is harder than it might seem to verify that the additives asserted to be most valuable, such as DES, do in fact offer large economic benefits. *See* Freedman, *supra* note 492, at 279 n.167, 274-76.

889.   The Saccharin Study and Labeling Act prohibits any regulation of saccharin other

above,[890] EPA has interpreted section 112 of the Clean Air Act to permit some balancing, despite its apparent contrary meaning. In terms of governmental process values, this decision would have been better made by Congress than by the agency, but as a matter of health policy it has been grudgingly conceded even by the environmental groups.[891] As for section 307(a) of FWPCA, in 1977 Congress amended the statute specifically to permit the consideration of economic factors.[892]

The major difficulty with the statutes that require balancing is that the usual broad delegation to determine a "reasonable" balance provides agencies with little meaningful guidance on the relative weights to accord economic factors and health and environmental interests. Rather than making this policy judgment itself, Congress has delegated the policy making role to the agencies.[893] The very existence of the toxic substances control laws indicates a national judgment that unregulated commerce does not protect health and the environment adequately. But the statutes do not indicate how high the agencies are to elevate these concerns above the level of attention they would otherwise receive.

On occasion, Congress is able to give explicit consideration to the risks and benefits associated with particular chemicals and to determine how the costs of regulation are to be allocated. Prominent examples are the 90 percent reductions in selected auto emissions mandated in 1970 by the Clean Air Act,[894] the regulation of lead-based paint,[895] the ban on polychlorinated biphenyls mandated by TSCA,[896] and the moratorium on banning saccha-

---

than labeling until spring 1979. Pub. L. No. 95-203, § 3, 91 Stat. 1451 (1977) (to be codified as a note to 21 U.S.C. § 348). The Act also calls for a study of the wisdom of the "health only" approach, both in the specific context of saccharin, and in the general case. *Id.* § 2(a)-(b) (to be codified as a note to 21 U.S.C. § 343). Section 2(a)(1) requires studies of:

    (B) the direct and indirect health benefits and risks to individuals from foods which contain carcinogenic or other toxic substances:

    . . . .

    (D) instances in which requirements to restrict or prohibit the use of such substances do not accord with the relationship between such benefits and risks; and

    (E) the relationship between existing Federal food regulatory policy and existing Federal regulatory policy applicable to carcinogenic and other toxic substances used as other than foods.

FDA is to report to Congress at the end of the period with the results of this and other studies. *Id.* § 2(c). At that time Congress may re-evaluate the food additives law.

    890. See text accompanying notes 401-409 *supra*.

    891. At an EPA hearing on whether to adopt the "zero-emissions" goal as general policy for hazardous air pollutants, Environmental Defense Fund attorney Robert Rauch indicated that the environmental group would concede that some balancing should be allowed, in exchange for a substantial increase in the number of substances that EPA would regulate. *Industry Supports EPA Approach To Control Of Airborne Carcinogens*, 1 BNA CHEM. REG. REP.—CURR. REP. 1989 (1978).

    892. See text accompanying notes 706-709 *supra*.

    893. *See, e.g.*, Industrial Union Dep't, AFL-CIO v. Hodgson, 499 F.2d 467 (D.C. Cir. 1974): "[OSH Act] sets forth general policy objectives and establishes the basic procedural framework for the promulgation of standards, but the formulation of specific substances provisions is left largely to [OSHA]." *Id.* at 474 (citation omitted).

    894. Clean Air Act § 202(b), Pub. L. No. 91-604, 84 Stat. 1676 (1970), amended by Pub. L. No. 95-95 (1977), now codified at 42 U.S.C.A. § 7521 (West Supp. 1978).

    895. 42 U.S.C.A. § 4841(3) (West Supp. 1978).

    896. TSCA § 6(e)(2)(A), 15 U.S.C.A. § 2065(e)(2)(A) (West Supp. 1978).

rin.[897] However, there are several reasons why direct congressional regulation of toxic substances is not an adequate control strategy. First, the number of substances is far too great for Congress to give many chemicals the amount of attention that the substances mentioned above have received. Second, there is a serious danger that these decisions would become more heavily politicized than they are when in the hands of administrative agencies.

Thus it falls to the agencies to develop clear policies on the balancing issue. They have not yet succeeded in doing so, either through statements of general policy or through individual decisions.[898] Nonetheless, some tentative initiatives in this direction are now discernible. For example, in its proposed cancer policy, OSHA has stated its intention to set a zero emissions standard for those carcinogens which have safer, "suitable" substitutes.[899] The criteria defining "suitable," however, remain to be articulated. OSHA, like the other toxic substances control agencies, has discovered that in this highly controversial field, attempts to be specific may be severely criticized, whereas more vague statements about the balancing of interests are more difficult to attack. Thus the agencies' incentives work against specificity.[900] Nonetheless, the development of more specific criteria for balancing judgments is an important goal.[901]

2. *Precautionary Regulations*

A necessary feature of adequate toxic substances control legislation is that it must permit regulation that is to some extent precautionary.[902] Often definite proof that a substance is harmful to health or the environment can be found only after unacceptable harm has already occurred. To prevent such harm from occurring, it is necessary to take action on uncertain, suggestive evidence.[903] To be sure, this approach is not without its costs. While a lowered standard of proof increases the chances that dangerous chemicals will be correctly identified, it also increases the chances that safe chemicals will be falsely labeled dangerous. To a point, the trade-off is advantageous; the harm avoided may be more valuable than the economic benefits lost.[904]

Nearly all of the health and environmental statutes authorize precautionary regulation. The statutes allow regulation of "risks,"[905] of sub-

---

897. Saccharin Study and Labeling Act, Pub. L. No. 95-203, § 3, 91 Stat. 1451 (1977) (to be codified as a note to 21 U.S.C. § 348).

898. With respect to OSHA, see Berger & Riskin, *supra* note 171. *See also* Karch, *supra* note 859.

899. *OSHA Cancer Policy Proposal, supra* note 252, at 54,148.

900. *See* NATIONAL ACADEMY OF SCIENCES, DECISION MAKING IN THE ENVIRONMENTAL PROTECTION AGENCY 32-33 (1977) [hereinafter cited as DECISION MAKING IN EPA].

901. *See id.* at 32-36.

902. *See* Ethyl Corp. v. EPA, 541 F.2d 1, 6-7, 13, 8 ERC 1785, 1786, 1791-92 (D.C. Cir. 1976).

903. See text accompanying notes 23-72 *supra*.

904. *See* Page, *supra* note 11, at 236-39.

905. *E.g.*, TSCA § 6(a), 15 U.S.C.A. § 2605(a) (West Supp. 1978); FEPCA § 2(bb), 7 U.S.C. § 136(bb) (Supp. V 1975); HMTA § 104, 49 U.S.C. § 1803 (Supp. V 1975).

stances that "may" be harmful,[906] that "endanger" health,[907] or that are not "reasonably certain" to be harmless.[908] All of these phrases free the agencies of the need to demonstrate actual, past harm in order to take protective action.[909] Some of the statutes spell out explicitly a necessary corollary—that after considering uncertain, suggestive evidence in the threshold decision whether to regulate a substance, an agency may consider such evidence in determining what action to take. These statutes state criteria such as that standards shall "provide an ample margin of safety to protect the public health,"[910] or that they shall assure the "highest degree of health and safety protection."[911]

After some division in the mid-1970s, the cases reviewing agency decisions are now united in confirming the precautionary intent of these statutes.[912] The cases reject the contention that under these laws agencies must show "actual harm" before they may take action; rather, the cases hold that the statutes give the agencies the authority to resolve uncertainties

---

906. *E.g.*, Clean Air Act § 112(a)(1), 42 U.S.C.A. § 7412(a)(1) (West Supp. 1978); SDWA § 1401(1)(B), 42 U.S.C. § 300f(1)(B) (Supp. V 1976); FDCA § 601(a), 21 U.S.C. § 361(a) (1970) (cosmetics).

907. *E.g.*, Clean Air Act § 211(c)(1), 42 U.S.C.A. § 7542(c)(1) (West Supp. 1978). *See* OSH Act § 6(c)(1)(A), 29 U.S.C. § 655(c)(1)(A) (1970) (exposure to "grave danger").

908. S. REP. NO. 85-2422, 85th Cong., 2d Sess. 6 (1958) (legislative history for the term "safe" in the Food Additives Amendment).

The one exception is the definition of toxic water pollutant, which states that such a pollutant "*will*, on the basis of information available to the Administrator, cause" specified adverse effects. FWPCA § 502(12), 33 U.S.C.A. § 1362(13) (West Supp. 1978) (emphasis added).

There was formerly another exception. Before passage of the 1977 amendments to the Clean Air Act, one requirement for designating an air pollutant for which an ambient air quality standard would be set was that the pollutant "has an adverse effect on public health or welfare." Clean Air Act § 108(a)(1)(A), Pub. L. No. 91-604, 84 Stat. 1676 (1970) (prior to 1977 amendment). This phrase was construed in dictum in *Ethyl Corp. v. EPA* to require a showing of actual harm. 541 F.2d 1, 14-15, 8 ERC 1785, 1792-93 (D.C. Cir. 1976). In 1977, Congress amended § 108 to allow EPA to set an ambient air quality standard for a pollutant without first showing that it has caused actual harm. Pub. L. No. 95-95, § 401(a), 91 Stat. 790 (1977). The section now requires only that emissions of the pollutant "cause or contribute to air pollution which may reasonably be anticipated to endanger public health or welfare." Clean Air Act § 108(a)(1)(A), 42 U.S.C.A. § 7408(a)(1)(A) (West Supp. 1978).

909. *See, e.g.*, Ethyl Corp. v. EPA, 541 F.2d 1, 13-32, 8 ERC 1785, 1791-1808 (D.C. Cir. 1976).

910. Clean Air Act § 112(b)(1)(B), 42 U.S.C.A. § 7412(b)(1)(B) (West Supp. 1978); FWPCA § 307(a)(4), 33 U.S.C.A. § 1317(a)(4) (West Supp. 1978).

911. OSH Act § 6(b)(5), 29 U.S.C. § 655(b)(5) (1970).

912. See cases cited in note 913 *infra*. This was also the primary issue in Ethyl Corp. v. EPA, 541 F.2d 1, 8 ERC 1785 (D.C. Cir. 1976), which concerned EPA's regulations ordering the removal of lead additives from gasoline as a health hazard. The court construed the phrase "will endanger" in § 211(c)(1)(A) not to require proof of actual harm; the court characterized this sort of regulation as precautionary. 541 F.2d at 12-32, 8 ERC at 1791-1808 (D.C. Cir. 1976).

In 1977, Congress amended § 211 to make the precautionary construction doubly certain. EPA now may take action against any fuel or fuel additive if an emission product "causes, or contributes to, air pollution which may reasonably be anticipated to endanger the public health or welfare." Pub. L. No. 95-95, § 401(e), 91 Stat. 791 (1977), codified at 42 U.S.C.A. § 7545(c)(1)(A) (West Supp. 1978). See note 908 *supra*.

in order to take protective action. In so doing, an agency is exercising a congressionally delegated power to make policy, rather than finding facts as would a district court.[913]

The cases describe the functional relationships governing decision making under uncertainty. The agencies may assess risks; this involves a joint consideration of the certainty, probability, and magnitude of a harm. A high probability of a relatively minor harm may justify action; so may a low probability of an extremely serious harm. Moreover, the more severe the

---

913.   The two key cases on this subject are Ethyl Corp. v. EPA, 541 F.2d 1, 8 ERC 1785 (D.C. Cir. 1976) and Industrial Union Dep't, AFL-CIO v. Hodgson, 499 F.2d 467 (D.C. Cir. 1974). In *Industrial Union*, which reviewed the OSHA asbestos standard, the court stated:

> In a statute like [OSH Act] where the decision making vested in OSHA is legislative in character, there are areas where explicit factual findings are not possible, and the act of decision is essentially a prediction based upon pure legislative judgment, as when a Congressman decides to to vote for or against a particular bill.
>
> [OSH Act] sets forth general policy objectives and establishes the basic procedural framework for the promulgation of standards, but the formulation of specific substantive provisions is left largely to [OSHA].
>
> . . . .
>
> [S]ome of the questions involved in the promulgation of these standards are on the frontiers of scientific knowledge, and consequently as to them insufficient data is presently available to make a fully informed factual determination. Decision making must in that circumstance depend to a greater extent upon policy judgments and less upon purely factual analysis. Thus, in addition to currently unresolved factual issues, the formulation of standards involves choices that by their nature require basic policy determinations rather than resolution of factual controversies. . . .
>
> For example, in this case the evidence indicated that reliable data is not currently available with respect to the precisely predictable health effects of various levels of exposure to asbestos dust; nevertheless, [OSHA] was obligated to establish some specific level as the maximum permissible exposure. After considering all the conflicting evidence, [OSHA] explained [its] decision to adopt, over strong employer objection, a relatively low limit in terms of the severe health consequences which could result from over-exposure. Inasmuch as the protection of the health of employees is the overriding concern of OSHA, this choice is doubtless sound, but it rests in the final analysis on an essentially legislative policy judgment, rather than a factual determination, concerning the relative risks of underprotection as compared to over-protection.

499 F.2d at 474-75 (footnotes omitted). The same court, reviewing EPA's gasoline additive standard, stated in *Ethyl Corp.*:

> Where a statute is precautionary in nature, the evidence difficult to come by, uncertain, or conflicting because it is on the frontiers of scientific knowledge, the regulations designed to protect the public health, and the decision that of an expert administrator, we will not demand rigorous step-by-step proof of cause and effect. Such proof may be impossible to obtain if the precautionary purpose of the statute is to be served. Of course, we are not suggesting that the Administrator has the power to act on hunches or wild guesses. . . . However, we do hold that in such cases the Administrator may assess risks. He must take account of available facts, of course, but his inquiry does not end there. The Administrator may apply his expertise to draw conclusions from suspected, but not completely substantiated, relationships between facts, from trends among facts, from theoretical projections from imperfect data, from probative preliminary data not yet certifiable as "fact," and the like. We believe that a conclusion so drawn—a risk assessment—may, if rational, form the basis for health-related regulations under the "will endanger" language of Section 211.

541 F.2d at 28, 8 ERC at 1804 (citation and footnotes omitted). *See also* Amoco Oil Co. v. EPA, 501 F.2d 722, 740-41, 6 ERC 1481, 1492-93 (D.C. Cir. 1974).

For cases from other circuits taking similar positions, see cases cited in note 860 *supra. See also* Reserve Mining Co. v. EPA, 514 F.2d 492, 528, 7 ERC 1618, 1642 (8th Cir. 1975).

possible harm, the less certainty the cases demand concerning the probability of its occurrence.[914]

Ultimately, if the statute requires, the product of this assessment must be balanced against the substance's benefits, which have been assessed separately in a similar fashion.[915] Although there is less case law reviewing the assessment of benefits, the same considerations apply concerning uncertainty.[916] The uncertainty concerning the economic consequences of a regulation often equals or exceeds the uncertainty surrounding health effects.[917] An agency must assess the certainty, probability, and magnitude of economic effects as well.

These functional relationships are extraordinarily difficult to pin down with any precision. Neither Congress, the agencies, nor the courts have found ways to make and state finely-tuned conclusions on the basis of information as uncertain as that characteristic of toxic substances control problems. This difficulty is not surprising; the descriptive language can be no more exact than the underlying information.

Some commentators have suggested, however, that the agencies' decision making under uncertainty is not as exact as it could be.[918] They have observed that the agencies and courts often use conclusory, result-oriented adjectives to describe risks and costs that could be described, at least roughly, in a quantitative manner. For example, automotive lead was termed a "significant risk" to urban children;[919] the pesticides aldrin, dieldrin, heptachlor, and chlordane were said to pose a "substantial likelihood of harm" to the public.[920] On other occasions, the agencies and courts use similar language to describe contrary conclusions; FDA permitted food additives to be marketed if they pose "no significant risk of harm."[921] The

---

914. See Ethyl Corp. v. EPA, 541 F.2d 1, 18, 8 ERC 1785, 1795-96 (D.C. Cir. 1976); Environmental Defense Fund v. Ruckelshaus, 439 F.2d 584, 595, 2 ERC 1114, 1120 (D.C. Cir. 1971); Wellford v. Ruckelshaus, 439 F.2d 598, 601-02, 2 ERC 1123, 1124-25 (D.C. Cir. 1971). *See also* Carolina Environmental Study Group v. United States, 510 F.2d 796, 799, 7 ERC 1675, 1677-78 (D.C. Cir. 1975); Reserve Mining Co. v. EPA. 514 F.2d 492, 519-20, 7 ERC 1618, 1636-37 (8th Cir. 1975).

915. See Environmental Defense Fund v. EPA, 465 F.2d 528, 539-41, 4 ERC 1523, 1530-32 (D.C. Cir. 1972); Environmental Defense Fund v. EPA, 548 F.2d 998, 1010-12, 9 ERC 1433, 1442-43 (D.C. Cir. 1977).

916. See, e.g., Industrial Union Dep't, AFL-CIO v. Hodgson, 499 F.2d 467, 478-81 (D.C. Cir. 1974); Society of Plastics Indus., Inc. v. OSHA, 509 F.2d 1301, 1308-10 (2nd Cir. 1975), *cert. denied* 421 U.S. 992 (1975).

917. See text accompanying notes 61-78 *supra*.

918. DECISION MAKING IN EPA, *supra* note 900, at 32-36.

919. Ethyl Corp. v. EPA, 541 F.2d 1, 12, 8 ERC 1785, 1790 (D.C. Cir. 1976) (affirming the EPA Administrator's construction of the "will endanger" standard and his analysis of the evidence).

920. See, e.g., Environmental Defense Fund v. EPA, 510 F.2d 1292, 1297, 7 ERC 1689, 1690-91 (D.C. Cir. 1975); Environmental Defense Fund v. EPA, 548 F.2d 998, 1005, 9 ERC 1433, 1436 (D.C. Cir. 1976) (both cases affirming agency findings of "imminent hazard" on the ground that substantial evidence showed that the substances involved posed a "substantial likelihood" of "significant harm.").

921. 36 Fed. Reg. 12,093 (1971) (codified at 21 C.F.R. § 121.1(i) (1972)). The regulation has since been amended to require "a reasonable certainty in the minds of competent scientists that the substance is not harmful." 42 Fed. Reg. 14,483 (1977) (codified at 21 C.F.R. § 170.3 (1977)).

commentators have urged the agencies to avoid these result-oriented terms and to try to state conclusions more precisely. Preferably, agencies would make rough quantitative, probabilistic statements, indicating the range within which the truth is likely to lie. This approach probably would sharpen evaluations somewhat, and it would decrease the chances that observers will be influenced by the choices of adjectives rather than by the data and policy considerations themselves.[922]

In general, in light of the ambiguity of these terms and the uncertainty of the underlying data, it would not be productive to attempt to distinguish fine gradations in the statutes' standards of proof. From time to time, cases have suggested that a "significant risk" is an event less certain than a "substantial likelihood," and that certain evidence could satisfy the former standard and not the latter.[923] It is difficult to imagine either an agency or a court reliably administering these fine differences. Perhaps for this reason, a later case from the same court specifically avoided making the particular distinction mentioned above.[924]

There is one exception to this generalization; in TSCA, Congress succeeded in creating two distinguishable degrees of uncertainty.[925] If a chemical "may present" an unreasonable risk, EPA must subject it to certain testing requirements.[926] But if EPA has "a reasonable basis to conclude" that the substance "presents or will present" an unreasonable risk, the agency may ban the substance or restrict its use.[927] Both standards are precautionary, since both use the probabilistic term "risk." One, however, implies greater knowledge than the other. The legislative history indicates that the former standard describes the situation when "there is a basis of concern, but . . . inadequate information to reasonably predict or determine [a substance's] effects on health or the environment."[928] This standard governs when EPA should require more testing. The second standard applies when sufficient information for safety evaluation has been compiled. This standard should be considered equivalent to those already discussed.

Recognition by the federal agencies that the statutes' standards of proof are for all practical purposes equivalent would make possible more frequent joint regulation of chemicals by two or more agencies. The doubt as to whether more certain evidence is needed to support regulation under some

---

922. Decision Making in EPA, *supra* note 900, at 32-36.

923. Ethyl Corp. v. EPA, 541 F.2d 1, 16 n.28, 8 ERC 1785, 1794 n.28 (D.C. Cir. 1976).

924. Environmental Defense Fund v. EPA, 548 F.2d 998, 1005 n.15, 9 ERC 1433, 1436 n.15 (D.C. Cir. 1976).

925. The observations in this paragraph are derived from Slesin & Sandler, *supra* note 11, at 365-67.

926. TSCA § 4(a), 15 U.S.C.A. § 2063(a) (West Supp. 1978). *See also id*. § 5(b)(4)(A)(i), (e), 15 U.S.C.A. § 2064(b)(4)(A)(i), (e) (West Supp. 1978).

927. *Id*. § 6, 15 U.S.C.A. § 2065 (West Supp. 1978).

928. H.R. Rep. No. 1679, 94th Cong., 2d Sess. 61 (1976) (Conference Report).

statutes than under others has deterred such cooperation in the past. Currently, a work group of the IRLG is conducting a comparative analysis of the
toxic substances control statutes.[929] The IRLG group would be the appropriate body to assert the statutes' agreement on this issue, as part of its effort to
increase cooperation and consistency among the four member agencies.

3. Allocating the Burden of Persuasion

The toxic substances control statutes differ in allocating the burden of
persuasion. Under some statutes, the government bears the burden of showing that the use of a substance should be controlled; under others the
proponent of a substance's use bears the burden of showing that it should not
be controlled. The difference governs who must produce data and how the
agencies must resolve uncertainties in close decisions. The latter element,
the ultimate burden of persuasion, is the focus here.[930] The different allocations of this burden reflect congressional policy judgments as to whether, for
particular categories of uses or sources of exposure, there should be a basic
presumption in favor of health and environmental protection, or in favor of
economic activity.[931]

Among the statutes applicable to VC, the allocations of the burden of
persuasion break down along the following lines. The proponent of use
bears the burden for pesticides, food additives, drugs, and medical devices.[932] The agencies bear the burden regarding toxic substances in the
workplace, air and water pollutants, drinking water contaminants, materials
in transportation, cosmetics, consumer products, and currently used chemical substances covered by TSCA.[933]

In close cases, the allocation of the burden of persuasion can significantly affect decisions. For example, under the Food Additives Amendment—a "health only" statute that places the burden on the manufacturer—
uncertain, suggestive evidence of harm may be sufficient to block a finding
that an additive is safe, even though the evidence would not be sufficient to
support a finding that the additive is unsafe.[934] In contrast, under the
provisions of FDCA dealing with cosmetics—a "health only" statute that
places the burden on FDA—on comparable evidence the agency would have
to reach the opposite result.[935]

---

929. *IRLG Work Plans, supra* note 850, at 7192.

930. The burden of production issue is complex and is peripheral to this Article's
concerns. For an illuminating discussion of the burden of production under FEPCA, see Note,
Pesticide Regulation: Risk Assessment and Burden of Proof, 45 GEO. WASH. L. REV. 1066
(1977).

931. *See generally* Krier, *Environmental Litigation and the Burden of Proof*, in LAW AND
THE ENVIRONMENT 105, 107-108 (M. Baldwin & J. Page, eds. 1970).

932. See text accompanying notes 489, 562-566, 780 *supra*.

933. See text accompanying notes 192-201, 369, 573-579, 621-623, 641-643, 662-663, 797
supra.

934. See Freedman, *supra* note 492, at 271-72. *See also* Certified Color Manufacturers Ass'n v. Matthews, 543 F.2d 284, 287, 297-98 (D.C. Cir. 1976), interpreting similar
provisions of the 1960 Color Additive Amendments, 21 U.S.C. § 376 (1970).

935. See text accompanying notes 573-577 *supra*.

The same impact is to be expected under the statutes that require balancing of health and economic interests. Under FEPCA, which places the burden on the registrant, evidence may be sufficient to preclude a conclusion under the substantial evidence test that a pesticide's benefits outweigh its risks, even though the evidence could not support the conclusion that its risks outweighed its benefits.[936] In contrast, under TSCA, which places the burden on EPA when regulating chemicals already in commerce, comparable evidence would lead to the opposite conclusion.

Surprisingly, the case study of VC does not supply striking examples of the burden of persuasion at work on the margin. Statutes that establish different burdens were directly juxtaposed in the control of aerosols. In this area, however, the outcome was so clear under all of the statutes that differences in the burden of persuasion were academic.[937] The burden of persuasion was an issue in the setting of OSHA's standard, the only VC regulations yet to be litigated on the merits. In *Society of Plastics*, the VC and PVC industries vigorously contended that OSHA lacked sufficient evidence to support its conclusions that a health risk existed at low exposures and that the standard was feasible. However, the court ruled that OSHA had adequately supported both conclusions.[938]

The burden of persuasion has had greater influence in proceedings over substances other than VC. The allocation of the burden may have been determinative in the early cases concerning the regulation of potential carcinogens. In the early 1970s, the idea was just beginning to gain acceptance in regulatory and legal circles that if a chemical induced cancer in laboratory animals, it should be considered to pose a human cancer risk as well, and that agencies need not await confirming human evidence before promulgating safety and health regulations.[939] Animal evidence played an important role in EPA's decision to end most uses of DDT in 1972.[940] The fact that the pesticide statute places the burden of persuasion on the registrant may have been essential to EPA's decision,[941] and to the District of Columbia Circuit Court of Appeals' decision to sustain the agency.[942]

Since then the sufficiency of such evidence standing alone has gained

---

936. *See generally* Environmental Defense Fund v. EPA, 548 F.2d 998, 1004, 9 ERC 1433, 1436-37 (D.C. Cir. 1977).

937. See text accompanying notes 607-608 *supra*. The burden of persuasion is important in determining whether VC from PVC food packaging may reasonably be expected to migrate into foods. This is a jurisdictional issue, however, rather than a substantive one; it determines only which section of FDCA applies to packaging. See text accompanying notes 495-496 *supra*.

938. Society of Plastics Indus., Inc. v. OSHA, 509 F.2d 1301, 1308-10 (2d Cir. 1975), *cert. denied* 421 U.S. 992 (1975).

939. *See generally* Karch, *supra* note 859.

940. EPA, *In re Stevens Industries, et al.*, 37 Fed. Reg. 13,369, 13,371 (1972).

941. *Id.* at 13,375.

942. Environmental Defense Fund v. EPA, 489 F.2d 1247, 6 ERC 1112 (D.C. Cir. 1973). Prior and subsequent pesticide cases emphasize that the burden of persuasion is on the registrant. *See* Environmental Defense Fund v. EPA, 548 F.2d 998, 1015, 9 ERC 1575, 1578 (D.C. Cir. 1977) (supplemental opinion) and cases cited therein.

greater acceptance.[943] In 1974, OSHA, which bears the burden of showing the existence of a hazard, set standards for 14 substances whose carcinogenicity was supported by studies on rodents.[944] The Third Circuit Court of Appeals held that this evidence was sufficient to support a conclusion that regulations were necessary to protect workers.[945] Thus it appears that the allocation of the burden is no longer determinative of this issue; the probative value of the animal tests is now considered great enough that decisions based on such tests no longer rest on the margin that the placement of the burden affects.

But although the allocation of burden of persuasion probably no longer determines the *qualitative* issue of whether a substance presents a human cancer risk, the allocation of the burden still would be expected to affect the *quantitative* issue of how stringent a standard an agency may set. For example, most agencies must show not only that a substance is dangerous at the prevailing exposure level, but also that the exposure reduction they require is warranted in light of its costs. This weighing of uncertain risks and benefits is essentially a matter of degree, and the exposure limit ultimately selected must be defended against relatively close alternatives along a continuum. The allocation of the burden may be expected to affect the stringency of the standard selected. All other things being equal, under FEPCA, EPA probably could set a lower exposure limit than could OSHA under its statute.

The cases to date have focused on the qualitative issues and generally have slighted the importance of the stringency question.[946] But there are reasons why such matters of degree probably will emerge soon as the dominant question for the agencies and the reviewing courts. First, the interested parties, the agencies, and the courts are becoming more sophisticated in their understanding of toxic substances control problems, and they are beginning to see shades of gray rather than just black and white.[947]

---

943. *See generally* Karch, *supra* note 859.

944. 29 C.F.R. §§ 1910.1003-.1016 (1978), promulgated at 39 Fed. Reg. 3756 (1974).

945. Synthetic Organic Chem. Mfrs. Ass'n v. Brennan, 503 F.2d 1155, 1158-61 (3rd Cir. 1974). Two other OSHA standards, for VC and for coke oven emissions, have been upheld on a combination of animal test evidence and evidence of cancer in humans. Society of Plastics Indus., Inc. v. OSHA, 509 F.2d 1301 (2d Cir. 1975), *cert. denied* 421 U.S. 992 (1975) (VC); American Iron & Steel Inst. v. OSHA, — F.2d —, 6 OSHC 1451 (3d. Cir. 1978) (coke oven emissions).

946. To a large extent the cases have focused only on the threshold issue of whether the need for any regulation has been shown. Rather than press a burden of persuasion argument, industries have argued for a high *standard* of proof. Most of the cases have resolved the issue by holding that a precautionary standard of proof applies, and the issue of the burden of meeting this lesser standard has not been addressed. *See, e.g.*, Ethyl Corp. v. EPA, 541 F.2d 1, 8 ERC 1785 (D.C. Cir. 1976), *cert. denied* 426 U.S. 941 (1976). See text accompanying notes 902-929 *supra*. Nor have the agencies been aggressive about meeting the matters of degree. EPA has not made extensive use of its authority to classify pesticides—*i.e.*, to restrict their uses short of completely cancelling them. *See* Schulberg, *supra* note 570. OSHA has largely avoided the matter of degree in its standards. *See, e.g.*, the preamble to the coke oven emissions standard, 41 Fed. Reg. 46,741, 46,748-51 (1976).

947. *See generally* Karch, *supra* note 859.

Second, as the agencies increase the number of substances that they regulate, pressure will grow to set priorities among substances and to be at least roughly consistent in balancing the risks and benefits of individual substances. The allocation of the burden of persuasion may become more important as more controversies arise involving these matters of degree.[948]

There are limits, however, to the control over decisions that can be achieved through the allocation of the burden of persuasion. An agency or a court cannot administer burden of proof rules without also applying a standard of proof rule and without measuring evidence against the standard. To the extent that the standard cannot be stated precisely and that the evidence is uncertain, it is difficult to determine whether the burden of persuasion has been met.

Ultimately, it is difficult to explain why Congress has allocated the burden of persuasion in the toxic substances control statutes as it has. Historically, food and drugs have been subject to more stringent public health regulation than other sources of exposure to toxic substances.[949] This reflects an understandable assumption that substances taken internally pose a greater hazard than other substances. Allocating the burden to proponents of the use of food additives, pesticides (which are used on foods), drugs, and medical devices probably reflects this assumption. There are anomalies, however. Drinking water would appear equally eligible for such treatment, but nonetheless the burden of persuasion in establishing drinking water standards is on EPA.

More significantly, the assumption that substances taken internally should be subject to more stringent regulations than other substances is itself of doubtful validity. The risks from the vast number of substances in workplaces, the air and water, and consumer products are now equally or more serious than the risks from substances taken internally. It would be appropriate to place the burden of persuasion on the proponents of using these substances as well.

4. Judicial Control Over Agency Decision Making

Some control over agency decisions involving uncertainty and balancing of interests can be found in judicial review, which is available directly

---

948. *See* Leventhal, *Environmental Decisionmaking and the Role of the Courts*, 122 U. PENN. L. REV. 509 (1974):

It is my feeling that the burden of proof concept will be relied upon increasingly in review of technically complex questions by courts which are reluctant, on the one hand, to interfere with the agency's expert manipulations of test data and, on the other, to defer blindly to whatever methodology the agency puts forth in support of its predictions.

Id. at 536. Judge Leventhal was discussing his use of burden of proof concepts to resolve the issue of the automobile makers' ability to meet the original 1975 emission standards established by the 1970 Clean Air Act. *See* International Harvester Co. v. Ruckelshaus, 478 F.2d 615, 643, 4 ERC 2041, 2056 (D.C. Cir. 1973).

949. The Food and Drugs Act of 1906, ch. 3915, 34 Stat. 768 (1906), the progenitor of

under the toxic substances control statutes or indirectly under the Administrative Procedure Act (APA).[950] The APA and the substantive statutes that set out their own procedures all commit to the agencies the assessment and weighing of evidence and making of policy in the first instance. The statutes give the courts a supervisory role in these matters; they are not to "substitute their judgment" for that of the agencies, but nonetheless they must keep agency decisions within certain outer boundaries of reason or rationality.[951] The question of where along this continuum courts should operate is commonly stated as the question of the proper depth or intensity of judicial scrutiny of agency decisions.

The depth of judicial scrutiny defines the minimum test of rationality that an agency's decision must meet. The minimum is important for two reasons. First, as a matter of substantive decision making, it sets limits on the inferences that an agency may draw from uncertain evidence. Second, as a means of managerial control over agency behavior, it establishes minimum standards for how careful and convincing agencies must be in the preparation of decisions.

Judges and scholars have found it difficult either to articulate how intense judicial scrutiny of agency decisions should be, or to describe how intense it is in given cases. Certain trends, however, are clear.[952] In the past, judicial scrutiny was relatively shallow. The agencies had the benefit of a presumption that evidence existed to support their factual conclusions.[953] Often the agencies needed to explain their reasoning and policy judgments to no greater extent than to state conclusorily that a course of action was "in the public interest" or furthered the objectives of the statute.[954] Courts

---

FDCA, was the first federal regulatory statute aimed at chemical contamination. The concern for drug safety has been held great enough under FDCA to warrant imposing strict criminal liability for certain conduct, regardless of a defendant's lack of conscious wrongdoing. United States v. Dotterweich, 320 U.S. 277, 280-81 (1943).

950. 5 U.S.C. §§ 701-706 (1970).

951. *See, e.g.*, Universal Camera Corp. v. NLRB, 340 U.S. 474, 491 (1951); Consolo v. Federal Maritime Commission, 383 U.S. 607, 619-21 (1966); Citizens to Preserve Overton Park v. Volpe, 401 U.S. 402, 415-16, 2 ERC 1250, 1256 (1971).

952. The following discussion of trends in judicial review relies heavily on chapter 29 of K. DAVIS, ADMINISTRATIVE LAW OF THE SEVENTIES 646-87 (1976).

953. *See, e.g.*, Pacific States Box & Basket Co. v. White, 296 U.S. 176, 185-86 (1935).

954. In Environmental Defense Fund v. Ruckelshaus, 439 F.2d 584, 2 ERC 1114 (D.C. Cir. 1971), Chief Judge Bazelon reviewed the old posture and stated the new trend:

We stand on the threshold of a new era in the history of the long and fruitful collaboration of administrative agencies and reviewing courts. For many years, courts have treated administrative policy decisions with great deference, confining judicial attention primarily to matters of procedure. On matters of substance, the courts regularly upheld agency action, with a nod in the direction of the "substantial evidence" test, and a bow to the mysteries of administrative expertise. Courts occasionally asserted, but less often exercised, the power to set aside agency action on the ground that an impermissible factor had entered into the decision, or a crucial factor had not been considered. Gradually, however, that power has come into more frequent use, and with it, the requirement that administrators articulate the factors on which they base their decisions.

Id. at 597, 2 ERC at 1122 (footnotes omitted).

would overturn decisions that were based on policy considerations not relevant or permissible under the applicable statutes; this was viewed as a question of law on which the courts were expert. But they would overturn decisions on factual grounds or on grounds of defects in reasoning only if the agency's conclusions were "entirely at odds" with the facts and logic brought to the courts' attention.[955] On these matters, the courts gave great deference to the agencies' supposed expertise.[956]

With the recent growth of health and environmental regulation and other modern social and economic regulation, this approach to judicial review was severely challenged. In the toxic substances field the subject matters are characterized by tremendous scientific, technological, and economic complexity which often is accessible only to highly trained experts. On the other hand, regulation necessarily takes place under substantial uncertainty, before the mechanisms of disease are fully understood, control processes are fully developed, and economic effects are fully divined.[957] Thus while expertise is necessary to reasoned decision making, it is not sufficient. Decisions must be based largely on assumptions made to resolve unknowns, and underlying these assumptions are policy judgments about whether any error in the agency's resolution of uncertainties should favor one or another interest group.[958] These mixed questions of fact-finding and policy-making dominate the ultimate decisions, and they are the most difficult to control through judicial review.

In response to this development, in the last decade courts have become

---

955. American T. & T. v. United States, 299 U.S. 232, 236-37 (1936).

956. *See, e.g.*, American Trucking Ass'ns v. United States, 344 U.S. 298, 314 (1953). *See also* Radio Corp. of America v. United States, 341 U.S. 412, 419-20 (1951), which was cited in the quotation in note 954 *supra* from *Environmental Defense Fund. See generally* K. DAVIS, *supra* note 952, § 29.01-1, at 654-56.

957. *See generally* Leventhal, *supra* note 948; Wright, *The Courts and the Rulemaking Process: The Limits of Judicial Review*, 59 CORNELL L. REV. 375 (1974).

958. Professor Davis calls this the distinction between "adjudicative" and "legislative" facts. The former are the concrete issues of past fact with which courts are familiar. The latter are more like legislators' policy-based judgments about the true state of facts when the reality is unknown. In most of the modern regulatory statutes Congress delegates to the agencies the authority to make such determinations of "legislative" as well as "adjudicative" fact. K. DAVIS, ADMINISTRATIVE LAW TREATISE § 15.03, at 353-63 (1958).

The legislative and adjudicative fact distinction is not easy to administer at the margin, and courts differ in their categorizations. Compare the treatment of medical uncertainties in Industrial Union Dep't, AFL-CIO v. Hodgson, 499 F.2d 467 (D.C. Cir. 1974), with that in American Iron & Steel Inst. v. OSHA, — F.2d —, 6 OSHC 1451 (3d Cir. 1978). In *Industrial Union*, the court characterized OSHA's conclusions about the carcinogenic risk from various levels of exposure to asbestos dust as a matter of legislative fact. 499 F.2d at 474-75, quoted in note 913 *supra.* In *American Iron & Steel*, the court treated OSHA's conclusions about the similar issue of the human cancer risk from coke oven emissions as a matter of adjudicative fact. — F.2d at —, 6 OSHC at 1456-57. The court in *Industrial Union* subjected the conclusions to the arbitrary or capricious test and upheld them. The other court subjected the conclusions to the substantial evidence test and also upheld them. In view of the doubts that the two review tests differ, see text accompanying notes 970-987 *infra*, the difference in characterization of an issue as a matter of legislative or adjudicative fact makes little difference in the result.

more active in their review of agencies' decisions. The trend has been led principally by the District of Columbia Circuit Court of Appeals, largely in the context of health and environmental regulation, although other courts and other subject matters have also played important roles.[959] The courts have deepened their scrutiny of agencies' factual conclusions, policy judgments, and reasoning, particularly with regard to technically complex, uncertain, and value-laden subject matters.[960] The basic conceptualization of the role of judicial review has remained constant and the statutory standards have not changed The courts continue both to express their role as guaranteeing that decisions are reasonable or rational and to reject substituting their judgment for that of the agencies. Nevertheless, many agency decisions that would have passed muster in the past would fail today, either because the agencies failed to support critical factual conclusions adequately or because they failed to explain adequately how the interaction of these conclusions and their policy judgments leads to their ultimate decisions. The outer boundaries of reason or rationality have been constricted substantially.[961]

Deeper judicial scrutiny has imposed certain minimum standards on agency decision making, in the interest of producing "reasoned" and "principled" decisions.[962] The agencies now must state the critical facts on which they rely.[963] They must explain the rationale for the methodologies by which they make predictions or extrapolations from data.[964] They must explain the assumptions they make to resolve unknowns and they must indicate the policies behind those assumptions.[965] The agencies must also explain the policies by which they balance competing interests.[966] In the notice-and-comment process or at a hearing, interested parties must have

---

959. The discussion below considers mainly District of Columbia Circuit cases. It is not meant to be an exhaustive treatment.

960. *See, e.g.*, Greater Boston Television Corp. v. FCC, 444 F.2d 841 (D.C. Cir. 1970); International Harvester Co. v. Ruckelshaus, 478 F.2d 615, 4 ERC 2041 (D.C. Cir. 1973).

961. Davis states that although the reasonableness of decisions remains the criterion, "what has happened in the 1970's is that the determination of what is 'reasonable' has been vastly elaborated, and in the process of elaboration the courts have sometimes increased the intensity of their review. In determining what rules are 'reasonable,' the courts did not until recently inquire into the factual basis of rules; now they often do." K. DAVIS, *supra* note 952, § 29.01-1, at 654-55.

In Citizens to Preserve Overton Park v. Volpe, 401 U.S. 402, 2 ERC 1250 (1971), the Supreme Court reaffirmed that the presumption of the existence of facts to support an administrative decision still stands, but that the presumption "is not to shield his action from probing, in-depth review." *Id*. at 415, 2 ERC at 1256. Davis states that although the presumption is still nominally in effect, it is on the decline. K. DAVIS, *supra* note 952, § 6.01, at 170.

962. Greater Boston Television Corp. v. FCC, 444 F.2d 841, 851 (D.C. Cir. 1970); Environmental Defense Fund v. Ruckelshaus, 439 F.2d 584, 598, 2 ERC 1114, 1122 (D.C. Cir. 1971); International Harvester Co. v. Ruckelshaus, 478 F.2d 615, 648, 4 ERC 2041, 2061 (D.C. Cir. 1973).

963. *See* K. DAVIS, *supra* note 952, § 6.01-2, at 172-76 and cases cited therein.

964. International Harvester Co. v. Ruckelshaus, 478 F.2d 615, 642-43, 4 ERC 2041, 2056 (D.C. Cir. 1973).

965. Industrial Union Dep't, AFL-CIO v. Hodgson, 499 F.2d 467, 475-76 (D.C. Cir. 1974).

966. *Id*.

notice of the key facts and issues and an opportunity to present contrary data, arguments about abstruse analytical methodologies, and arguments about the policy matters at issue.[967]

These minimum standards have improved the fairness, openness, and ultimate quality of agency decision making. Missing facts, gross flaws in reasoning, and statutorily irrelevant or prohibited policy judgments tend to come to the courts' attention. Perhaps most important is the self-disciplinary effect on the agencies. Many of these defects come to light in the decision making process. Gaps can be remedied or conclusions altered prior to the issuance of final decisions.[968]

But while more intensive judicial review has brought these benefits, it does not permit close control of the agencies' factual conclusions and policy judgments.[969] The agencies still have wide latitude in drawing their conclu-

---

967.   Portland Cement Ass'n v. Ruckelshaus, 486 F.2d 375, 392-393, 5 ERC 1593, 1604-05 (D.C. Cir. 1973).

In the 1970s the courts were developing two conceptually distinct means of accomplishing the end results described above. One means is "substantive" review, in which the court examines the record of a decision for adequate support and explanation and typically remands for further proceedings if the record is found inadequate. *See, e.g.*, *Portland Cement*. *See also* Associated Industries of N.Y.S. v. United States Dep't of Labor, 487 F.2d 342, 353 (2d Cir. 1973). The other means was "procedural review," in which the court would order an agency to use adversarial techniques (such as cross-examination) in excess of what is required by APA § 553 when the court believed these procedures to be necessary to air the issues adequately and to generate an adequate record. The implication was that better results would flow from better procedures. *See, e.g.*, International Harvester Co. v. Ruckelshaus, 478 F.2d 615, 649, 4 ERC 2041, 2061 (D.C. Cir. 1973) (opinion of Leventhal, J.); *id.* at 652, 4 ERC at 2062-63 (concurring opinion of Bazelon, C.J.). *See* Williams, *"Hybrid Rulemaking" under the Administrative Procedure Act: A Legal and Empirical Analysis*, 42 U.CHI. L. REV. 401 (1975), and cases discussed therein. *See also* Natural Resources Defense Council v. Nuclear Regulatory Comm'n, 547 F.2d 633, 644, 653-54, 9 ERC 1149, 1157, 1165-66 (D.C. Cir. 1976) (opinion of Bazelon, C.J.); *id.* at 655-57, 9 ERC at 1167-69 (separate opinion of Bazelon, C.J.), *reversed sub nom.* Vermont Yankee Nuclear Power Corp. v. Natural Resources Defense Council, 98 S. Ct. 1197, 11 ERC 1437 (1978).

This line of cases came to an abrupt halt with *Vermont Yankee*. In this case the Supreme Court held that while agencies may adopt procedures in excess of those required by APA § 553 of their own accord, the courts have no power to order them to do so, except possibly in unspecified, "extremely rare circumstances. The Court reaffirmed the propriety of substantive review, but held that procedural matters were the responsibility of Congress and the agencies. *Id.* at 1202-03, 1211-14, 11 ERC at 1440, 1447-50. The Court endorsed the view expressed by Judge Wright, *supra* note 957, at 386-88, that ad hoc procedural review would encourage the agencies to be cautious and to err on the side of using excessively formal procedures; this would lead to a loss of the advantages of notice-and-comment rulemaking. *Id.* at 1213-14, 11 ERC at 1450.

Prior to the Supreme Court's decision in *Vermont Yankee*, Judge Friendly had expressed doubt that outcomes would differ if courts were restricted to substantive review alone. Practically speaking, agencies may still have to adopt some adversarial procedures in order to generate a record that will withstand substantive review. Friendly, *Some Kind of Hearing*, 123 U. PENN. L. REV. 1267, 1313-14 (1975).

968.   For a strong endorsement of the self-disciplinary effect, as well as the general value of current review practices, see Pederson, *Formal Records and Informal Rulemaking*, 85 YALE L.J. 38, 59-60 (1975).

969.   This would be true at least so long as the bar against substituting judgment is respected. If it were not, then it would be necessary to control the courts' decision making. See Judge Friendly's warning that it may be difficult for courts to avoid intruding too deeply into

sions, within which there is room for widely differing regulations.[970] The limits of judicial control are illustrated by two related problems that currently beset judges and scholars: whether there is a difference between the standards of review established in the APA and other statutes, and how much deference to give agency fact-finding, policy-making, and reasoning under the more deferential standard (assuming the standards differ).

The toxic substances control statutes establish three nominally distinct tests for judicial review.[971] Under some of the statutes agency decisions must be upheld unless they are "arbitrary, capricious, an abuse of discretion, or otherwise not in accordance with law."[972] Under other statutes decisions must be upheld if supported by "substantial evidence" in the record of the decision.[973] Two statutes, the Food Additives Amendment and FHSA, establish a third test; a decision is to be upheld if it is supported by "a fair evaluation" of the record before the agency.[974]

The substantial evidence test is conventionally thought to call for deeper scrutiny than the arbitrary and capricious test.[975] Both tests call for a weighing of evidence both for and against a conclusion. The former test is said to require "such relevant evidence as a reasonable mind might accept as adequate to support a conclusion."[976] The latter test is said to call for a somewhat lesser degree of rationality.[977] The fair evaluation test has never

---

agency decision making, in Associated Indus. of N.Y.S. v. United States Dep't of Labor, 487 F.2d 342, 354 (2d Cir. 1973).

970. Pederson, *supra* note 968, at 49-50; Wright, *supra* note 957, at 392.

971. There are two exceptions which require *de novo* court actions. First, unlike sections pertaining to other regulated items, FDCA §§ 601-602, pertaining to cosmetics, include no provision for the issuance of regulations. FDA therefore must regulate cosmetics through proceedings in district court, in which the agency must prove to a court that the cosmetic or a contaminant of it "may be injurious to health." FDCA §§ 302, 601-602, 701, 21 U.S.C. §§ 333, 361-362, 371 (1970).

Second, EPA may issue a proposal order blocking the marketing of a new chemical if the information submitted by the manufacturer is not sufficient to enable the agency to determine whether the substance will pose an unreasonable risk. The order becomes final unless the manufacturer objects within 30 days. If there is an objection, EPA must seek an injunction from a district court to make the order effective. In order to prevail, the agency must show the court that it has not received sufficient information to permit "a reasoned evaluation" of the chemical's effects and either that it "may present an unreasonable risk of injury to health or the environment" or that there may be substantial human or environmental exposure. TSCA § 5(e), 15 U.S.C.A. § 2604(e) (West Supp. 1978). In both cases, the district court decides the issue *de novo*.

972. 5 U.S.C. § 706(2)(A) (1970). For example, this is the standard of review under the Clean Air Act. *See, e.g.*, Amoco Oil Co. v. EPA, 501 F.2d 722, 731, 6 ERC 1481, 1486 (D.C. Cir. 1974). The 1977 amendments to the Clean Air Act now state explicitly that the arbitrary or capricious test is the standard for review. Pub. L. No. 95-95, § 305, 91 Stat. 685 (1977), adding § 307(d)(9), 42 U.S.C.A. § 7607(d)(9) (West Supp. 1978).

973. *See, e.g.*, OSH Act § 6(f), 29 U.S.C. § 655(f) (1970).

974. FDCA § 409(g)(2), 21 U.S.C. § 348(g)(2) (1970); FHSA § 3(a)(2), 15 U.S.C. § 1262(a)(2) (1970).

975. In Abbott Laboratories v. Gardner, 387 U.S. 136 (1967), the Supreme Court stated that the substantial evidence test affords "a considerably more generous judicial review" than the arbitrary or capricious test. *Id.* at 143. See K. DAVIS *supra* note 952, § 29.00, at 646-52.

976. Consolo v. Federal Maritime Commission, 383 U.S. 607, 619-20 (1966).

977. Wright, *supra* note 957, at 392.

been judicially construed, but the legislative history indicates that Congress desired courts to scrutinize decisions more intently than they would under the substantial evidence test.[978] Presumably, however, this test also stops short of permitting substitution of judgment. The result is a supposed hierarchy of the three tests where conceivably a decision could be held to pass the arbitrary or capricious test but to fail the substantial evidence test, or to pass these two tests but to fail the fair evaluation test.[979]

Recently, however, doubts have grown that the differences between tests can be administered with any consistency and reliability. In most cases the issue is avoided; the courts tend to define the arbitrary or capricious test and the substantial evidence test not with respect to each other, but in comparison with the alternative of substituting their own judgment for that of the agencies.[980]

In cases under at least one statute, however, the issue has been taken up. OSH Act establishes essentially informal rulemaking procedures for the development of occupational standards, but it also establishes the substantial evidence test as the standard for judicial review.[981] In early cases the parties, hoping to capitalize on the supposed difference between the tests, strenuously debated whether the specified test applied or whether the specification of informal rulemaking meant that the arbitrary or capricious test should apply. The Second Circuit held that the substantial evidence test applied but stated:

> While we have felt constrained to determine and sustain the applicability of the substantial evidence test, it may well be that the controversy is semantic in some degree, at least in the context of informal rulemaking, and that it lacks the dispositional importance that respondents imply. . . . In WBEN, Inc. v. United States . . . , while we applied to F.C.C. rulemaking the "arbitrary and capricious" standard . . . , it is hard to see in what respect we would have treated the question differently if we had been applying a "substantial evidence" test. . . . While we still have a feeling that there may be cases where an adjudicative determination not supported by substantial evidence . . . would not be regarded as arbitrary and capricious, . . . in the review of rules of general applicability made after notice and comment rulemaking, the two criteria do tend to converge.[982]

In a similar OSH Act case, the District of Columbia Circuit stated essentially that the label attached to the review standard would not "affect the

---

978.   See the language of the committee reports, quoted in note 490 *supra*.

979.   *See* K. DAVIS, *supra* note 952, § 29.00, at 646-52. Davis does not discuss the "fair evaluation" test, but it fits easily into the hierarchy he describes.

980.   *See, e.g.*, Environmental Defense Fund v. EPA, 489 F.2d 1247, 1252, 6 ERC 1112, 115-16 (D.C. Cir. 1973); Ethyl Corp. v. EPA, 541 F.2d 1, 34, 8 ERC 1785, 1809 (D.C. Cir. 1976).

981.   OSH Act § 6(b), (f), 29 U.S.C. § 655(b), (f) (1970). TSCA embodies this combination as well. TSCA §§ 6(c), 19(c), 15 U.S.C.A. §§ 2605(c), 2618(c) (West Supp. 1978).

982.   Associated Industries of N.Y.S. v. United States Dep't of Labor, 487 F.2d 342, 349-50 (2d Cir. 1973) (footnotes omitted).

rigorousness of our review to the extent the Government seems to suppose, or that petitioners purport to fear.''[983] At least one judge, in a case arising under FDCA, has asserted outright that the tests are identical: "In essence I think that when an agency engages in substantive rule-making, it abuses its discretion (or acts arbitrarily or capriciously) if its actions are not supported by substantial evidence.''[984]

The difficulty of finding the decision which could survive review under the arbitrary or capricious test but fail review under the substantial evidence test is increased by the play in the two tests. The intensity of judicial scrutiny in a given case is difficult to specify, since it depends heavily on the facts of the case and on the court's characterization of the facts. Nonetheless, the depth of scrutiny under either of the tests appears to vary considerably.[985] Even if the review tests differ on an abstract level, it is likely that in practice they overlap to the point of being indistinguishable.

The problem of describing and administering distinctions between these tests applies as well to purported differences between these tests and the fair evaluation standard. In fact, the legislative description of the fair evaluation test closely resembles the conventional statement of the substantial evidence test.[986]

In sum, it is not productive to make distinctions between the judicial standards of review applicable to the health and environmental statutes. In a practical sense, the agencies' options are no wider under one test than another, and their treatment of uncertainty will not differ under one or another of the tests. Since the tests coincide in practice, they should be acknowledged to coincide in theory.[987]

Despite the fact that in practice the review tests are converging, Congress continues to differentiate among them. Most recently, in the 1977 Amendments to FWPCA Congress specified the arbitrary or capricious test as the review test for designations of substances as toxic pollutants,[988] and the substantial evidence test as the test for review of the standards set for those pollutants.[989] It seems that Congress still wants the courts to give

---

983.   Industrial Union Dep't, AFL-CIO v. Hodgson, 499 F.2d 467, 473 (D.C. Cir. 1974), citing the Second Circuit case discussed above.

984.   National Nutritional Foods Ass'n v. Weinberger, 512 F.2d 688, 705 (2d Cir. 1975) (concurring opinion of Lumbard, J.).

985.   *See* K. DAVIS, *supra* note 952, § 29.01, at 653-54.

986.   *Compare* the language from the committee reports, quoted in note 490 *supra*, *with* Universal Camera Corp. v. NLRB, 340 U.S. 474, 477-78, 487-88 (1951).

987.   Davis discusses the convergence of the arbitrary or capricious test with the substantial evidence test, but ultimately he declines to support acknowledging their coincidence. He suggests a number of propositions that the Supreme Court "might safely adopt" for clarifying when each test applies. These propositions, however, do not address whether the choice of tests will yield different results in cases. *See* K. DAVIS, *supra* note 952, § 29.01-4. Acknowledging that the tests have the identical effect would be preferable to perpetuating distinctions without meaning.

988.   FWPCA § 307(a)(1), 33 U.S.C.A. § 1317(a)(1) (West Supp. 1978).

989.   *Id.* § 307(a)(2), 33 U.S.C.A. § 1317(a)(1) (West Supp. 1978).

agencies more deference in some decisions than in others. But if the courts and 'the agencies cannot administer the difference, then the distinction is fruitless and should not be perpetuated.

The problem of describing the deference due to the agencies' conclusions drawn from uncertain facts is no easier once the coincidence of the tests is acknowledged. The only point of definite agreement among courts is that they are not to substitute judgment.[990] Since determining the minimum rationality necessary to support an agency decision is a problem of degree, this point of agreement does not help much. The Supreme Court has said that the reviewing court must make a "searching and careful" inquiry into the facts and must assure that all the "relevant factors" have been considered.[991] Two of the judges of the District of Columbia Circuit have coined their own terms. Judge Leventhal would require that an agency take a "hard look" at the factual issues.[992] Judge Wright urges that this standard is too intrusive, and that the arbitrary or capricious test is "undemanding," that it "subjects a rulemaker to only the most rudimentary command of rationality," and that the weight assigned to various factors in a decision is "of virtually no concern to the reviewing court."[993] Judge Friendly of the Second Circuit sees the differences between these positions as "in some degree semantic."[994] In *Ethyl Corp. v. EPA*,[995] the most recent major case on the depth of judicial scrutiny, Wright and Leventhal were able to agree fully on a common analysis of the agency's action.[996]

Regardless of formulas, the scrutiny actually applied varies from case to case.[997] It depends in part on the judges' perceptions of how careful the agency has been.[998] It may also depend unavoidably to some degree on whether the judges are sympathetic to the goals of the regulatory program they are reviewing.

Without question, judicial review of toxic substances control decisions allows careful advocates to prevent decisions from being based on grossly unsupported factual assumptions, impermissible or irrelevant policy considerations, or grossly illogical or incomplete reasoning. But within these

---

990.   *See, e.g.*, cases cited in notes 951, 962 *supra*.

991.   Citizens to Preserve Overton Park v. Volpe, 401 U.S. 402, 416, 2 ERC 1250, 1256 (1971).

992.   Greater Boston Television Corp. v. FCC, 444 F.2d 841, 851 (D.C. Cir. 1970). *See also* Leventhal, *supra* note 948, at 511.

993.   Wright, *supra* note 957, at 392. *See also* Ethyl Corp. v. EPA, 541 F.2d 1, 34-37, 8 ERC 1785, 1809-11 (D.C. Cir. 1976).

994.   Friendly, *supra* note 967, at 1313.

995.   541 F.2d 1, 8 ERC 1785 (D.C. Cir. 1976).

996.   *Id.* (opinion by Wright, J., concurred in by Leventhal, J.) *See also id.* at 68, 8 ERC at 1837 (statement of Leventhal, J.).

997.   *See* Universal Camera Corp. v. NLRB, 340 U.S. 474, 488-89 (1951) ("A formula for judicial review of adminstrative action may afford grounds for certitude but cannot assure certainty of application.").

998.   K. DAVIS, *supra* note 952, § 29.01, at 652-54.

outer boundaries, close, reliable judicial control over agency decision making should not be expected.

CONCLUSION

The VC case study in Part II has illustrated the fragmentation that
besets the federal government's toxic substances control efforts as they are
now organized. It also has illustrated the factual uncertainties and value
conflicts inherent in individual control decisions.

Better coordination of the government's efforts is essential to regulating individual substances effectively and to dealing with the tremendous
number of substances that merit regulation. The effectiveness of the current
coordination initiatives depends largely on the willingness of all the agencies to yield some of their current jurisdiction and on the willingness of the
agencies more interested in reform to pull along those less interested. The
incentive to do so lies in the potential for sharing information and expertise
and in the prospect that by acting consistently, and even jointly, they will
have greater credibility with the public and the courts. The possibility of
presidential reorganization is also an incentive for cooperative efforts.

Health and environmental groups, unions, and other advocates of more
effective and efficient regulation have an important role to play in fostering
the coordination efforts. They must publicly emphasize the reasons for
cooperative measures. They must apply persuasive political pressure on the
agencies to adopt such measures, and on the President to exercise the
reorganization threat toward that end.

Ultimately the effectiveness, efficiency, and fairness of individual
decisions depends on political factors. The advocates of better control can
use legal tools to assure that uncertain evidence of harm is considered, that
economic balancing takes place only where it is allowed by statute, that the
burden of persuasion is actually placed where the statute puts it, that the
agencies have considered the relevant issues and evidence, and that they
have explained their factual conclusions and policy judgments rationally.
Inside these outer boundaries the inferences made from uncertain information and the balances struck between competing interests depend on the
orientation of the agency and on the persuasiveness and political power of
the advocates on all sides.

Coping with the number of chemicals to be evaluated for possible
regulation depends on similar factors. The agencies must coordinate their
activities on individual chemicals so as to avoid wasting resources on
duplicated work that otherwise would be available for action on other
substances. As the agencies begin to regulate more substances, the need will
grow even greater for the development of consistent approaches to assessing
and weighing risks and benefits, to promote more efficient use of resources
devoted to health and environmental protection. The agencies will need to
develop better means of assigning priorities among substances that are

candidates for regulation and of determining what degree of regulation to impose in given cases. In these general policy decisions, as well as in decisions specific to particular chemicals, there are choices to be made about how to resolve uncertainties and to balance interests. The advocates of better control need to press the agencies to address these issues more closely, and they need to participate heavily in the proceedings leading to their resolution.

The vinyl chloride episode is only a forerunner of problems that will be encountered hundreds of times in the implementation of the toxic substances control laws in the coming decade. The episode teaches important lessons about the character and magnitude of the problems, and about some of the responses and areas needing further work. These lessons must be observed as the serious work of toxic substances control begins.